ADELAIDE

Independent Monthly Literary Magazine
Revista Literária Independente Mensal
Year III, Number 15, August 2018
Ano III, Número 15, agosto de 2018

ISBN-13: 978-1-949180-21-3
ISBN-10: 1-949180-21-2

Adelaide Literary Magazine is an independent international monthly publication, based in New York and Lisbon. Founded by Stevan V. Nikolic and Adelaide Franco Nikolic in 2015, the magazine's aim is to publish quality poetry, fiction, nonfiction, artwork, and photography, as well as interviews, articles, and book reviews, written in English and Portuguese. We seek to publish outstanding literary fiction, nonfiction, and poetry, and to promote the writers we publish, helping both new, emerging, and established authors reach a wider literary audience.

A Revista Literária Adelaide é uma publicação mensal internacional e independente, localizada em Nova Iorque e Lisboa. Fundada por Stevan V. Nikolic e Adelaide Franco Nikolic em 2015, o objectivo da revista é publicar poesia, ficção, não-ficção, arte e fotografia de qualidade assim como entrevistas, artigos e críticas literárias, escritas em inglês e português. Pretendemos publicar ficção, não-ficção e poesia excepcionais assim como promover os escritores que publicamos, ajudando os autores novos e emergentes a atingir uma audiência literária mais vasta.

(http://adelaidemagazine.org)

Published by: Adelaide Books, New York
244 Fifth Avenue, Suite D27
New York NY, 10001
e-mail: info@adelaidemagazine.org
phone: (917) 727 8907
http://adelaidebooks.org

FOUNDERS / FUNDADORES

Stevan V. Nikolic & Adelaide Franco Nikolic

EDITOR IN CHIEF / EDITOR-CHEFE

Stevan V. Nikolic
editor@adelaidemagazine.org

ASSOCIATE EDITOR

Raymond Fenech

MANAGING DIRECTOR / DIRECTORA EXECUTIVA

Adelaide Franco Nikolic

GRAPHIC & WEB DESIGN

Adelaide Books DBA, New York

CONTRIBUTING AUTHORS IN THIS ISSUE

Alexandra Lapointe, Annabelle Blomeley, Maureen Hossbacher, John Tavares, J.R. Night, Katherine Steblen , Gabriel Sage, Evan Massey, Shawn Van Horn, John Wells, Carolyn Soyars, Larry Smith, Paul-John Ramos, Bettina Rotenberg, Leslie Kain, Dave Gregory, Sean Brzoska, Cindy Adams, E. P. Tuazon, Alexa Findlay, Jose Recio, Andrew Mitin, Robert Perron, Toni Morgan, Janel Brubaker, Steve Coughlin, Nicolette Munoz, A. M. Palmer, Victoria Endres, Matthew Ross, Shirley Palmerton, Justine Cadwell, Andrea Bernal, Endika Sangroniz, Debra Brenegan, Jack Brown, María Agustina Pardini, Austin C. Morgan, Jack Conway, Mike Li, Martin Willitts, Felix Purat, Tee Jay Holland, Linda Casebeer, Rafiki Chemari, Tony Tracy, Reuben Ellis, Antoine Airoldi

CONTENTS / CONTEÚDOS

Editor's Notes
Stevan V. Nikolic

WHENCE WE CAME FROM

Naquela sexta-feira à noite	That Friday evening
À medida que as luzes se acendiam	As the lights turned on
Ela saiu	She walked out
E deixou no passeio	And left on the pavement
As suas pegadas	Her footprints
Como notas de música	Like music notes
De uma sonata ao luar	From moonlight sonata
Desde então, carrego nos meus lábios	Since then I carry on my lips
Um beijo tão glorioso como a Via Láctea	A kiss as glorious as Milky Way
E procuro a palavra	And I am looking for a word
Que descreva a sua magia	That will describe her magic
Eu nasci naquela noite	I was born that evening
Na estação de comboios de Faro	On the Faro train station
Um orfão sem passado	An orphan with no past
Enganado pelo futuro	Deceived by the future
Acusado pelas minhas próprias palavras	Accused by my own words
Amaldiçoado para amar	Cursed to love
Sem descanso	Without ceasing
Deusa encantada de saudade	Enchanted goddess of longing

MY FRIEND SINDSMAN
by Alexandra Lapointe

Neither the day before nor the day after were of much significance. It was only the day I met Sindsman that I can vividly recall. I was sitting on my porch rather typically for a Thursday evening. I was inspecting the overgrown strings of grass that stood erect against the rotted wood of my mother's house. Interestingly, I didn't care much for the grass, but rather the assorted insects residing among it, living or dead.

As I probed around the damp grass with my gentle fingers, I heard heavy footsteps approaching. I looked up to see Sindsman, whom I had not met previously. From a young, rather underdeveloped boy's perspective, Sindsman looked grotesquely large. I would have said at that moment that he was the ugliest thing I'd ever seen. His ears resembled the size of watermelons, and his overbite was so severe that he was practically incapable of closing his mouth. Sure, as a kid who had barely enough meat on my bones to feed a mouse, I was certainly intimidated by the surrealistic creature. He was easily triple my height; I had to crane my neck up towards the sun to get his head into view. But once I did I didn't look away. He looked at me delicately and outstretched his grubby hand.

"I's Sindsman." His substantially debilitating lisp made it difficult to decipher his words. I nodded my head, not yet comfortable with speaking myself. My hand cautiously shook his lanky fingers. Sindsman leaned backwards and smiled, exposing his plaque-filled, crooked teeth.

"Come wif me" Sindsman said next, wasting no time. My concentration on the grass had already been disrupted so I stood up and followed Sindsman as he sauntered down the street. I followed him until my house was clear out of view and the woods were quickly approaching. He stepped into the wall of trees and was immediately engulfed by the shrubbery. I'm not entirely sure why I didn't hesitate to follow Sindsman, but nevertheless I ended up in the center of the wooded area surrounding Willow Pond. The ground was soggy, making it difficult to walk with the mud suctioned to my damp sneakers. Sindsman effortlessly walked around the north side of the pond and pulled back a wall of vines to reveal a dilapidated treehouse. The softness of the dirt and the rotted planks of wood it was constructed with made me question how it was still standing, let alone able to hold the weight of Sindsman. He didn't seem to have the same skepticism and rapidly climbed the contorted ladder. Once he was safely inside, he poked his head from above the sloppily formed wall looked at me.

"Come join da party." Sindsman said. I walked up to the ladder. It was taller than I had originally thought. I gripped it with both my palms and shook it to check its stability. It wobbled faintly but I figured if Sindsman could climb it, a ninety-pound kid could manage. Up I went, attempting to suppress my nervous shaking. Sindsman must've been irritated with my slow pace and grabbed my waist to hoist me up himself. My feet landed hard on the floor of the treehouse and the whole structure wobbled slightly, making me panic. I looked around, noticing a thick tree branch extending about four feet above where the treehouse ended. Sindsman reached up and rested his arm on it.

I peered through the wooden planks and looked out into the cluster of trees. The only thing I heard besides Sindsman's heavy breathing was the birds chirping invisibly among the foliage. The woods seemed eerily tranquil, as if it was patiently waiting for Sindsman's next move, as was I. He seemed to possess vivacious energy which was unsettling for me as I awkwardly stood next to him in anticipation. When he was satisfied with the duration of his silence, he bent down and picked up a small plastic bucket that was resting at his feet. He peered inside it and smiled, offering me a glance. I leaned towards him and saw a pile of misshapenly lumpy toads. They were laying on top of each other, defeatedly squirming around their counterparts' muddied skin. Their repulsive stench jerked my head backwards. I looked at Sindsman quizzically.

"Watch dis," Sindsman said. Concerningly, my eyes followed him as he walked over to the ledge of the treehouse and reached his hand into the bucket. He removed a writhing toad and raised it above his head. In one methodical motion, his arm violently extended towards the ground and he released the toad. I watched it fly through the air for the few seconds that it was airborne. Then, it abruptly hit the ground, exploding into a pancake of skin and guts. Although I was far enough away from the collision to not be affected by the splash, I still wiped my face with my hands in case of a stray drop of blood or piece of intestine.

"Cool right?" I heard Sindsman say. I glanced up to see him reaching back inside the plastic bucket.

"Don't," I said, holding my hand out in an attempt to stop him from murdering another. His eyebrows lowered, almost as if he was perplexed by my disapproval.

"It's okay, boy. Froggies likes it." He picked out his next victim, raised his hand, and threw it with enough force for a cloud of displaced air to smack my face. I chose not to look this time, but hearing the splat was just as disturbing. I turned towards the ladder and grabbed it with both of my palms. Instantaneously, I felt a hand on my shoulder.

"Wait," Sindsman said. "My turn." I decided to give him one last chance to convince me to stay. He grabbed the tree branch above his head and hoisted himself on top of it, until he was straddling it like a horse. He looked at me and smiled, as if he was confident that his plan would catch my interest. The desperateness that welled up in his eyes started dripping down his entire face. I could see it transform his body. He wanted someone to play with, someone to impress. I'm not sure why I was the one he chose. I might have simply been the first person he saw on his morning recruitment run. Or he could have been stalking me for days, deciding if I was qualified to accompany him on his toad-tossing adventures. Either way, I could feel how meaningful my presence was to him, so I stayed.

He shimmied his way up the tree branch until he was hovering over the edge of the pond, his feet swinging from side to side. I wanted to speak up and ask him what he was doing. I wanted to tell him to come back to the safety of the treehouse, so we could go back into town together. Yet my mouth remained shut. Despite his jittering limbs he managed to slowly stand upright on the branch. Then, without a warning or any final words, Sindsman jumped.

I wasn't sure what to make of the abhorrent scene that unfolded in front of me. Sindsman's body had hit the ground with substantial force. The bloodcurdling sound of breaking bones was louder than the thud of his impact. His legs laid in the dirt, twisted in disfiguring directions. He wasn't moving. I didn't hear a moan or a scream. Even the birds overhead had either flown away in fright or fell silent. I ran to the ladder and flung myself to the ground, stumbling towards his body. His face was facing me, although half of it was buried in the dirt. He had landed on the edge of the water and I watched at trickles of the pond water and mud seeped into his nostrils and eyes, which were wide open. The smile remained on his face, even after being compressed by the impenetrable earth. Laying at his feet were his victims, as if he had meticulously constructed a mass grave.

The horrific sight made me grimace. I looked up and tried to remember which way we had come from. Walking around the pond, I made my way out of the woods and back to my front porch. Sweat was dripping down my back like the beads of water collecting inside Sindsman's nose. Sitting on my porch, seemingly intentionally, was a brown, bulbous toad. I kicked it.

About the Author:

Alexandra Lapointe is a recent college graduate who writes fiction short stories in her spare time, and is currently working towards finishing a science fiction novel. She resides in Rochester, New York with her family.

THE SINGING SCALLOP
by Annabelle Blomeley

The Singing Scallop Restaurant held its fifteenth anniversary on the day Hurricane Robert starting raining down onto the town of Winnie Shores. Out the windows, customers could see what looked like ten foot waves, with nothing but gray clouds off in the horizon.

The Singing Scallop herself looked like it could be blown away if someone sneezed in its direction. The walls were aged wood, and the roof was made of shiny tin. Colorful signs and knick-knacks covered the walls, both inside and outside, making it look like an antique store from a distance. The building had started off small, but after years of growing and growing, the restaurant now had three add-ons, each one looking slightly different than the last. The first main room was called the Jellyfish Room, because ribbons and dried seaweed hung from the ceiling like tentacles. The second was the Stingray Room with a giant stuffed Stingray on the wall named Sting, the third was the Scallop Room, and the fourth was the Gift Shop.

The Singing Scallop was known for her authentic "beach bum" vibe, various types of fried fish, stellar views of the ocean, and tastefully made side dishes. But most of all, she was known for being named after scallops but then not selling scallops. It was a nice contradiction that tourists loved mentioning when they went home after vacation.

Despite the hurricane, dozens of people were crowded in each of the Singing Scallop's creaky rooms. The regulars stayed in the Scallop room; they were comprised of local fisherman and the owners of the town's notorious tourist traps. The Tourists themselves stayed in the Stingray and Jellyfish Rooms; and as Bill the

Regular said, "They're quaking straight outta their flip flops 'cause of this tiny-ass Hurricane."

And they were scared, no matter how many fried shrimp and crabcakes that they crammed into their mouths. Their eyes looked like they were at a tennis match, going from the window to the TVs that hung on the walls. They were watching a weatherman with gel-slicked brown hair and a gray suit. He was frantically pointing to the eye of Hurricane Robert.

"Don't you worry," the owner, Ruth, told the customers, shaking her head and putting her fists on her hips. "The Singin' Scallop ain't never fallen to a couple of raindrops and sea breezes." She then laughed, her hearty giggles filling the room.

Ruth herself was middle-aged, with dyed bleach blonde hair and brown roots. She had laugh lines and her skin was tan from the sun.

"Are you sure we'll be okay?" a little boy whimpered beside her, rocking back and forth on his feet nervously.

Ruth turned to him and smiled. "Where ya from?" she asked, kneeling down and putting her elbows on her knees.

"Tennessee," the boy said, looking at his mom anxiously.

"Well, lemme show you something that you can't find in Tennessee," Ruth said, taking the boy's hand and bringing him over to the corner of the Scallop Room, where a large aquarium stood. Green grass was floating rhythmically in the water and if you looked hard enough, you could spot some shells sitting at the bottom.

Ruth glanced into the water for a couple of seconds before reaching her hand in and pulling out the biggest shell, which snapped shut when her finger touched it.

"This here is Verlon," she said. "He's my most favorite scallop that I've ever caught."

"There's a scallop in there?" the boy asked, eyeing the shell.

"Well, yeah!" Ruth answered. She motioned for the boy to watch, and then set the scallop back into the water. Right as it touched the surface, the shell opened up and by snapping up and down, swam straight back into the grass.

"There's tons of other scallops in there: Jane, Albert, Bernard, Matilda. But Verlon's been here for years," Ruth explained. "He was supposed to be dead by three Christmases ago yet he keeps on fighting." She looked at the boy. "If Verlon can make it, so can we."

The boy smiled and walked back to his parents, who were both eating french fries while looking anxiously out the window.

Ruth sighed and walked up to some of the Regulars, who were all eating shrimp smeared in butter and laughing at each other's jokes.

"Can't believe Verlon's still kicking, Ruth," Amos said, in between mouthfuls of homemade chips and hushpuppies. He was sitting with his pals, all of whom came to The Singing Scallop every Monday, Wednesday, and Friday. They told Ruth that on Mondays they needed a pick me up, on Wednesdays they were celebrating half the week being over, and on Fridays they just wanted some food.

"Does he still hum to you, Ruth?" Jack asked, twirling his fork in his hand.

Ruth turned and shrugged. "Not as loud as he used to." She smiled sadly and walked away, swinging open the doors to the kitchen. She shuffled over to the corner of the room where another aquarium stood in the back. Ruth always said that having scallops in the kitchen would bring good luck to the restaurant, so she kept a couple near the prep table. When she made it to the tank, Ruth closed her eyes and put her ears near the bucket, trying to focus on

listening, yearning to hear the hum. She blocked out the sound of the dishwasher and the sizzle of food being fried, until she heard a tiny song erupt from the basket. It reminded her of all the years past.

Ruth first went scalloping when she was about to turn thirty-six. She was working at Daisy's Diner as a waitress, and the local scalloper had just finished dropping off that day's scallops.

"You should come with us some time," the scalloper said, dropping a box in front of Ruth's feet. "The scallops are mighty feisty this time of year."

And so Ruth went scalloping, and as she sat on the scalloper's boat, she realized that she didn't know how to scallop and she didn't know the people she was scalloping with. They all wore scuba suits, and Ruth wore her bathing suit. They all knew what they were doing, Ruth did not.

The scalloper threw some goggles, flippers, and a bag at Ruth, and told her to hurry on up because it was about to rain. Scallops don't like the rain.

"Now ya just dive into the grass at the bottom right there," the scalloper said, pointing to the bottom of the water. "And when ya see a scallop, grab it and put it in the bag."

Ruth stood at the edge of the boat, looking down at the water. She nodded at the scalloper, even though her stomach was churning and she felt cold.

"Well, then go!" the man said, nudging her from behind right as she jumped in.

Ruth hit the water, warmth overcoming her body and her hair floating around her. She looked around and saw the bottom of the boat: a figure looming overhead like storm clouds. She turned around and saw nothing but blue and gray water, tiny particles floating in front of her nose.

Suddenly she became aware of the burning in her lungs, and frantically started splashing around. Finally she kicked up and popped into the surface, sputtering and coughing.

"Oh, shit! You didn't tell me you didn't know

how to swim!" the scalloper yelled at Ruth from above.

Ruth looked up, treading water and fumbling with her goggles. "I can swim!"

"Then swim!" everyone on the boat screamed.

Ruth frowned and taking in one more breath, pushed down into the water. A calmness washed over her. No one was yelling at her, no one was looking at her.

So Ruth dove down deeper until she made it to the green grass that swayed in the waves. She looked around, pushing away the leaves, finding nothing in the bush. Ruth stopped to gather her senses, and just as she was about to go up for air, she heard a tiny voice, humming in the distance. She turned her head to the left, towards the song, and swam over to it. Frantically searching for the singer in the grass. The hum got louder and louder the more Ruth looked. And just as her lungs almost gave out, her hand moved a leaf. Sitting in the sand was the scallop.

Ruth grabbed it and started to swim towards the surface, feeling the shell's ridges push against her palms. As she popped out of the water, she held the scallop up into the air.

"I got one!" she screamed at the boat, smiling and laughing to herself.

The scalloper appeared on the boat. "Good job! Now go get more." He turned around and left Ruth's view. Frowning, Ruth grabbed the bag that hung on her hip, and carefully set the scallop inside.

And with that, she went straight back in. This time she followed hum after hum after hum. The scallops sounded like an underwater choir, each one hitting a different note and coming together to harmonize. Ruth grabbed scallop after scallop until her bag was about to burst. She looked at the last scallop in her hand. Its shell was a pale pink, with brown stripes going down the side. Ruth smiled and let it go, watching it flutter back down into the grass.

With the last of her strength, Ruth swam to the surface. She reached for the boat's ladder and pulled herself up, humming under her breath.

Hoisting her bag up, she fell onto the boat's deck, and tried to catch her breath.

"What in the hell?" the scalloper said, walking up to Ruth. "Did ya put rocks in the bag or something?"

Ruth looked up, confused. "No, these're scallops!"

"Good Lord above! I ain't never seen anyone get this many scallops during one trip! Are you messing with me?" the scalloper cried, grabbing the bag that Ruth held out in front of her. He opened it gently and Ruth watched his eyes grow wide.

"How in the world?" he murmured, gazing among the piles of scallops in the bag.

Ruth sat up and leaned against the railing of the boat as the scalloper turned to her. She shivered as it started to rain, water hitting her face and getting stuck in her already damp hair.

"How did you do it?" the scalloper said softly, not once taking his eyes off of the bag.

"You can hear 'em," Ruth said, wringing out her towel.

"Hear what?"

"The scallops! They sing!" Ruth exclaimed, grabbing a scallop out of the bag and putting it up to her ear. "Well, I mean, they do underwater." Ruth could hear nothing but the crash of waves and the murmur of the boat's engine.

With this the scalloper looked up. "You can't hear scallops!" he laughed. "Are you crazy?" He patted Ruth on the back and walked away giggling under his breath.

Ruth shrugged and they sat in silence for the rest of the ride. She watched as they anchored and moored, finally hopping onto the deck and taking her bag of humming scallops along with her.

"Order for table eight!" one of the cooks yelled, snapping Ruth out of her daze.

"I'll get it!" she said, grabbing two of the plates and balancing them on her forearms, and holding the other two in her hands. She started to walk, opening the door with her back and strutting all the way back to the Jellyfish Room. As she set the plates down on the table, the little boy from before tugged on her white apron.

"How did you meet Verlon?" he asked quietly when she turned around. His parents were arguing whether or not to take the chance and leave or stay and wait it out. From the tv on the other side of the room, the weatherman told everyone to stay put and get to high ground.

Ruth looked at the boy. "I was out scallopin' in my brand new boat a couple of years back. It was right when this place finally took off," she started, gesturing to the restaurant. "My bag was almost full, ya see, and so I was only trying to find a couple more because although they don't move much, scallops need a pretty big tank to live in. So I listened and listened until I heard Verlon singing his pipes off over by a rock." Ruth stopped for a moment to wave at one of the regulars, who was putting his raincoat on.

"Imma get home, Ruth! Thanks again!" the man said, opening the door. A blast of wind slammed the door shut and everyone jumped.

"Be safe, George!" Ruth yelled, turning back to the boy. "Anyways, so I went to the rock and found Verlon perched on another smaller rock. I remember thinking, How in the world can this one scallop sing better than my entire church's choir?" Ruth laughed and the boy smiled.

"And so I put him in the bag, went all the way back to the restaurant, and I swear the whole time Verlon just sang and sang in the back of my truck! I'm surprised he didn't die from overexertion or some crap like that!" Ruth continued to pause so she could laugh, her eyes twinkling in the fluorescent lighting.

"Scallops sing?" the little boy asked, pushing his hair back.

"Of course!"

The boy smiled as his parents waved him over. Ruth stood back up and looked around, swinging back and forth on her heels. The sky was darker now, almost as dark as Jane the Scallop's stormy gray shell. The waves were getting

scarily close, stopping mere inches before the walls of The Singing Scallop. The rain was coming down hard, as if Ruth was staring straight into a waterfall. Every couple of minutes the floors would shake from thunder and the lightbulbs would flicker. Children were crying and parents kept their heads in their hands.

Suddenly, the weatherman showed up on all the screens, his brown hair looking slightly more unkempt than usual. "We are now under a state of emergency. Everyone evacuate to either high ground or further inland, and never drive your car into a flooded area..." he said, pointing with his hand to the big swirl of a storm on the green screen behind him.

Ruth looked away, blocking out his warnings to the best of her ability. But the words "get out now!" repeated in her head over and over again.

"Ruth!" a man yelled from the other room. All the customers looked up, fear etched across their faces.

Ruth ran to the door of the Scallop Room, putting her hand on the old wooden door frame and stopping. On the opposite side of the room, the floors glinted with water, and the window laid in pieces on the ground. Wind whistled through the cracks and gusts of the cold hit Ruth and the Regulars in the face, making goosebumps stand up on their arms.

"Dammit," Ruth muttered, staring straight into the sea, which was now right out of her window.

The Regulars grabbed their jackets and leftovers. Jack walked to Ruth, putting his hand on her shoulder.

"I'm going inland to stay with my brother and his family. He's a fancy doctor so he's got two guest bedrooms. I'd be happy to drive ya up there, Ruth," he said, watching the waves outside the window get closer and closer. "I can even wait for ya to kick everyone out."

Ruth turned to him and smiled. "It's fine. Thanks for offerin' though."

Jack grinned. "Be safe, Ruth."

Ruth only nodded, staring as the water splashed against the floor like it was beating a drum. To get her mind off of it, she walked to the kitchen, where the cooks and waitresses were huddled and anxiously talking.

"I'll let y'all out soon. Don't you worry," Ruth said, grabbing a sponge and starting to wash the dishes that had piled higher than she had ever seen them before.

It took her awhile, but by the time the dishes were done, all of the waitresses had packed up their bags and the cooks had hung up their aprons. They were silently shuffling out the door, covering their eyes with their hands to avoid the wind and rain.

Ruth wiped her hands on her pants and walked into the dining rooms. She saw the little boy wave goodbye, as well as most of the tourists and even the Regulars. Only a handful remained, and they were all leaving.

Ruth now stood in The Singing Scallop alone. She went and grabbed her phone, along with her jacket. And then she went back into the Scallop Room, surrounded by water and the leftover food of the customers. More windows had been knocked out, so much that she felt like she was standing outside. Her ankles were completely covered in seawater and the bottom part of her pants were soaked. Ruth sat in one of the chairs and leaned back, crossing her legs and putting her hands over her stomach. She sat there and lost track of time, watching as the chairs' legs were covered by water, as napkins floated on the surface, even as the tvs finally went out and the weatherman's cries to evacuate were hushed. The sky was dark and for awhile, it scared Ruth. She had never seen a sky that dark before, even on a normal night she could see the moon and stars.

There was a silence that engulfed the room; nothing but waves splashing against the walls like torpedoes. In the distance, Ruth could see a wave coming towards her. It was higher than the others and looked stronger, too. It seemed like a dream, like there was no way it would actually come and hit the Singing Scallop.

Ruth stood up and watched as it got closer and closer. Ten feet away, six, four, three, zero. It passed by all the broken windows, heading straight towards the Scallop tank.

"No!" Ruth screamed right as the water made impact on the glass and everything shattered. The water spilled out of the tank like a waterfall and one by one the scallops started raining down into the ocean.

"Verlon!" Ruth sputtered, diving into the water and swimming to the edge of the building. Her eyes burned with salt, but she spotted Verlon's black stripes fluttering further out into the sea. His song flooded the water, so much that the waves couldn't be heard anymore. All Ruth could hear was Verlon, whose voice was getting further and further away.

About the Author:

Annabelle Blomeley is studying creative writing at the Alabama School of Fine Arts in Birmingham, AL. She has been published in Cadence Literary Magazine and Aura Literary Magazine's Fall Issue.

FINER THINGS

by Maureen Hossbacher

Even in retrospect, Wesley Byrne is disinclined to acknowledge the cliché of his affair with Ellie. He was past forty and starting to bald. Ellie Mattisen, his secretary then, was twenty-five. She had honey-blond hair and green eyes that sparkled like the cellophane grass in an Easter basket. That was nearly 30 years ago. Wes refuses to taint his memories with the excuse of midlife crisis. He simply believed that he had found his one true love in Ellie. Bliss, however, was marred by complications: he was married to someone else, to Kathryn, the daughter of the man whose law practice he was destined to inherit. He also had two young sons and a house that was almost paid for. Still, he was ready to chuck it all for love of Ellie.

But Ellie wouldn't have him. In the end she said he was a louse to want to divorce his wife. Ellie was a girl with lofty ideals.

*

When Ellie is shown into his office she is wearing a stylish white blazer over a navy blue dress. Her hair is short, still blond. She looks at least a decade younger than Wes had anticipated. They shake hands and embrace, cheek barely brushing cheek.

"You're looking lovelier than ever, Ellie," he observes. Indeed she is sleeker, more delicate. She still moves with the grace of a dancer, the career to which she aspired but never achieved, as far as he knows.

"I'm still a nut for exercise," she tells him.

"Well, let's see what we have, here," says Wes, relieving her of the leather portfolio tucked under her arm. When they take their chairs on opposite sides of his large, mahogany desk, the clot of nervousness in his chest dissipates. Over the years their only contact has been a string of Christmas cards, mostly hers, sent to his office address. On his few in response, he was careful to write nothing but his signature. Some of Ellie's included a "Dear Everybody" letter, the last one bearing tidings of the demise of Peter, her second husband, and this is the event which has finally reunited them. Widows are C. Wesley Byrne's specialty. Though he's more or less retired and his son now heads the firm, he likes to keep his hand in by assisting with probate matters. As he leafs through the papers Ellie has brought him, she chatters about the incompatible relationship between herself and her late husband's attorney, which she had already explained to Wes when she telephoned a week ago. His task is merely to tie up loose ends and he does not plan to charge Ellie a fee. From what he sees so far, there is nothing here to challenge his expertise, but he examines each document carefully and mutters a steady drivel of legalese. He has all intentions of detaining her until lunch time and has made a reservation at Gabrielli's , where the food is excellent and the tables well spaced for privacy.

*

When noon finally arrives, Ellie easily accepts his invitation to lunch, as if she had expected it. Heads turn as Wes proudly escorts her through the outer offices. In the crowded elevator she positions herself in front of him, leaning her back lightly against his chest. She is not wearing perfume. Her hair smells like the fur of a fastidious cat. She is taller than he remembers. But no, more likely he is shorter, gravity having worked its way on his aging frame. Unlike Ellie, he has never been a nut for exercise.

Though the restaurant is a short walk, Wes has arranged for his car to be waiting. He wonders whether Ellie will appreciate this, or will she think his ostentation has grown worse with age. Surely she remembers how once he tried to win her by promising that if she'd marry him, she could devote herself entirely to dancing, his money would open doors for her. With exquisite magnanimity, he promised, too, that he would set her free the instant she grew tired of him. Oh, he knew, even then, they wouldn't have lasted long together, she'd eventually outgrow her dependence on him. Ellie was offended. She said he couldn't buy her. By that time, of course, a younger and properly eligible rival was lurking in the wings. The first husband. He was a gym teacher or basketball coach, or some such thing, as Wes recalls. He warned her she'd rue it if she married the fool; she was meant for finer things. Ellie said, "You don't know what the truly finer things in life are, Wes. You don't understand that money can't buy them." Those were her exact words, on the day she left his employ and him. He will never forget the sincerely compassionate smile on her face when she walked out the door.

*

At the restaurant Wes begins to relax after a gulp of champagne. Ellie had asked for a glass of white wine. Rejuvenating a bit of his old verve and chauvinism, he ignored that and ordered instead a bottle of Veuve Clicqot. She takes a sip and smiles approvingly. The hand caressing the fluted glass is impeccably manicured. She used to bite her nails. Maturity seems to have wrought perfection.

Ellie says, "I noticed the Wesley Byrne junior on your letterhead. How nice."

"My son is in court today, or I would have asked him to join us," Wes lies.

Ellie peruses the menu, selects the broiled sole, claiming,"I have to watch my figure." She lays the menu aside and asks, "Is your other son a lawyer too?"

"No, Donald tried his hand at acting for a while, but now writes screenplays for television and seems to like that quite well. And then . . . there's Annie, our youngest--"

"A daughter? I don't remember you having a daughter."

"Well . . . Annie was a bit of a surprise to Kathryn and me. She's in California, at UC Berkeley, working on her Masters in Anthropology, or Folklore, or some sort of combination of those. She'll be an adjunct instructor in the program next semester, and has her eye on a PhD. She loves school. And your daughter--?"

"Miranda. She's a dancer. We started her young with ballet but she grew bored with it, said it was too confining. Contemporary dance is her passion, choreography especially. She'll be doing a residency next month at Jacob's Pillow in the Berkshires. I'm very proud of her." As Wes refills Ellie's glass and his own, Ellie adds, "So you and Kathryn are still together."

Wes nods.

"And how is Kathryn?"

"Oh, thriving, thanks. She had heart surgery a few years ago, but she's in excellent health now, knock wood. She let her hair go gray after that, when she discovered her feminist consciousness -- or I should say when our daughter, Annie, discovered it for her. The result of all this consciousness raising is that Kathryn went back to school. She was a nurse, you know, when I met her -- LPN. Now she has her RN and she works part time as a hospice nurse. She enjoys it."

"Really. Sounds grim, but of course it is a special calling."

"Well, it's part time, and a lot of it involves setting up care plans and monitoring the aides. She's especially good with families, with helping them cope, you know. And then there's her cat breeding business, a joint venture with a neighbor friend. At the moment our daughter's room is serving as the nursery for six Abyssinian kittens. Abyssinians are a noble breed, you understand: it would be un-thinkable to shunt the little dickenses off to the basement."

Ellie laughs in the most endearing way. "Heaven forbid!" she exclaims. "Miranda wanted a Bengal kitten once. The breeder wanted Nine Hundred Dollars!. We ended up with a pretty tabby from the local animal rescue."

*

By dessert, they are mellow enough to speak of the past. Ellie murmurs, "We had some wonderful times together, didn't we, Wes? I was so infatuated with you. And lord, how you spoiled me." She nibbles a chocolate truffle. "Mmmm . . . this is positively evil."

"You can afford the calories," he assures her.

"Thank you," she says. "Believe it or not, I still take dance classes just to keep in shape.. Now that I think of it, I was pretty pudgy in the old days, wasn't I?"

"No, Just pretty."

"And I thought you were the suavest thing on two feet."

She is bolstering an old man's ego, but Wes savors it, tells himself there's a morsel of truth at the core of her blarney.

They linger over coffee. Espresso with a dash of Anisette. She used to like that. Still does. He orders a second for her, but not for himself, heeding the inner admonition that another dose of liquor-laced caffeine could be lethal.

*

When they get outside, the afternoon is brilliant and warm, the trees along the avenue newly sprouted into full, green bloom. And the scent of urban Spring, fresh and musty at the same time, is very strong. Ellie removes her jacket, drapes it over her arm. She suggests they walk back to the office, where her own car is parked. Wes obliges, tells his driver to go.

They stroll along wordlessly for a minute, until Ellie says, "Remember the Comerford? That was such a lovely old hotel. The bar, with all that etched glass and those wonderful chandeliers. Last time I was in town -- oh, a couple of years ago -- I was meeting a friend for a matinee and I thought we could meet there, but it didn't exist anymore, I discovered."

They have stepped from the curb and Wes is guiding her across the street, as gentlemen do (or used to) with his hand gently touching her waist. Through the thin fabric of her dress, the benefits of regular dance workouts are revealed to him. Wes is not sure whether it is this contact, or the residual effects of the champagne, or her mention of the Hotel Comerford that is causing the stirring in his loins. The Comerford was once their trysting place. "Yes, it's been torn down," he says. "Not too long ago. Three, four years, maybe." He had watched its demolition on the evening news telecast. His wife, Kathryn, was sitting across the room, on the antique chair with the needlepoint seat, her bare feet resting on its matching footstool. He stole a glance in her direction. Their old cat Bonkers, since deceased, was sprawled down the length of her jeans-clad thigh. Kathryn, oblivious to the TV, was holding an open paperback in one hand and scratching the cat with the other. It occurs to him, now, as he strolls along with Ellie, that he hasn't seen a dress on Kathryn in years, and that includes her nurses's whites: polyester tunics and trousers.

Too soon they have reached Ellie's car. Wes knows she is going to kiss him goodbye, and she does . . . on the cheek. He finds it curious and vaguely disappointing that the touch of her lips is not unsettling. The last time she kissed him goodbye, he wept.

It is not his habit to work past noon, but when Ellie departs, Wes returns to his office. He leans back in his comfortable leather chair and hoists his feet up on the desk, the way he used to do, when he was younger. And suaver.

Wes sighs. Loneliness suddenly grips him, like a cramp in his heart. He would love to be able to tell someone about this day. About the way Ellie looked. How she hinted that a cinder of his former charm glimmers yet, if only faintly. The telling, however, would require an empathetic listener, a confidant possessed of sensitivity and insight. Ordinarily, that would be Kathryn.

Encapsulated in his soundless, dustless tower, Wesley Byrne stares out his office window at a familiar battalion of buildings, the heads and shoulders of the city, standing stiffly at attention, like the pipes of a silent calliope.

About the Author:

Maureen Hossbacher is the author of the poetry chapbook Lesser Known Saints (Finishing Line Press). Her fiction is included in The Next Parish Over: A Collection of Irish American Writing (New Rivers Press). She holds an MFA in Creative Writing from City College of New York and taught writing as an Adjunct Lecturer in the CUNY system for 20 years, primarily at Hunter College. Retired from teaching, she's now at work on a novel. A member of Irish American Writers & Artists, Inc., she participates in the organization's twice monthly salons in NYC, reading her poetry and fiction and occasionally hosting.

THE NIGHT MAINTENANCE MAN

by John Tavares

Occasionally, when she felt lonely and depressed on graveyard shifts at the hospital, June had late night trysts with the night maintenance man in her locked broom closet and cleaning supplies room, which was surprisingly spacious. Amidst shelves with rolls of paper towel and toilet paper, rags, scrub pads, spray bottles, brooms, and mops, near the emergency department fire exits, she found surprising gratification in orally pleasuring the night maintenance man. His kisses, caresses, and hugs she found affirming, a relief. Divorced, in his early sixties, a recovering alcoholic, curious about her relationship with Wayne, the night maintenance man also asked her about Doctor Spirit, for whom he sometimes did handyman jobs at her three-bedroom house near the hospital.

Meanwhile, Wayne worried about June being friends with Doctor Spirit. He didn't want his girlfriend socializing and partying with Doctor June, or plain hanging around the family physician. Doctor Spirit earned a shitload of money and had too many hoity-toity, high net worth friends for his liking.

"High net worth?" June demanded, with a sense of outrage and indignity. "What is that supposed to mean?" June protested she earned a union wage, making more in hourly wages than some community college or university graduates she knew earned and had plenty of perks and benefits, like prescription drug coverage, sick days, and extra vacation time. Wayne, though, constantly reminded June she was just a high school dropout and a lowly cleaner in the regional hospital in Beaverbrook.

Wayne was on disability; he suffered a cardiac condition, a congenital heart defect, and angina pectoris whenever he strenuously exerted himself physically, at work or during exercise or even recreation, sometimes even when he was eating a heavy meal or sleeping restlessly. When a bout of angina struck, he sometimes feared he was having a heart attack and panicked. Since Wayne came from a German immigrant family of workaholics, his heart condition and chest pains didn't stop him from taking odd jobs, or occasional handyman work with the night maintenance man, which didn't involve considerable physical exertion, as a taxi dispatcher, a store clerk, or even a ward clerk at the hospital, renowned as a centre for rural medicine. At times, he even helped the night maintenance man when the hospital supervisor, who didn't need to worry about the two difficult personalities getting along, summoned him for a casual shift.

Invariably, though, a pattern established itself where he became frustrated with a problem at work or more likely flabbergasted at a person, a co-worker, customer, or, worse yet, a supervisor. Subsequently, he lost his temper, had a huge outburst of anger, or a massive outburst of bile or argumentation and verbal abuse. Immediately afterwards, he apologized and tried to make amends, but it was usually too late, since he frightened and scared co-workers, so he was forced to return to disability insurance, either because he aggravated his heart condition or suffered a full-fledged attack of angina, bordering on a heart attack. Usually, one of his angina attacks, with its abrupt chest pains, sweats, and dramatic display of symptoms, was enough to disturb and frighten co-workers in and of itself. Consequently, supervisors or bosses were likely not to call him back to work; he was on probation, a temporary worker, or working casual, and workplace bosses in Beaverbrook were renowned for their conservative attitudes and work ethics and simply didn't like to take chances. Still, June ignored his advice and exhortations.

June continued to spent time around Doctor Spirit because they had such a good time together, dancing, drinking, partying, shopping. June often didn't have enough money to shop for luxury and high-end brand names like Doctor Spirit, but she often bought her gifts because June made for such a trustworthy friend, something of a soulmate, and fun loving. Besides, even though June didn't use illicit drugs, and had to be persuaded to utilize prescription drugs when she was ill or in pain, she loved beer and rye, vodka, and gin. She knew where to draw the line, but she also knew, through friends or friends of friends, where to score some pot or even coke, which Doctor Spirit liked when she was stressed or needed to smoke or snort some stuff or do a few lines.

June especially liked and admired Doctor Spirit's collection of jewellery. Wayne leaned back in Doctor June's comfortable reclining chair, in front of her massive high definition wide screen television, watching reruns of a crime drama series from her collection of DVDs. Meanwhile, June dusted, swept, and cleaned Doctor Spirit's home, one of three houses she owned: in Winnipeg, where she was born and raised; Thunder Bay, where she attended medical school; Beaverbrook, where she wanted to practice medicine for the rest of her career. Doctor Spirit herself was working at a nursing station and clinic up north, treating indigenous patients at an Oji-Cree reserve of Tea Lake and the Cree reserve of Tobacco House. Wayne didn't understand how Doctor Spirit could have such an eclectic and expensive collection of aboriginal art and artifacts and jewellery, especially living in a town with such a high crime rate. In fact, although Beaverbrook didn't make any lists of violent cities, because of the rural municipality's relatively small size, Wayne, who grew up in Southern Ontario county renowned for its Mennonite

community, thought with all the murder, assaults, and sex offenses, Beaverbrook had to be the most violent small town in the province.

Still, June told her Doctor Spirit kept her large jewellery collection as a long-term investment. June especially admired her beautiful large pearl necklace. Around the time June complained she couldn't survive the long winter and chilly spring of Northwestern Ontario in general and Beaverbrook in particular and would succumb to cabin fever, and longed for a cheap beaches vacation in Cuba, she received an invitation to her niece's wedding in Winnipeg. Determined to go all out, loosen her inhibitions, in attending the wedding, June bought an expensive tailored gown, designer shoes, and high-end brand name lingerie. She almost maxed out on her credit cards. Wayne kept shaking his head and gruffly exhaling; he didn't even want to join her in attending her niece's wedding; she was making such a humungous deal out of the occasion, blowing the event out of proportion, trying to present an image of herself manufactured, artificial, fictitious. Wayne thought nobody looked better than June and liked to brag she was built better than a brick outhouse, but he also thought she dressed down better than anybody and still looked hot. With her curvy figure and cleavage, she could get away with wearing the same tank top and pair of faded blue jeans for a more than a week without anyone noticing.

Wayne wanted June to take Doctor Spirit to the wedding, but June, consuming a few beer and shots of vodka, became defensive and argued and fought with him, insisted he accompany her. June didn't want to give people, friends, and relatives the impression she was a lesbian, if she brought Doctor Spirit.

"I thought you told me Doctor Spirit wasn't a lesbian."

June was also very defensive about her relationship with Doctor Spirit and was adamant and insistent and argumentative Doctor Spirit wasn't a lesbian. Doctor Spirit liked to smoke pot and do a few lines of coke the odd time, when she was stressed or needed energy to party, but "she isn't a lesbian."

Despite Wayne's insistence June invite Doctor Spirit, June, who eschewed unconventionality, insisted it was proper and normal if she went with her boyfriend. Seeing how June admired her clothes and wardrobe, and how they were virtually the same size and measurements, Doctor Spirit asked her if there were any clothes or fashion items she wanted to borrow. June was so relieved she asked if she could borrow her necklace of gleaming satiny pearls, strung together with a gold braid.

"That's all?" Doctor Spirit asked.

"Yes," June said, surprised that Doctor Spirit didn't express any concern or reservation.

"Done deal."

Worried and concerned, Wayne asked, "How much does a string of pearls like that cost?"

"Probably about a hundred and fifty thousand dollars."

Wayne gasped. "Leave it alone, June; they're too expensive."

But June donned the luxurious string of pearls, shimmering, gleaming, and felt like magic. Wearing the string of pearls, she felt like an entirely different woman, like the chief executive officer of the hospital, for which she worked as a cleaner for the past two decades, or like the mayor of Beaverbrook. Even though Wayne thought the pearl necklace was loud and ostentatious, even a bit gaudy, for a wedding, he did admire the transformation that took place in June; for a change, she wasn't grimacing, grinding her molars, and her brow wasn't wrinkled with worry or concern. She wasn't fretting and preoccupied with worries about the hospital, workplace politics, arguments and personality conflicts with co-workers and crew bosses, and, best of all, she wasn't obsessed with money, and making certain all the bills were paid and on time, and actually, preferably ahead of time. Still, he almost thought it was the height of folly wearing such ostentatious pearls like that to a wedding.

In his judgement, it was a mistake for her to wear the pearls to the wedding. He thought this belief was confirmed when he noticed what a big distraction the pearls were at the wedding, diverting the attention of well-wishers and attendees, when wedding guests should have been directing their gaze and compliments towards the bride and groom. Now Wayne started to worry.

Meanwhile, anxious about his appearance and dress, worried about the way he looked, Spirit forced Wayne to follow her advice and made an appointment with him with her hairstylist to have his long, scraggly hair, which was greying and whitening, styled and his beard trimmed. Wayne usually avoided the barber or hairstylist because he occasionally suffered a distressing and seemingly unprovoked attack of angina in the chair. When they finally drove to the Winnipeg in her beat up pickup truck, Wayne thought it ironic. Even though they were dressed elaborately and ornately, very formally, particularly for residents of Beaverbrook, they stayed at the cheapest accommodations they could find in the west end of Winnipeg. They roomed at a grungy motel at the far end of broad, wide Portage Avenue, near a strip joint, a porn shop, a used bookstore, and airport motels, where jetliners and aircraft constantly flew overhead to take-off and land at Winnipeg International Airport. Earlier, while they rode in her four-wheel drive truck along the TransCanada highway, he took several photographs of the pearls with his cellphone. The wedding was a stupendous success, from everybody's perspective, although Wayne was annoyed at how June seemed to upstage everybody with her gown and particularly the string of pearls. Wayne became annoyed with all the compliments about the pearls. He also annoyed June when he kept reminding her she couldn't really fess up to the true owner of the pearls.

Then there was a hostage-taking incident in the hotel, according to one group of guests. No, there was a fire in a washroom, according to another group of guests. To avoid bad publicity, since this was the second incident involving a customer with a firearm or bathroom fire caused by a discarded cigarette butt in two months, hotel customers were moved by a shuttle bus to a more comfortable and luxurious hotel downtown, apparently owned and managed by the same hotel and motel chain.

Wayne and June couldn't return to sleep, though, because they started arguing. June insisted Wayne was jealous of her looks and appearance.

"No, June, I admit it, you're a sexy looking woman. You have a pretty face and an attractive body. I don't know why you don't look after yourself better, because at home you're always wearing torn jeans and my denim and plaid shirts, which are way too big for you."

The couple continued to argue, as, looking as if they had attended a formal royal reception for the Prime Minister and Queen in the ballroom of the Fort Garry hotel, the couple went to a twenty-four hour coffee and doughnut shop near Portage and Main. When the argument still hadn't exhausted itself, they went to the restaurant for iced tea on the Esplanade Riel alongside the Provencher Bridge over the slow flowing muddy waters of the Red River. Then they walked downstairs and down a flight of escalators into the underground pedestrian concourse at Portage and Main.

June became nervous as, lost, they circled around and around in the underground concourse, through the brick corridors and passageways and steel and glass doors, up and down stairwells and escalators, backtracking, trying to find the exits at the northeast corner of Portage and Main, searching for a shortcut and the subterranean concourse entrance to their hotel. Shortly after midnight, there was a large group of indigenous youth lounging in the concourse, waiting for the last Winnipeg Transit bus, to take them to their homes near the railyards, taverns, pawnshops, service stations, used car dealers, and parking lots and big box stores in Transcona. Nervous in the summer city night, though, June didn't want to ask the group of indigenous youth for directions.

"Don't they have anything better to do than lounge and loiter? It always bothers me when I see those people hanging around in the doorway of the pool hall, video arcade, or liquor store in downtown Beaverbrook."

"Yes, June, we're so well to do, upper class," Wayne said, clucking, clicking his tongue.

When they arrived back at the hotel room, June noticed the pearl necklace was missing. In a panic, they backtracked, retraced their tracks and followed their footsteps, walking back along the route they took along the concourses, sidewalks, and streets of downtown Winnipeg. June thought one of the indigenous youth deftly snatched the pearl necklace, but Wayne thought she was the victim of her own biases. The youth didn't get near her, never mind the pearl necklace, and Wayne engaged in a friendly chat and conservation with them. They filed a police report with the Winnipeg Police department and attached a few photographs, detailed close-ups, monochromatic prints, of the pearl necklace, printed from the scanner and fax machine in the hotel lobby, which Wayne took with his smartphone.

June begged the police officers to treat the theft of the pearl necklace with the utmost discretion and secrecy. She provided them with detailed descriptions of the First Nations young men, with their tattoos, piercings, hoodies, bandannas, baggy jeans, high top sneakers, sweats, and steel toe boots. But Wayne argued with her and protested the accusations, saying they had no evidence the necklace was stolen, adding June was starting to sound racist saying the indigenous youth had taken the string of pearls. Willing to admit he didn't recall totally accurately, because, against doctor's orders, he drank several beer and whiskies at the wedding reception, he demanded what would teenagers want with gaudy pearls anyway? The underground concourse would have probably had closed circuit video surveillance evidence if anything untoward happened. They stayed an extra four days in Winnipeg, searching for the necklace, but the pearls didn't turn up anywhere they searched. June insisted on checking all the pawnshops, thrift shops, consignment stores, and jewellers in Winnipeg, along Main Street, and around the exchange districts, downtown, and especially near the casinos.

"I can't see anyone being so foolish as to take an expensive necklace to a pawnshop on Main Street, unless, unless—"

"Don't you dare say it. You're full of bull sometimes."

Wayne tagged along and followed her around the city in dismay and frustration. Then June realized she needed to return home for work as a cleaner at the hospital. By Wednesday, after walking endless miles in downtown Winnipeg and making countless pay phone calls, after visiting pawnshops and consignment shops along Main Street and Portage Avenue and around the Exchange District and the casinos for the necklace, she surrendered her intensive, tireless search. Wayne figured she was finally acting rationally about the loss, until she made the decision.

"I'll have to buy her a new string of pearls."

"You're crazy. How are you going to be able to afford pearls?"

"I'll borrow the money from the banks. I have a personal line of credit. I'll use my credit cards."

"Just wait. Why don't you simply come clean with Doctor Spirit? Tell her what a shitshow the weekend turned into after the wedding. She'll understand."

"Are you being sarcastic? She bought the jewellery for an investment."

"Then she must have insurance."

"No. I don't want to sacrifice our friendship."

Wayne tried to dissuade June and argued with her, telling her she was acting foolhardy, out of excessive pride. Still, June visited banks, payday loans offices, mortgage companies. After endless trips to bank branches, credit union offices, and mortgage and loan companies, following endless walks and hikes along Winnipeg streets, during which she broke the heel on her shoes and bought a new pair of walking shoes, June lined up and cobbled together financing for a new string of pearls. Wayne grudgingly accompanied her to the most expensive jewellery store in Winnipeg. He watched incredulously as she bought a pearl necklace identical to the one she thought was stolen from her. She borrowed to the maximum against her credit cards. Without consulting with Wayne, she borrowed to the limit on his credit card as well. The credit card charges led to a huge row and argument, during which June backhanded

him on the cheek, breaking his front tooth, which bothered him because he didn't like making trips to the dentist and he was proud of what good care he took of his full mouth of shiny, white teeth. Then, after a trip to several banks and credit unions, June took out a second mortgage on her home. She even got two different payday loans, at exorbitant rates of interest, from cash stores downtown, around Portage Avenue and Main Street. June shouted she considered herself an honorable woman and it was shameful and embarrassing if she didn't live up to her obligations.

"The clasp broke and you dropped the string of pearls without noticing," Wayne said. "That's my theory."

To replace the pearl necklace she was confident was stolen from her, June bought an identical looking pearl necklace from a jeweller, whose elegant hands moved like a magicians' beneath the bulletproof glass counter. June thought he wore the finest suit she ever saw on a man, and his luxuriant dark hair had a fashionable contemporary hairstyle, with a stripe of grey hair running from the back of his head to his forehead, which reminded her of the pattern on a skunk's fur coat, at the most expensive jeweller in Winnipeg. Wayne couldn't believe her actions or understand her willingness to assume the tremendous burden of debt and onerous interest payments, all for the sake of a pearl necklace. When they arrived home, June returned the pearl necklace without comment to Doctor Spirit, except for profuse expressions of gratitude.

Over the following months June took extra shifts at the hospital to help pay off the payday loans, the credit cards debt, the bank loans, the personal line of credit, and even the second mortgage. The credit statements that arrived in the mail each week boggled Wayne's mind. Then June sought additional work and started moonlighting at part-time jobs on weekends and during the evenings and late nights. She cleaned office buildings downtown and washed dishes after hours at restaurants. She dispatched taxis and drove taxi-cabs, school buses, chartered buses, and delivery motor vehicles. She took whatever extra part-time jobs she could find, aside from her job cleaning in the hospital, to pay off the loans and personal lines of credit and credit cards bills as quickly as possible. She no longer had time for the simple pleasures they both enjoyed. Previously, Wayne enjoyed taking a drive to Dryden to shop with June at the Walmart superstore and eating hamburgers at the A&W restaurant on Highway 17 and sundaes and milkshakes at the Dairy Queen in Dryden. He even enjoyed strolling along the boulevard and thoroughfare to Robin's Donuts or Tim Horton's in Beaverbrook for coffee and doughnuts, even though the walks occasionally left him gasping and short of breath and the doctor ordered him to drastically reduce caffeine, sweets, and high cholesterol food. His favorite activity with her was watching movies on television, videotape, or DVD, but now with the unending saga of paying for the lost pearls she possessed no free time to spend with him. She just worked. After he argued and quarrelled with her about the long hours she laboured and the fact they never spent time together, he lost his temper and exploded. She wound up calling the police. Later, even though she called the emergency police line, and was called to testify against him, she refused to take the stand in court against Wayne. She then described him to the crown prosecutor as her former boyfriend and long-time lover, the man she still hoped to formally make her husband. After he took anger management courses, the crown prosecutor agreed to drop the charges, even though June never intended to testify. He did feel personally betrayed when she called the police and that helped him decide.

He benefitted immensely from the personal coaching and counselling sessions. Still, he decided it would be best for them both if he moved out of her house, and went their separate ways. The day he moved she sobbed and cried and tried to restrain him add prevent him from leaving. When she continued to beg him to return and said she wanted to have his baby, Wayne thought,!, and her pleas fell on deaf ears. After moving out of her house, he found his own apartment in a small social housing complex, where he could read his paperback books, novels, and watch movies online in peace. Finally, Wayne started exercising regularly at the local gym, and managed to lose

plenty of weight. Eventually, the surgeon and cardiologist were convinced he would survive and he had open-heart surgery, including catheterization, a stent, and valve replacement. He even started jogging on the treadmill at the park and recreation department fitness centre. After he lost fifty pounds and took a course and passed an exam, he managed to find work as a security guard at the hospital.

He worked nights at the hospital. Since he worked the graveyard shift, he mainly stood behind the main desk at the entrance and spacious lobby of the hospital, checked personal and corporate identification, and signed in guests. June often dropped by after hours, after her own late afternoon and night shifts and between part-time jobs, to visit him. She begged him to return, to come back into her life, since she nurtured the dream of getting married to him, in an official ceremony, even if it was merely a justice of the peace or another municipal official at the town hall.

Several years after she lost the pearl necklace, she had only a few thousand dollars left on the "pearl" loans and second mortgage to pay off. She looked haggard and tired, dressed in loose worn, ripped work clothes, whereas in the past she liked to wear tight clothes, form fitting boldly colored uniforms, which accentuated and flattered her figure, now thin and bony. She let her once well-tended wardrobe go ragged and hardly washed now, except when a supervisor warned her about her appearance, her scraggly hair, or body odour.

Months and years of long hours, endless workdays, and hard labour to pay off loan payments and high interest wore June down. She no longer possessed the leisure time to party—never mind socialize—with Doctor Spirit. One night Doctor Spirit was invited to a presentation and dinner in the boardroom of the hospital to listen to a speech delivered by the premier of the province of Ontario and the Beaverbrook regional hospital CEO. Meanwhile, June chatted with him at the front desk when Doctor Spirit arrived. In fact, Doctor Spirit kept walking back and forth between the boardroom, in the administrative section of the offices, and the intensive care unit because she was literally caring for a patient. She feared this patient to whom she had gotten close might be dying.

June joked: "You're not wearing your pearl necklace tonight."

"Of course, not," Doctor Spirit snapped. June gazed at Wayne: neither ever observed Doctor Spirit grow impatient or short-tempered or snap before so they both barely contained their surprise. Tired, carrying her high heels and stethoscope in her hands, Doctor Spirit replied, "Those pearls were fake. These so-called pearls are made from cheap synthetic glass. The premier would see these pearls are fake. Anyway, they were a gift from my former boyfriend, who was a stalker and domestic abuser and a con man." Neither June or Wayne, neither of whom had ever seen Doctor Spirit look so bitter, could believe their senses. "I only keep those fake pearls as a reminder of how evil and phony and what great con men can be. The man who gave me those fake pearls was a jeweller in Winnipeg. He had the most beautiful hands, which always wore fancy, sparkling, expensive-looking jewellery. He looked like a male model, except he had this

thick dark hair with a grey pattern like a skunk pelt. He kept telling me pearls are timeless, immortal—they'll be your legacy to your niece and nephews. When I had this so-called pearl necklace appraised and authenticated by virtually every authority on pearls I could find in Toronto, though, every last one of them assured me, along with the jewellers I saw in Montreal, they were genuine fakes, not worth more than a few hundred dollars. They're made from some cheap synthetic glass or material—but the ex kept trying to reassure me they were genuine, timeless pearls from Tahiti, or some South Seas islands. From the way he talked, you'd think pearls were the ticket to an afterlife."

Wayne sputtered on his takeout coffee. Doctor June, worried Wayne was asphyxiating, tried to ascertain if he was choking, but he assured her he was all right. He assured her he never felt better, but June looked stunned.

"After Doctor Spirit left, they argued, oblivious to the occasional visitors, patients, and medical staff. Wayne insisted she tell Doctor Spirit precisely what happened and request the return

of the genuine pearls. June wearily no longer even regarded as a friend but more as a workplace acquaintance and superior. The night maintenance man, at the other end of the spacious lobby, working on a faulty air conditioning and air filtration unit, incredulously eavesdropped on the lively argument, as they rehashed the whole history of the pearls.

Then Doctor Spirit's pearls went missing. Relieved of the burden, she mentioned the loss, jokingly, in passing reference to June, who tiredly mopped the women's washroom and scrubbed the toilets. June couldn't believe how cavalier Doctor Spirit was about having her house broken into and the pearls stolen, even if she believed they were fake. June couldn't contain her anger or control herself and blamed Wayne. But the night maintenance man, who overheard the contretemps between Wayne and June, still sometimes did odd jobs for Doctor Spirit. He fixed the plumbing in her bathroom several months earlier and knew where she kept a spare house key. Doctor Spirit suspected it might have been the dog walker, because she left the door unlocked for her, but she didn't care either way and thought, goodbye and good riddance. The night maintenance man left the pearls in the bottom of a tacklebox in his unheated garage. He forgot about the necklace, since he had absolutely no use for a jewellery and had no idea how to sell or fence them and unlock their value. Several month afterwards, when the night maintenance man left his trailer and boat parked at the boat launch, a teenage angler stole his tacklebox. He kept the tackle and tacklebox, and from the boat launch tossed what he considered a bizarre discovery of costume jewellery into the lake. Although June was hoping to marry him officially, after she originally tried to blame him and insisted he return the pearls to their rightful owner, Wayne ended up refusing to speak with her again.

About the Author:

Born and raised in Sioux Lookout, Ontario, **John Tavares** is the son of Portuguese immigrants from the Azores. His education includes graduation from 2-year GAS at Humber College in Etobicoke with concentration in psychology (1993), 3-year journalism at Centennial College in East York (1996), and the Specialized Honors BA in English from York University in North York (2012). His writings have been published in various magazines and literary journals. Set of his short stories has been broadcasted at the Sioux Lookout's CBLS/CBQW radio.

THE FOX AND ITS CATCHER

by J.R. Night

Oh, he would get him today. Months had passed, and he had maintained this charade long enough. All students were required to eat their lunch in the cafeteria. But, no, not this student, this particular student thought he was above it all. The school security guard would sometimes catch a glimpse of him here and there: the flash of grey faded sneakers before they pivoted into the next hall; the whipping of a backpack before it vanished into the boy's restroom; and a locker slam before the disappearing flight up the staircase. Each time at lunch, without fail, the student evaded him.

But not today. Today, he had crafted, what he thought, was a rather clever and well-thought-out plan. He reflected on how the only times he would ever capture an immobile image of this creature was when on hall duty. He would see him sitting in the back of the classroom, slumped low, arms tied across his chest, just simply radiating trouble.

So, today, he decided he would stand outside his class, wait until the bell rang, and then guide this little rule-breaker right to the cafeteria to eat just like everybody else. That was his self-proclaimed brilliant master plot.

At half past eleven, the hall flooded with students. Be it luck or the mystical accuracy that comes with focus, the security guard distinguished the rabble-rouser's black hair in an instant. The slippery animal was moving much swifter than the rest, zigzagging through the crowd with an expert ease. The guard set off, attempting to echo the student's trajectory, but failing to match the fluidity in which he did it. As the rest of the students drained the hall and cleared his line of sight, the guard felt his

heart sink when he saw the student several feet away turning a corner into the hallway that lead to staircases.

The guard dropped his shoulders, crestfallen. The student would no doubt fly downstairs since the upward one was closed off because of water damage. Once there, he would be downright untraceable in the maze that made the basement floor.

It was during this thought process that the guard paused, his eyes bulging. His spirits suddenly soared as he bolted at an electric speed. The student had been in class when the janitor was closing off the staircase; He would not know it was closed until he made it all the way up and would then be forced to make the journey back downstairs, costing him a decent chunk of seconds. Seconds that the desperate guard now hoped to fill.

He took a chance, and plunging to the nearest downwards staircase, he begged lady luck to let him meet the student. In a matter of seconds, the guard arrived. And there the boy was, frozen, startled for a second, but not wholly surprised.

"What are you doing here?" said the guard. His eyes twinkled with an air that could only be called tunnel vision.

"Nothing," said the student.

"The cafeteria is the other way, son," said the guard.

"Okay, thanks. I'll head there."

"How about I help you get there since you seem to be lost already."

The student's mouth shut a little, tightened, and then he said, "Okay."

The guard was delighted.

As they walked up back toward the cafeteria, the student said nothing. He opened the door and let the student in. He closed it, capturing him, the fox at last inside its cage. He gawked through the small window of the door to watch his wonderful prize. He turned away and threw a fist into the air, grinning for all he was worth.

He wanted to give one last look at his victory before he went on with his job, wanted the glorious sight of him sitting there. He pressed his stubby nose to the window and his smile fell.

He abandoned the door and went careering down the hallway at the side of the cafeteria. He shouted right when the boy was closing the back door of the cafeteria.

"What are you doing? Get back in there!" thundered the guard, all patience within him gone. "I've had enough. We're going to get in line, you're going to get your food, and you're going to sit down until – the – bell — rings. Got it?"

The boy said nothing, continued to say nothing when they got in line, and picked nothing to add onto his plastic tray. The guard, fed up, began to stack items on his tray: an apple, some tater tots, and a box of chocolate milk.

The boy mumbled something.

"What?" said the guard.

"I haven't got any money."

They had reached the cashier. The guard looked down at the boy and saw for the first time the red that marred his complexion.

Flustered himself, he told Paloma, the register lady, he would pay her back. The student seized the tray as though it were an extra limb he did not know what to do with.

As they left the food counters, the guard, his voice several decibels lower, said, "Okay…go on and sit with your friends."

"I don't have anyone to sit with," said the student, still holding his stiff limb.

The fox and its catcher locked eyes for a long moment.

No words passed between them. In the next seconds, the red tray exchanged hands and the boy fled for the backdoor, and while the guard followed him out into the hall, he did not pursue him any farther. Instead, he watched his prey, with his grey faded sneakers and frayed backpack, dash down the hall, and turning at the end of the corner, he vanished from sight.

About the Author:

J.R. Night is a recent graduate from The University of Maryland with a degree in English Language & Literature. You can find more of his work at The Dime Show Review, The Drabble, and The Ogilvie.

SECOND SIGHT

by Katherine Steblen

"Kids are back," said Jerry, wiping gummy residue from his eyes. Leaves were mashed against his face from where he'd passed out the night before in a whiskey haze, marks of stems tattooed across his ruddy cheeks. "Ross, the kids!" he repeated louder, pushing the reclined figure next to him, his street-buddy wrapped up in a blanket.

Ross rolled over and looked up into a pleasing silhouette, backlit by the morning sun—an hourglass shape of a girl. For three days in a row she'd shown up at Buena Vista Park, bringing sandwiches. She was accompanied by a couple of other kids who looked to be her age, each of them wading through the humped forms of sleeping men, rousing them and offering food. Ross guessed she was in her late teens, early twenties.

The girl towered above him, dangling a brown paper bag aloft.

"Breakfast?" she asked, swinging the bag to and fro, a starburst in her blue eyes. She made a pretty picture with her lovely wide mouth and cascade of beige freckles across her nose. A doll of a girl, thought Ross, someone he imagined had a pretty name like "Rosie."

"Lay it on me," he said, his voice sounding like gravel shaken-up in a can.

He was a big man. Most days he woke up with a storm of hunger thundering across his belly. A chef by trade, he was used to three squares a day and then some, but after several months of living in the park, his robust girth shrank. He still appeared big, but his belly was now concave.

"Much obliged," said Ross, tipping an imaginary hat. He looked at the shining face of his benefactor. She appeared pleased, almost grateful, to have him accept the bag. He smiled broadly in a show of large teeth, yellowed at the edges. He hurriedly opened the bag and wolfed down everything inside it—a sandwich of peanut butter and jelly spread thick on grainy bread, a shiny apple, and a bag of Cheeto's. There was even a tiny bottle of vodka, the kind people drank on airplanes to take the edge off. Ross took a sip, hiding the rest for later.

In a dainty gesture, the girl scooped her gauzy skirt around herself and sat down. Ross knew she expected conversation in exchange for the food. He didn't mind; he missed the company of women. Maybe she was doing research on the homeless in San Francisco. There'd been others coming around asking questions, but none of them brought food and they weren't worth his time. Rosie was different somehow—not here as a voyeur, it didn't seem so; she looked him straight in the eyes.

When she'd first strolled into their midst, Ross felt a flicker of protective caution. It's not the old men he feared might hurt her, but the younger ones, like Jupiter. Most of those boys were sleeping it off in the am. but sometimes Jupiter was still tweaking. No amount of liquor quelled his craziness, spouting random phrases that sounded like hammers striking metal. Ross heard one of the research-kids call it "word-salad." Jupiter looked wild sometimes, his pupils expanding to fill his eyes so that the blue looked black. Ross knew to be alert when Jupiter's eyes become a solar eclipse. He'd growl at

Ross, The fuck they want with me? He said it even when no one else was around, only the two of them under a tree, sharing a joint.

Ross guessed that people thought all the homeless were like Jupiter, but it wasn't like that. Some just had a bad turn and no place else to go.

"How long you been living outdoors?" asked the girl.

Ross laughed. "You mean homeless? How long I been homeless? It's okay to say it." He tapped his chest. "Home's in here now. I got tossed off that gerbil wheel with no regrets. Should'a jumped off long ago."

"What'd you do before... this?" She gestured to the demolished blankets and battered duffle bags, empty bottles and paper wrappers scattered in disarray.

Ross leveled his gaze and thrust his neck forward so that his face nearly touched her nose. She didn't flinch. "I was a bum!" he said, emphasizing the last word. His eyebrows looked unruly, with sprouts of white curling this way and that. Once he'd been vain enough to pluck those long hairs, but now he let them be. All of his features were large—his eyes, his mouth, his nose.

The girl laughed uncomfortably, shook her head and squinted at him. "Aren't you a bum now? Don't you think that sleeping outside makes people think you're a bum? That's sort-of the definition of one, isn't it?"

Ross clarified: "I don't mean that kind of a bum, sleeping on the ground and what not. I mean I was an asshole to people, a complete asshole." He hadn't expected to be living outdoors, but the motorcycle accident had left his right arm paralyzed. He could no longer slice, chop, or dice; could no longer smack people in the head, or play pool; couldn't make a living doing what he knew how to do. "I once thought the world owed me something. If it wasn't handed to me, I'd steal it; screwed friends over and didn't give a shit; fucked women I didn't care about; busted-up faces in bars after too many shots of Tequila." He exhaled loudly, as if in regret, or maybe just tired after stringing so many words together first thing in the morning.

The girl nodded. "What'd it feel like?" she asked.

"What'd you mean?" said Ross.

"What'd what feel like? Busting heads?"

"No, I mean, what'd it feel like to be a bum, on the inside? I heard you say what it looks like, but what'd it feel like?"

Ross sat back. No one had ever asked him a question like that before. He took a deep breath. "I once found an old can of Planter's Peanuts. You ever see their logo—spiffy dude in a top hat, holding a cane? That was me—good looking, buff, drove a Harley, always had cash, a big roll of it; pissed it away every weekend. Anyways, I opened that can of nuts ready to cram a handful into my mouth and the thing was crawling with worms; I mean cocoons, moths hatching out, just everything alive in there; all that shit living down in the dark. That was me, on the inside." He looked at Rosie's slender leg, imagined running his sandpaper palm up the inside of her pale thigh; but no, he wouldn't let himself do that to Rosie.

"I feel that way too," she said. "Like people see me all sparkly but there's nothing in here but shadows." She put her hand to her chest.

"How can that be, darling?" laughed Ross. "Shadows? What'd you ever do to anybody?"

"I don't know." She drew her knees up and wove her arms in a loop around her legs. "I just feel that way all the time." Her voice caught raspy, mid-sentence.

"Look at what you do for people. I'd 'a woke up hungry if it weren't for you," said Ross. "Why you bringing us food? You're good to do it."

"I do it," she said, "to feel worthy."

"Worthy?" Ross pulled a rubber band off his wrist and tied back his long hair into a ponytail. He'd adjusted to using only one hand for everything and was about as proud of that as he'd been about anything he'd mastered his whole life. His hair used to be a deep chestnut brown, but after the wreck, his head was shaved and it had grown back in slate-gray. He remembered the vanity of it, combing out that thick mane in front of the mirror each day. Now he couldn't remember the last time he'd seen his own reflection. "Why you don't feel worthy, girl?" he asked, looking her way, seeing how she seemed to shrink into herself.

The girl shrugged her shoulders despairingly. "I just, I guess—I don't know why." Her voice strangled, choking out the sentence. She turned to face him, looking startled, lost.

He longed to cradle her head against his chest but knew enough not to touch a girl like Rosie. He hoped she'd grow up lucky enough to have men know when not to touch her. He tried to make his voice into an embrace, to hug her with words, but all that came out was, "Yeah, yup, it's okay; you're okay, honey."

A silence settled over them. Ross tried again. "You know, I think some folks just come out feeling like they're not good enough. They spend their lives trying to resurrect themselves when, all along, they're the good ones; the best ones, really. Other folks come out and strut around like cocky roosters, but they ain't worth shit. You care about people, Rosie."

She startled at the name that wasn't hers, but didn't correct him. Maybe he thought she was someone else, a girl from his past, somebody better than the person she felt herself to be. She liked the name; the way it rolled out on his tongue, rich and round-- it made her feel beloved.

Ross went on: "What's life anyway, than just our thoughts strung together 'til the day we die? I knew guys who had it all: money, families, houses, and they were all a bunch of sorry-ass sons of bitches, always moaning about something. I was the same way." He thought about how things had been for him. Who the hell did he think he was at 49 years old, swooping around those loopy turns on highway one? What pissed him off that night and every night before it? He'd been saying F-you to life for years, daring it to take him, then finally his bike careened out of control. He was lucky to be alive, and now, living hand to mouth, he was more content than in those restless, bile-fueled

days when he'd had rolls of cash. How could that be? How could sleeping out here on the ground be better? He used to smolder, remembering a bunch of shitty things threaded together by a strand of "what ifs"—what if he'd stayed in school? What if he'd never taken that first drink? What if his old man hadn't been such a flaming asshole? Now his thoughts were strung together like white lights. He wanted Rosie to feel like she mattered. In the old days, he'd have run his hands up and down her body like mallets tenderizing a slab of meat. But it wasn't like that now—he saw people in new ways, he listened to them; he belonged to a community; they helped each other. He remembered when Gerry stole a roll of hotdogs and Robby snatched a hibachi from someone's back porch, and they'd had an impromptu cookout. Everyday brought new gifts. He was grateful for warm nights, sweatshirts, and food; nothing was taken for granted.

His head began to ache, the gnawing for nicotine starting to grind. He looked around for butts on the ground but found none.

"You wouldn't have a cigarette on you, dear, would you?" asked Ross, half-joking. To his surprise, Rosie produced a pack from somewhere inside her embroidered bag. She lit one for him, and then one for herself, tiny brown sticks that smelled like cloves. They sat for a while, puffing companionably, neither one needing to speak.

"Rosie, look over there," said Ross in a hushed, reverent tone. He pointed to a tree about twenty feet away. "Look! It's moving. See all the life going on in that tree?"

"Yeah, uh-huh," she murmured. Ross saw her expression and laughed out loud. She was humoring him. He realized he sounded like Jupiter, hallucinating.

"No. Look closer, Rosie. See it?"

She squinted at the tree, reaching into her bag for a pair of glasses. Without them, she was practically blind, couldn't see further than five feet in front of her. He was right, the tree was moving! Butterflies and bees lit on peach-colored blossoms. Dozens of humming birds zipped and hovered among the branches, so rapidly they were hard to see unless someone stood there for awhile, looking. How could she have passed by this spot so often and never noticed?

They stared at the tree and the birds, feeling the sun's heat edged with the coolness of a breeze, letting the day's gifts wash over them.

About the Author:

Katherine Steblen is a mother, artist and counselor who has always been interested in learning about people's lives. Writing fiction has been a way to explore the many facets of the human psyche. Kathy's work has been published in "Everyday Fiction," and "100 Word Story."

BAD DAYS COME IN DOZENS

by Gabriel Sage

I've always gotten lost or mistaken directions. It's been happening as long as I can remember. My internal compass completely broken – a sundial at night. I was once traveling in Spain and found myself terribly adrift in the thick slices of the night, tragically lost somewhere between getting out of a cab, and getting into my little hostel room with the bunk beds, lime green walls and broken ceiling fans. Disoriented under the deep velvet sky, pushing through the dark air and red wine, I wandered into the only establishment that seemed open, and squeezed into the stool of another bar instead of cramming dormitory style into my room. Inevitably, I would have to ask for embarrassingly simple directions, but I would start with another glass of crimson red Spanish wine.

It arrived and without looking up, I swirled the sanguineous liquid in the glass, it spun like water in a drain and I thought of the communal shower in what would be, at this hour, an empty bathroom. I didn't have to check what time it was; it was too late to still be out with an early train to catch in the morning. I glanced around the bar to find that it was just that – a threadbare and simple room with a low, rectangular bar top obtruding up from the floor. The dimly lit interior matched that of the twilight just outside the door, and I was still caught in the curtain folds of misdirection.

Upside-down glasses lined small wooden shelves that were crudely secured to the walls, alongside a large dirty mirror framed in a once extravagant but now dilapidated silver frame. Besides the bar there were a few vacant tables pushed up against the far wall, a chalkboard with an illegibly hand written menu, and a girl

washing dishes with her hair in an effortless top knot and her aproned back towards me. When the dished had been cleaned, and eye contact received, my drunken attempt at getting directions garnered me an invitation to her flat just upstairs, very easy to find, with private bath and much better company.

I couldn't have realized it at the time, but while my misadventures in the wanderings of a directionless fool got me nowhere geographically, they seemed to take me everywhere in life. After all, was is being lost if not the precursor to being found? Plus, it was finding myself more misplaced in San Francisco than I should have been for a Bay Area native, that I met Samantha, and ultimately moved to Los Angeles where my destiny would outlast my doom.

While most of the kids in my high school spent their weekends driving up the coast to SF from Santa Cruz - hoping to get away with using fake ID's, smoke cigarettes far enough away for the smell to dissipate before returning home, or find any general and questionable things to do – I was in a pool, swimming head first into the cerulean chlorine water, competing in swim meets. I suppose that's what made SFU appealing to begin with. While my graduating class set off to see new cities, for me, San Francisco still felt big and bright, teeming with possibility.

So when I eventually moved there and started school, my inherent lack of direction, coupled with my deprivation of even the slightest familiarity in my surroundings, left me more turned around than usual.

The day I met Sam I became her boyfriend within a matter of seconds, and it had nothing to do with love at first sight.

It was my second week in school and I was attempting to make my way back to campus when I turned a corner I thought would lead to me to the Muni train station, but instead just opened up to another narrow street lined with jewelry stores. I walked in the unfamiliar landscape until I looked up at a brick building covered in chipped black paint interrupted by a large glass window tenuously holding on to old rotted wooden molding with weathered red paint. The exposed interior revealed a jewelry store gleaming with silver. Above the door, in brick letters, a sign read, The Rock N Roll Circus. Inexplicably intrigued I decided to enter, and at the very least ask for directions.

The inside was much larger than I had anticipated from the small storefront, and glass display cases lined the walls and divided the floor space so as the sun hit the front window, light streamed in and reflected every surface. Bright white and amber splashes gleamed from ceiling to floor in between the occasional rainbow refracting on the wall. The surreal shimmer flickered through the store's interior, and just as my eyes began adjusting to the dancing light, I made out the sound of angry voices bursting from what seemed like a back office. I took a step closer but walked directly into the sharp edge of blinding sun, unable to make out the source of the voices. In a flash of light, the door flew open, cracking violently against the wall, and a girl about my age stormed out, as pretty as she was angry, followed by a terribly gross middle aged guy dressed in nineties rock attire with aggressively thinning and unfortunately long hair.

"It is true and you're mad and that's why you're acting like a kid!" She was loud for such a small and cute girl, and with her hands in fists raised above her head she brought them down by her sides and leaned into it, using the momentum to launch her words at the creep. "You know what? I'm honestly done. I don't need this!"

He immediately fired back, "Are you kidding me Sam? Who even cares? You wanted it the whole time." He reached down and grabbed at his package through uncomfortably tight leather pants. "Please, do me the favor and leave."

He used his free hand to point at the door and it was there, in the middle of the shop and at the end of his heavily jeweled finger that they found me. The moment lingered, caught between the rays of light, then dissipated into a sticky awkwardness before quickly turning tense.

"Is this fucking him?" the creep asked, still holding his package, biting through the silence. She had been staring straight through me for the entire duress of this uncomfortable ménage. Her eyes played hopscotch from me to him, and then back again before she said, "Yep. Here he is."

"What?" and a blank stare is all I managed before she crossed the room, took my hand in hers and kissed me on the cheek.

"Meet my boyfriend. Here to pick me up from this shit hole," she said, already pulling me towards the door.

"Wait, I- what?" again I tried but failed, rendered speechless from confusion.

We were practically out the door when she abruptly stopped, flipped up the bird, fired off one more round of insults directed the old man's libido, and said good-bye to The Rock N Roll Circus; we were on the street before he had a chance to reply.

We walked almost a half a block in silence still holding hands, both seemingly stunned when I finally stopped us, "So, uh, what the hell just happened?"

"Oh my god, I am so sorry, but thank you for saving me, you're kind of my hero now. That asshole thinks he can do whatever he wants but fuck him!" she stood on her toes and yelled the last part back down the block with a strange contorted grin. "It's just I've been working there almost two years and he- so many times I wanted- ugh, it's a really long story."

"No offense," I offered, "but it seems like the story of some strange sexual scandal with that old guy back there."

I probably shouldn't have been so bold judging by her reaction. She made a face that I at the time read, you think I would hook up with a creep like that, but years later I would learn really meant, I may have given him a few blow jobs but I'm definitely not telling you about it. I tried to backpedal, "Look sorry, I don't know what I'm talking about. Just trying to lighten up... whatever that just was. I'll tell you what; we can go back there in the middle of the night and rob that place blind. I've always wanted to be in a jewelry heist. You'll drive the van."

Her smile returned and she laughed. "It would be easy. I know the alarm codes."

"There we go. Look at that. I've become your boyfriend and partner in crime and I'm not sure I even know your name. I'm Elliott by the way." I reached my hand out to exaggerate the ignored formalities.

"Nice to meet you, Elliott. I'm Samantha." She took my hand and gave it one large cartoonish shake. It jingled and I noticed her fingers and wrist covered in silver jewelry.

"So, since we've become so close already maybe you can do me a favor? I'm trying to get to back to campus and I'm not sure where the train is. You want to point me in the right direction?"

She looked me over and giggled, "College boy, huh? I'll tell you what; I'm parked just up the street and heading to my girlfriend's house for a party in Park Merced. Why don't you come with? I definitely owe you a drink, and after I'll give you a ride back to campus?"

"Definitely," I replied probably too quickly and eager. I took a half step and offered her my elbow.

I didn't make it back to campus for two days. I had boarded the Samantha City party-train; a one way trip to the world of nightlife, narcotics, and name brand fashion with a quick stop for sex in semi-public places.

After I finished my first year I moved off campus and into Sam's apartment. It wasn't until a year after that when she moved to New York for modeling or molly-ing or whatever that I finally got off that party train. It was a wild ride and a crash-course on living you can't enroll in.

I went to just enough actual class to keep my grades from showing how much class I wasn't actually going to. The rest of the time we tore down the city. Sam took me to the front of all the lines at clubs in downtown and showed me the liquor store behind the gas station where an employee discreetly distributed party favors and contraband. From there I was lost only in her, never without direction again because we were together, and I had nowhere else I wanted to be, plus, she knew every corner of SF. We pushed her white VW Passat up and down every hill that twisted landscape of a city could throw at us. I usually drove while Sam rode shotgun acting as the joint rolling copilot. The last time I was in that car we were of course fighting, something had become an increasing relationship ritual.

"There's another place my friend's promoting at we should go to," she told me one night as we were supposed to be leaving a party heading home so I could get some sleep for a midterm in the morning. She didn't look up from her phone, a sign I knew all too well to mean she was ready to be met with intransigency.

So I gave it to her, "Aw come on. I got that test tomorrow. I need to go back and crash."

I knew you would say that. You never want to do anything fun," she had turned in her seat completely to face me, "Why do you even care about one test? You are always talking about how you don't even know what to do for a major next year, so it's not like it matters anyway. Especially when I take us to LA!"

She wasn't necessarily wrong about any of it. I was very much going through the motions of school at that point and fantasizing about moving down to Los Angeles with her was one of my frequent favorites. We spent many drug induced sleepless nights floating our own version of the modern American Dream back and forth across our pillows. Her with her modeling or blogging career that could finally flourish, and I - with my newly earned degree – indulging whatever entrepreneurial endeavor I was currently captivated with; our own sort of debaucherous F. Scott and Zelda Fitzgerald love affair.

We would pack up the car, just like in a song, and peel down the California Highway. Taking the scenic 1 and planning only on stopping to adopt a puppy en route until we were too stoned to drive and would end up pulling over to get ice cream and take the dog for its first walk. Eventually we would get to Hollywood or maybe Venice Beach and unpack our bags and then our lives into a small studio. We played each other countless reels of fantastic home videos projected from our imaginations with every alternate beginning and ending we could think of. There was an unadulterated freedom and optimistic excitement in the wide-open possibility. We found a liberty in the uncertainty that in our youthful exuberance we turned into dreams but would eventually fade into distant memories in old minds incarcerated by pragmatism.

Driving with Sam glaring at me felt like I was being blinded by the high beams from an on-coming semi-truck. So I spoke without turning my head, "Are you kidding me? What does that even mean, take us to LA? You're going to take us to LA? This isn't about us. You want to go and you expect me to follow you! It's all about you- it's always all about you."

"Noo," she said drawing out the word with just enough inflection to peel the skin from my bones, "I fucking love you, and that's why I'm going to take care of us and I just want you to have some fun and not worry so much."

"You're going to take care of us how? Just because you did a bunch blow in the bathroom back there does not make you the celebrity you think you are Samantha." She paused briefly so I darted my eyes from the road to meet her halogen stare, which had now been replaced with the wattage of something more like stadium floodlights.

"Well I'm more of a celebrity than you'll ever be," and with that she reached across the car and jerked up on the emergency brake quickly sending the Passat lurching and swerving. We violently passed from of our lane before fishtailing into a street lamp and crashing to a complete stop.

I've been in a car accident before – I was driving with my sister back from a trip to visit her girlfriend in Seattle and we got rear ended pretty hard by an older woman, clearly lost in the open space, and truly, she had an accident. This could hardly fit into that same category. This was an all-out kamikaze collision, and I had certainly never been in one of those.

"Are you crazy?" I sat frozen with disbelief, "I can't - I mean, who even does shit like this?"

I burst out of the car not bothering to close the door. And despite the dramatic and angry effect I was intending, I couldn't help turning just enough to look back and check if she was all right. I saw her taking off her seatbelt and sliding into the driver's seat as I moved on for what I told myself would be the last time, even if that meant becoming lost all over again, trying to walk from where ever we were, alone.

If our previous fights toyed with the fine line teetering between insanity and passion, we had finally broken the boundary. When I heard her start the car behind me I reinforced my decision to stay on foot, and keeping my head down, continued to walk. The car engine revved but I thought nothing of it. Hands pushed deep in my pockets against the October chill I waited for the car to speed past me, contemplating yelling something profane as it did - except that I would never get the chance. By the time I felt the vehicle encroaching and come up behind me, I was already being plowed over.

She drove straight into me- colliding with my left side and hurling me over the windshield and onto the crumbling pavement of the road. She hadn't built up enough speed to inflict real damage but when I struck the ground the air absconded from my lungs and I struggled to catch my breath against the overwhelming sharpness in my chest.

I honestly wasn't sure if she meant to hit me or if she just lost control in her anger; she was never phenomenal behind the wheel, but as I lay on the ground I hardly cared either way. The pavement was dense underneath me and I slid my vision from the dampening evening sky back to the road to see the car come abruptly to a halt fifteen feet from me and the reverse lights flicker. My initial thought was that she was coming back to finish me off, but as I sat up, the parking lights clicked on and the brake lights off and she stepped out of the car. I threw my hands in the air akimbo and shouted at both her and the night. She didn't react in the slightest. Usually, she is snapping her fingers and shifting her hips in the opposite direction of her head as her Puerto Rican sass crosses with her New York attitude, but now she just stood still, staring at me the same way she had the first time I met her. And just like that, she scurried back into the car and drove off without a word. I lay back down and laughed into the darkness. "I'm calling a cab."

Thirty-five minutes later, I was in the back of a yellow taxi and faced with the only question I truly couldn't answer, "Where you heading, brother?"

I thought about going back to the apartment like I had originally wanted, Sam never came back on nights we fought anyway, but it didn't feel right anymore. I should have gone home. I had a midterm in the morning. But ironically, I didn't care about the test at all anymore, and even if I went home at this point, I would be showing up to class tired and moderately hungover tomorrow - so why bother? I had unmade my bed and now I had nowhere to sleep. The city felt stale and I was too used to seeing things through the eyes of a girl. I had been broadsided in every sense and the façade of not caring was already beginning to crumble under the weight of my inauspicious thoughts. I could go to Park Merced, but prospecting for another party seemed like a halfhearted and threadbare mission at best. Plus, there was always the ostensible chance I would walk into a party Sam was already attending.

Yo man, you okay? No offense but you kinda look like you just got hit by a semi."

You have no idea."

"I hear that buddy. Bad days come in dozens. So where can I take you?"

I hadn't been in this city two years but there was no place I could go that wouldn't remind me of her. I thought about Santa Cruz and the ocean. I thought about swimming – the sound of the lapping water washing out my head and brain. I wished there was somewhere to swim.

It didn't matter though, tonight not even cold water would cool my boiling blood; I could probably jump in a pool and end up sitting in a hole full of steam.

"You know, just take me to the train," I heard myself say, "I'll figure it out from there."

The cab was a Prius and we whirred away with the crunching gravel loud beneath the tires before the engine kicked on. As we pulled onto the road, out of the window I saw the small depression at the base of the streetlamp, indented from where the Passat had hit, leaving it slightly bent and casting a crooked glow on the scene.

That twisted light followed me all the way to the train station, into the nearby liquor store, and eventually back to the apartment where I stayed to brood. I made it to the test, but didn't pass. A few days later I would return to the apartment to find the windows open and stark daylight plastering the walls of a bare room, everything miraculously empty of all Sam's belongings. Clouds passed overhead and everything went dim.

In retrospect, it couldn't have gone any other way. She had always been a bird in flight - exempt of the expectations that caged in everyone else. There was never going to be a long talk in a coffee shop, something about it's not you it's me and that I'm a great guy. She left my life in the same flash of blinding light that brought her into it, and even after the wind picked up and the sun came back through the window, I was still standing in a shadow.

About the Author:

When Gabriel was in his early and formative salad days, he was given a book of poetry on fire by his father. Nothing was the same for him. What sparked a voracious appetite for reading turned into an affinity for the written word, and Gabriel is now both a student of English Literature and a writer. One word at a time, he hopes to create a body of work that will influence the world in the same way that first book of poems did his.In an attempt to bridge the ever widening divide between the literature intellectual studying classical structure and verse with the raw artist who embodies modernity by painting free verse on the walls of the city, Gabriel Sage's work attempts to speak to the array of readers that exist today. With a deep appreciation for the seminal writers that shaped the craft of English, Gabriel hopes to write with both tradition, and a unique view of the world that can only be achieved by a millennial living neck deep in today's strange culture.

BLUE FEATHERS

by Evan Massey

Sharon wanted to go out west to try her hand at movies. She told me she was done with school.

"It's not for me," she said.

She said, that she had wasted two years of her life and wasn't going to waste another two, she had other things she wanted to do: travel, see the world, stuff like that.

The number one thing was to be in movies. She had read about girls from small, nowhere towns going out west and hitting it big, becoming stars, names in lights kind of thing.

Sure, I tried stopping her, of course. I talked to her about the potential dangers a young girl could face out there. You know, the what-if's, trying to sway her. I told her she could come back and stay with her aunt and I, figure things out. The thought of her being alone and halfway across the country scared the hell out of me. But she was twenty, hard headed, and wanted nothing to do with what I had to say.

I wasn't surprised with her decision, not at all. Sharon had always wanted to be an actress of some kind. In our home movies she'd always find herself in front of the camera. She'd burst into song, singing at the top of her lungs, or she'd start reciting lines from famous actresses from films she'd seen. Every picture the girl took she posed some kind of way, tilting her head to one side, placing a hand around her face, or putting a hand on her hip, etc.

"It's your decision," I said to her. "I don't agree with it, but it's your decision."

"I'll call and write when I can," she said.

Sharon stuffed her car with bags and clothes and drove halfway across the country.

When she got there, Sharon said she was going to start off with modeling first to figure out her angles and what not. She had to find a good photographer who could take good head-shots for her comp cards. I'll have to ask her again what all that meant. She had to get them done and shop them around to agencies for jobs and auditions.

After a while, she'd drive back and forth from California to Nevada for photo shoots. I sent money every month to help her get along. In exchange for the money I sent, Sharon would send photos of herself. They were well-done photos like the ones in the magazines and TV ads—quality stuff. In some of the photos it was just her face from the neck up, looking straight on, staring at something off to the right or left or else behind the camera. In other photos, Sharon posed in these little bikinis at some beach lying on the sand with pouted lips or in the water flipping her hair a certain way.

"She's got the look," my sister said, looking over one of the bikini photos in her hand.

Sharon was sitting on her knees in the sand with her hair hanging to one side as she focused on something off camera. She had on this little, yellow bikini. The bottom was tight and thin, hugging her thighs.

I shook my head.

"Why can't she take a decent picture?" I said. "Where in the hell are her clothes?"

"This is what they have to do," my sister said.

"They want to see her range."

They'll see her range all right," I said.

You don't get it," she said.

"No. I don't."

Sharon wrote after a time and said that things were going well. She had taken a good number of quality pictures and she was going to send them to agencies. She was excited about her prospects. I was excited too, reading her letter. She also asked me to increase the money I was sending so she could pay the photographer and the portfolio people. I had to pick up extra shifts at work.

We spoke on the phone soon after that.

She said she hadn't heard from any of the agencies yet. "It takes time," she said. But the wait was killing her. If she didn't get any call backs from the agencies or from any of the auditions, she had a backup plan. Sharon came into contact with a guy out there who specialized in entertainment.

"He can help me," she said. "He'll be like my manager."

He knew people and had connections up down the west coast and some contacts in New York, though his hub was out west. But that's only if everything else didn't work.

"Last resort," she said. "Fingers crossed."

Sharon said that only one of the agencies called. They told her that it was between her and another girl and that it was difficult. They went with the other girl. But they told Sharon that she had something and to keep looking.

"She was skinnier," Sharon said, guessing that was the reason.

So, after hearing that news, she got in touch with that entertainment guy, Ronnie, that was his name. A real sleazebag, I tell you.

Anyway, Sharon and Ronnie got in business together. He had written up a contract for her to sign. He promised her money and fame and made it sound nice. She signed it.

He made her lose weight. She got down to one twenty, the lowest she had ever been. She was doing low-rent photo shoots for no-name brands and most times she didn't get paid for it. All the money went to Ronnie and he shared some with Sharon when she absolutely needed it. It wasn't the big leagues, but it was something, she said, something to help her get there. Ronnie told her that things like this take time, sometimes a lot of time, several years if she was lucky.

"I don't like this Ronnie guy," I said to her over the phone. "You shouldn't have signed anything."

"He only wants to help," Sharon said.

"Sure," I said. "But watch this guy."

"Ronnie's fine," she said. "He's got me doing other things, making me more marketable, he says."

"Like what?" I said.

"Dancing," she said.

"What kind of dancing?"

"Just dancing," she said. "Don't worry, it's harmless."

When Sharon wasn't posing in front of the camera, Ronnie had her dancing. For a while she danced at shows in Vegas in front of small crowds. Then she got good at it and went from doing small gigs to big shows with more dancers, many of whom went to school for it. Sharon learned a lot from them.

She sent a picture of one of her outfits. She was wearing a shiny two piece with silver sequins, top and bottom, with these big blue feathers sticking up in the back from her waist. The blue feathers also stood up from this thing she wore on her head. It looked ridiculous. I couldn't get over it. But Sharon looked as if she was having fun out there, smiling big in that picture with other dancers in the same outfit.

"I'm a Las Vegas Showgirl!" she said. She was excited. "It's happening!" she said.

She'd have two or three shows a night. Sharon would go from one show to another, making several hundred dollars in one night sometimes. Some went to Ronnie, the other half went to her, that was the deal, she didn't mind it. I did.

But she was happy and I was quite happy for her. She said she finally felt like she was doing something. She felt like she was on her way. I took it as a sign that things were looking up for her.

Then the shows died down.

Ronnie got in trouble with one of the show managers, a top guy who ran things, I forget his name. But it was something about money coming up missing, Sharon told me. They couldn't make the allegations stick. Nevertheless, he couldn't get her booked anymore, anywhere. That was the end of that.

But Ronnie still wanted her to dance. He told her that dancing was big, bigger than modeling. She could make more money dancing, he said. She was more profitable, he told her.

This Ronnie, I tell you, if I had the chance.

He had my daughter dancing at clubs first. She'd dance inside of cages with other girls, dancing all night and into the morning in those clubs. It would get hot in there, she said, and she'd work up quite a sweat. She did this for quite some time and she was making decent change. But it didn't match her blue feather days.

Then this sleazeball told Sharon that she could make even more money if she willing to, "step it up a notch," his words. My Sharon started dancing at private events and parties along with her club dancing. It would be her and a handful of other girls from the club that would go and dance for parties of men, and sometimes for women who'd like that kind of thing.

"Look, but don't touch," she said. That was one of the rules that Ronnie had established for the men and the women at the parties. Sometimes those rules were broken. Ronnie kept saying he'd deal with it. It kept happening. But Sharon said she made more money from those events.

"It's not ideal," she said. "But it's money and I need that right now."

"I'm coming out there," I said. "I don't like this."

"No," she said. "I can handle it."

"No. I'm coming to get you," I said.

"Stop," Sharon said. "I have it under control. Don't come."

We went back and forth on the matter and finally I decided to stay put.

But I kept a bag packed.

Even with all of this dancing going on, Sharon continued to send out her pictures and things and found time to audition. She did this all without Ronnie's knowing. Out of fear, she said. Something had made her fearful of Ronnie. She saw Ronnie drag a girl, Misty, from one of the parties for not dancing enough and complaining about being too tired. When she saw Misty again, her face was swollen up pretty bad. Ronnie didn't seem the same, she said. He began to be controlling, always asking where Sharon and the girls were, taking away their phones for punishment, and making the girls stay later at the private parties. She said it got bad.

But some of her secret auditions went well and she got call backs, but nothing panned out, nothing stuck. She kept sending pictures. She kept trying. She tried getting back on to be a showgirl again. That attempt failed, too. People would hear that she was still associated with that Ronnie character. That scared them off, she said. They took down her number just in case. We'll call if we ever get low on girls, they said.

"They're never low on girls," Sharon said when she called. "I won't hear a thing."

Sharon said that one night it all came to a head.

After dancing at one of those private parties, a party for a retiring policeman, Ronnie flipped. He had found out that Sharon was sending off her pictures and auditioning, all without his knowledge. They went at it and had words. They got loud with each other. Things got physical.

She called me as soon as she had the chance.

"I wanna come home," she said. She was frantic, breathing heavy, and I could hear in her voice that she had been crying.

"What happened?" I said. "What the hell happened?"

"Nothing," she said. "I wanna come home."

"Please come home," I said.

The phone clicked.

She didn't leave the house for a couple of weeks. She ate a lot and gained back the weight she had lost and more. My sister and Sharon sat around the house all day and smoked cigarettes. There would be more buds in the ashtray—that's how I found out. Sharon's smoking was news to me. I asked her about it, she told me she'd picked it up out there. All the actresses, models, and dancers she knew smoked, so she tried it and would smoke here and there. She said she was trying to kick it.

"It's a bad habit," she said, "but it helps."

We had talks some nights after I'd get off work. Sharon waited for my sister to go to bed before we'd have these talks. We'd meet at the kitchen table. I'd fix up some coffee or tea for us and we'd talk about everything, anything. Some nights we'd be up late in the kitchen talking things out. That's when she told me about all of it, everything that happened out west, the stuff I didn't know, filling in the gaps with parts she purposely left out.

Sharon said she was ashamed. She was ashamed at what she had done and the things she had gotten into. But she was more ashamed that she didn't get to do what she wanted, the being in movies thing, the reason she went out there in the first place. She was disappointed and she asked me if I was disappointed in her.

"No," I told her. "Not at all."

But it was as if I said yes the way she looked down at the table.

She had a little money left over from her time out there. She used that money to take up classes at the community college across town. I helped her with some of the tuition. She thought she could pick up where she had left off, but she took it slow, taking two to three classes to help get herself back into it. She also picked up a job at the roller rink.

"It's good being busy again," she said. "Helps me take my mind off of things."

While Sharon was at work one afternoon and I had got off pretty early, she got a phone call from Nevada. My sister and I were in the kitchen, smoking and playing cards when the phone rang. Nevada read on the caller ID. I picked it up and a man's voice asked for Sharon. I asked how he got the number, but I didn't let him answer. I told the son of a bitch to never call here again and that if he did, things wouldn't be good for him. Then I slammed the phone back. My sister asked who it was and I didn't know, but I could imagine.

Sharon had to work late the same night Nevada called. We missed our nightly talk. So we took it up on the porch the morning after.

It was a crisp morning, dew stuck to the grass, the sun crept up behind the trees. Sharon was in her red roller rink uniform and khaki's, gearing up to leave. I was in my pajamas as we sat on the porch sharing the ashtray and sipping coffee.

I told her about the time her mother got up on stage at a karaoke bar and sang.

"Was she good?" Sharon said.

"Not at all," I said, "but I couldn't tell her. I just let her keep on. People even clapped afterwards."

Sharon and I laughed.

Then we got quiet.

There was this blue jay that had landed right in front of us on the porch, flitting around on its little legs and twitching its head at us. You know birds, curious creatures. It bounced around some more then it took off. It flew away somewhere in a hurry, flapping its wings quick.

We sat there in silence. I turned to Sharon.

She followed that blue jay up into some tree and out of her sight. But she kept her eyes up there, considering something, her cigarette burned in between her fingers.

I went to tell her another thing that her mother did, but I didn't, I kept shut.

She finished her cigarette and pressed it out in the ashtray.

"I have to go," she said. "See you tonight?"

I nodded.

Sharon got up and got in her car. She backed out of the driveway. She honked twice, we waved. That's when I recalled that day she went out west. Nothing could stop her, the big smile she carried, the way she packed up her little car all the way to the back windshield. She couldn't see me waving that day, telling her to come back.

About the Author:

Evan Massey is a short fiction writer from Richmond, Virginia. In the fall, Evan will be studying for his Creative Writing MFA at Virginia Tech. His works have appeared in Populi Magazine, Literally Stories, and Brilliant Flash Fiction. He loves soccer and wine and hopes to one day own a bloodhound.

GRACELAND

by Shawn Van Horn

Sometimes, on the worst days, I walk the paved trails that snake through Graceland Cemetery. No king rests there, just thousands of us everyday paupers. Graceland calms me when I need to slow everything down. Standing there, I am never sad, never scared. I do not fear the end that we all must face. I accept it. Dare I say I embrace it? It instills in me a respect for life I desperately need. I never feel more alive than when in the midst of so much death.

How morbid it is to even think it, but I fit in there. It is not a hopeless thought. I do not wish for death. But we are the same, the dead and I; all of us quiet and alone and mostly forgotten. I can comprehend their world. My own I think I will never understand. I know what to expect. I know what goes on. The world of the dead never ever changes. This is not the view of a hopeless cynic though, for there is life there also, so much of it, abundant in buried memories.

I'm close to an atheist anymore. I do not blame that on a god. I blame that on a lifetime of living amongst his image. Even if my faith is diminished, still the cemetery is my church. It has a spiritual feel I cannot find anywhere else. And I've looked everywhere else.

I doubt I could find it in even the oldest, most famous of churches. I can't feel religion. The hypocrisy, the politics, the televangelists selling bottles of miracle water on my TV at 5 a.m. I can't feel any of that. At Graceland, standing on a step to somewhere else, is where I find god in all its brilliant mystery, the mystery you must succumb to in order to solve. It is reality in its purest form. It is not subject to opinions. Winners can't rewrite history. It is unalterable.

And there's nothing the world can do to take that feeling away from me. They could charge admission at the gate. They could hold political rallies on the steps of mausoleums. The could slap Pepsi stickers on the gravestones, even drop a Wal-Mart right in the middle of the place, and still they couldn't alter the control it possesses on me. It makes me happy. Dead people make me happy.

Today is another one of the worst days. They come more and more frequently, become harder and harder to take. Three kids died in a fire last night. It's in the paper, front page, headline in that big, black font reserved for only the really bad news. I show the paper to coworkers, tell them what I think. They do not care. There's a deadline tomorrow. It's important, they say. They are lost in computer screens. Walking the halls, I say hi to seven people who do not say hi back. I count them off. Four do not even make eye contact. This happens everyday.

Ellen breaks down over that son of hers. He brings her so much grief. We are alone in the stairwell and she cries. She says sometimes she doesn't want to live anymore. What am I to do with this? I'm no good at these things. I don't know what to say. I just say it'll be okay. Everyone says that. Even the people who don't say hi would say that.

Frank in Marketing loses seventy-five cents in the vending machine. It doesn't spit out his Fritos. So he spits. And curses. Kicks a wingtip at the side of the machine, leaving a dent as a reminder of unreceived Fritos. He storms out.

It is building up. I wish it doesn't. I wish what builds up is apathy. I wish that I only want to go home. But I don't. I can't breathe. I have to calm down. I have to go there. I know Jenny will be mad. I never call first. Dinner will become cold.

I drive with my seat belt off, my window down in bitter November. The wind like white noise fills my ears. I love it. My tie tosses about. I am on the road to Graceland. I'm so close. I'm almost there. I can make out the black iron gates in the far distance. They welcome me.

A red light. Damn. Red lights make me edgy. I cannot stand being still. I must always go, must always move. I tap my fingers on the wheel. A big, blue boat of a car idles in front of me. A silver Jesus fish hangs off center on its massive bumper. The stiff curly white hair of an elderly woman barely peeks over the leather headrest. The light turns green. The boat idles still. I honk my horn. Short. Short. Long.

C'mon! Go, go, go!

She goes. She goes oh so slow. I want to pass but double yellow lines on asphalt won't let me. A barrier of centimeter thick paint traps me. Stay inside the lines my art teacher told me in kindergarten. In first grade. In senior year.

Move!

I accelerate to within a few inches of her, then back off. Jesus fish disappears then reappears. This is not who I am. I am becoming one of them. Still...

Hurry up!

Such slow motion. Bit by bit we close in on Graceland. I can read its name on the brick wall. My heart pounds hard. I want to be there. And now even slower we go. Break lights on the boat flash on and off. Is this ship lost at sea?

Get off the road!

She is not lost. A blinking turn signal tells me so. She's going to Graceland too. It comes to me. The captain of the boat is a lonely widow off to visit her husband. I hang my head. I have become one of them. But it's not too late. I can force the wolf away, become the sheep again. Give me grace.

I reluctantly follow her through the black gates. She veers to the right, I to the left. Let her mourn in peace. Let me find mine.

The cemetery is a barren land save for the gravestones bobbing out of the ground like buoys in a sea. A perfect place for a boat to go. My ritual sets in and I begin to relax. I coast and read the names. Julia Evers. 1908-1998. Was she thankful for her long life? George and Wanda Fields, buried side by side. Wanda died first, George a year later. Of a broken heart? Was their love that strong? I wish I could ask them what their first kiss was like. Dr. Chen. My doctor when I was a kid. Dead at forty-eight. Hanging Christmas lights, fell off a ladder, broke his neck. Brad Raney. I still remember the day he didn't show up for school. They found his Camaro wrapped around a tree two blocks from home. How did his parents feel? How do they feel now? Does the mourning ever end? Or diminish?

I wonder what final moments were like. In each name I read I try to find the pain or the peace, the fear or the acceptance, the heaven or the hell, the enlightenment or the nothingness that comes with the end. I am surrounded by those who went through the final curtain. I am envious of the secret they carry. Are they envious of me?

My last stop is always the same. Rick Wade. My entire life I knew him, though never too well. He was a family friend. When I was young he would come over and play his guitar for everyone. Beatles songs mostly. I watched him, wishing he was my dad, even as I sat next to my own. To my toys drums I'd go when he left, imagining the band we'd have. Years went by, he came over less and less until he didn't anymore. That's how life goes. A few years after he didn't anymore the phone rang. Good Friday. Mom answered. I watched her face grow sad. She hung up, told me about Rick's stroke. He was too young for a stroke. I wept. I have lost grandparents. For them I have softly cried. For some reason, for Rick, I wept.

I look out the car window at his gravestone. Is it wrong to say it always makes me happy? He has been gone a decade, still it's always decorated. Always there are several vases of fresh flowers. Today there are balloons, wind chimes, candles. He is loved. He is celebrated. I step out and walk to where he rests. I speak to him sometimes. Or is it god? Whose face do I see in the granite of Rick's stone? Am I hoping someone will answer?

Today I am silent. I right a vase of dandelions that has fallen over. I turn and begin to walk back to my car. I trip over something. A rock? I fall, muddying my knees. I get back up, a hole in my Dockers. I'm not going to spit and curse about it. I look back to see what fell me. It was a rock indeed. Smooth and rectangular, a slab lying flat, hidden in high grass. A marker. The simplest one I've ever seen. My dog got a better send off. It seems so alone. No flowers, no decoration of any kind. No one celebrates whoever lies beneath. It is out of place. No wonder I have never noticed it before.

I bend down to read the chiseled name. My head swirls at the recognition and I grab onto my muddied knees to stop from falling again. Mary Keller. I knew her once long ago and I know how she ended here. I had forgotten all about her. I am saddened that everyone else seems to have forgotten her too. But this I already knew.

For a few months after high school I worked as a janitor. I had no idea what to do with my just begun life. Mary Keller had plenty of time to figure that out but apparently she never did. She was easily forty and my coworker at a factory in town. And an awful woman she was. She rarely spoke to anyone unless it was to complain. She never smiled. She was lazy as well. No one liked her. Many said bad things about her. I am ashamed to admit that at times even I joined in with the wolves. I went out of my way to avoid her. Mary Keller wanted no friends so she had no friends. She barely seemed to exist.

And then one day she didn't. Like the boy who didn't show up for school, Mary Keller didn't show up for work. And no one noticed. No one cared. I cared, begged my lower case god for forgiveness, when I read the paper the next day. Like today, there it was, that big, black font.

TWO DEAD IN APPARENT MURDER-SUICIDE

Here is the apparent: A man came home angry and prepared with a gun in his hand. He ended his girlfriend's life, then ended his own. The police had been called to the house several times over the years. "Domestic disputes". The man had a criminal record. He was a mechanic. The girlfriend was a janitor. Neighbors said she kept to herself.

Another story a few days later, in a smaller font, somewhere in the back of the paper. No one claimed the woman's body. She had no family and no friends. And she was from a different state. Kentucky, I think. There was no funeral. She was no one. She only sold some newspapers.

There really is a pauper at Graceland. Here she is, six feet under where I stand. It feels meaningful to be here. I was supposed to find her.

I'm sorry.

These are the words that come to mind. I don't know why. What am I sorry for? For not being nice to her? For being like everyone else? For forgetting her? For being like everyone else? I'm sorry for everything, me and everyone else. I am a sheep. I want now to always remember her. Her life feels worth it if someone remembers. I do not know what to remember. She was simply a mean, quiet woman to me. I think I will remember her circumstance. A lonely woman far from home, an abusive man her only friend in the world. I'd be mean and quiet too. What is the point? Not to judge? To know circumstance? To be a sheep among wolves? I think so.

I feel better. Reconnected. Centered again. I kneel at Rick's grave, take one of his flowers, and place it on Mary's slab. I hope that's okay to do. I pull out the high grass around it. I can see it better now. Others will see it too. Rick's widow perhaps the next time she comes out to see him. She might notice his neighbor for the first time. But I doubt she'll remember her. That has become my task. My lesson. I will learn it well.

I walk back to my car. The boat slowly passes me by. The captain looks out at me. She smiles.

She lifts a frail hand and waves. I wave back. I smile for the first time today. The smile lingers even after the boat is gone. I sit behind the wheel of my own boat. I am no longer lost at sea. People make me happy.

I take off my tie. I whistle. I can still whistle. How the dead must envy me. I drive away and I am thinking. Tomorrow will be a better day. It'll be okay. I'll tell Ellen that again, maybe more. And when I get home I'll tell Jenny I'm sorry I was late.

About the Author:

Shawn Van Horn currently resides in Sidney, Ohio. He has had stories and poems published in Our Time is Now, Wilmington Blues, Fourth & Sycamore, and The Oddville Press. He has written two novels and just started on his third.

A FEW DOZEN EGGS

by John Wells

He is standing in the batter's box in Oriole Park at Camden Yards facing Roger Clemens wearing a Baltimore Orioles uniform. The bases are loaded in the bottom of the ninth with the Orioles down 8-4. He slashes a vicious line drive to deep right field. The right fielder races to the ball, but it ricochets crazily off the wall and rolls toward the right field foul line. He barrels around the bases, crossing second, heading for third. The third base coach frantically waves him in as he rounds third, sprinting for home. The right fielder chases down the ball, heaves it to the second baseman, who spins and hurls the ball toward home plate. The crowd is going ballistic as the throw and the runner reach the plate at the same time. He slides head first, instantly buried under a mushroom cloud of dust. Lying on top of home plate, he looks up at the umpire who shouts, "You're out!" Then the umpire turns into a phantom, ghost-like figure with a blueish opaque face and long stringy gray hair.

"Hey Mister, are you okay?"

Jimmy West rolled over on his side, staring up at a skinny kid wearing a Boston Red Sox hat, clutching a baseball bat and glove. For a second he thought it was his brother Michael waking him up for baseball practice. Rubbing his bleary, bloodshot eyes he looked around to see where he passed out. The surroundings were familiar; he was lying in the grass near home plate of his former Little League field.

"Yeah sure," he muttered to the kid who was standing in front of two other boys carrying gloves.

"We thought you might be dead." said another kid.

"Or maybe you're a bum," added a third. "Are you a bum?"

Jimmy realized what he must look like. A homeless tramp interrupting Saturday morning practice.

"No, I'm not a bum, at least not all the time. I guess I was out, huh?"

"We have practice," said the kid in front

"I know," said Jimmy. "I was just leaving."

Nauseously dizzy, and fending off a wave of embarrassment, Jimmy struggled to a sitting position, crossed his legs, and rested his hands on his knees. The kids already turning to leave; Jimmy calling out, "Hey kid, come back! Let me see that glove."

The kid did an about-face, took a few steps, and held out his glove.

"This glove is Japanese and has no name on it," said Jimmy, flipping the glove back to the kid.

"Who cares?" said the kid, "It cost fifty bucks."

"Who's your favorite player?"

"Manny Ramirez."

"Well, you should have bought a Manny Ramirez model."

"Why?" asked the kid.

Jimmy rubbed his temples with his fingertips. "Never mind."

"Hey, is that your bike over there?" asked the kid.

"Yes."

"Looks old."

"It's a Schwinn. Best bike ever made."

The three boys retreated to the dugout. Jimmy eased himself off the turf, brushing grass clippings from the front of his Orioles T-shirt. As he took a step, a sharp pain stabbed his lower right leg. He lifted his pants leg, revealing a nasty red and purple bruise the size of a softball. He had no idea where it came from. Shambling awkwardly to his bike, he felt unsettled and shaky as if he was walking on ice skates for the first time. He glanced over at the boys sitting glumly on the dugout bench looking like three boys holding bibles trapped in a church. He knew they pitied this old, clumsy local loser, aware of his amplified self-consciousness slowly downsizing into compressed self-loathing.

Feigning dignity, he walked more erect, lifting his head to the skies as if he was on a mission from God. A shaft of sunlight poured through a tear in the sky blurring his vision. He forced his body to stride effortlessly across the field pretending to be a real athlete heading for the dugout. He wanted to cry out, "Hey, kids! I was a hero on this field many times, and when I was your age I was the best Little League player in town! You kids don't know it, but in 1981 I hit a grand slam home run right over that fence to win the annual All-Star game against the Fighting Tigers across the river!" Jesus, he thought, lowering his head to the ground, Calm the fuck down; there is no greater sin than self-pity.

Limping noticeably, the strained journey toward the bike seemed to take forever, the whole time Jimmy fighting off an anarchic impulse to fire a bullet in his aching head. Finally, he arrived at the Schwinn surprised at how exhausted and washed-out he felt. He picked up the bike thinking, This is one helluva way to start the day.

Six hours later, Jimmy was still nursing a hangover and sweating profusely as he rode along in his manager Larry Garner's partially primed orange GTO, on his way to his niece's seventeenth birthday. He stuck his arm out the window, a hot breath of sticky humid air flowing over his fingertips.

"They made these cars with air conditioning, you know," said Jimmy.

Larry shrugged. "Guys back then didn't give a shit about air conditioning. They wanted speed...and more speed—and to look damn good getting it."

Jimmy glanced back at the cracked, sun-faded brown leather upholstery. "If you ever fix up this jalopy, it'll be worth big bucks."

"Then what? It's not for sale at any price."

"Oh, I forgot," said Jimmy. "You're independently wealthy."

"On the salary you pay me? Forget it, boss."

"Let's not discuss anything connected to the Red Hawks."

"I don't blame you there."

Jimmy absentmindedly dipped his head into his open palms, massaging his forehead. "Man, I still have a headache."

"Look at the bright side," said Larry. "You don't look bad for a guy who slept in a field all night."

Jimmy peered out the window at endless acres of farmland littered with huge bales of wheat-colored hay rolled up like cinnamon rolls, barely visible through shimmering pale blue vapors. "You'd be amazed what a shower and a change of clothes can do."

Larry grinned. "I wouldn't know. I haven't had my summer shower yet."

"I can almost believe that."

Did you tell them you'd be late?" asked Larry.

"No."

"You need to get a cell phone."

"Why?"

"Well, for one thing, you could call them...let them know."

"I have one at home...and the bar."

"Right."

"It works, doesn't it?"

Larry shrugged again. "If you call being in last place working," his voice rising above John Mellencamp's "Blood on the Scarecrow" blaring out of the cassette player. He reached over, turning down the music. "You say this kid had a Jap glove with no name on it?"

"Not only that, but he had an aluminum bat."

"That's pitiful."

"Christ Larry, they don't even know what a line drive sounds like."

Larry pointed to the package on the passenger seat. "What did you get her?"

"The Willie Mays biography, and a card."

"The rookie year one?"

"Yeah."

"She'll love it."

"There are only two real baseball fans in the family."
"Who's the other one? Stuart?"

"Right," said Jimmy. "Stuart is more fanatical than you or me. He thinks no players should be in the Hall of Fame before Jackie Robinson. He thinks they don't count because they didn't face the best competition."

"He's got a point," said Larry.

"Maybe, but I don't think you're going to keep Ruth or DiMaggio out of the Hall. It's totally unreal."

"He's what? Twelve? Who the hell is realistic at twelve? At least he's got a brain and opinions. My kid doesn't know what year the War of 1812 was fought, for Christsakes."

Jimmy grinned and turned John Mellencamp back up. "Exactly what year was that?"

The two men cruised along twisting country roads slicing through picturesque rolling green hills dotted with grazing cattle, horses, and sheep, a glistening translucent haze reflecting off the Blue Ridge mountains in the distance.

Larry turned left into West Heaven Farms, easing the GTO down an asphalt driveway lined with a shady interlocking of maple and horse chestnut trees, flickers of fading sunlight glinting off the GTO's windshield. They reached the West homestead, a two-story grand colonial brick mansion perched high on a hill overlooking miles of lush fertile farmland. Larry pulled the car beneath an arched portico supported by four white twisted rope stone pillars with Tuscan style caps. Several luxury autos were parked in an adjacent parking lot.

"Here you are, partner," said Larry. "Have a good time. Say hello to the rich folks for me."

"I will. Thanks for the ride," said Jimmy, grabbing the gift and opening the door.

"Hey boss," said Larry. "Try not to get wasted tonight and pass out on any more baseball fields. It's bad for your image."

Smiling sheepishly, Jimmy uttered, "Hey, maybe that is my image!"

Jimmy watched Larry continue circling the horseshoe-shaped driveway before ambling along a Mexican ceramic walkway leading to an impeccably landscaped French Vanilla stone patio decorated with an abundance of sunflowers, woodland orchids, marigolds and golden asters. Beyond a gray stone retaining wall bordering the patio, he spotted the quietly rusting equipment of his childhood playground. The swing set, monkey bars, see-saws, and faded green plastic slide now seemed like abandoned relics of a mining ghost town in the Old West.

Allison West and Todd Cummings were lying naked in her bed, sucking in deep inaudible breaths, their bodies still glistening with sweat from the aftermath of sex. A CD by The White Stripes playing low on the stereo.

"That was a great birthday present Todd," said Allison, leaning over and giving him a light peck on the cheek.

"My pleasure," said Todd, nodding his head toward the window. "Did you hear a car pull up?"

Allison chuckled. "No Todd, I was busy."

"Maybe we should get dressed. I mean, your parents and all…"

Allison raised up, grabbed her long hair, twisting it into a bun in the back of her head. She leaned back on the pillow. "Don't worry, they never come in here unannounced. It's off limits….besides, the door is locked."

Todd glanced at the door as if someone had knocked, and then pulled the covers up.

"What's the matter, Todd? Afraid of getting caught?"

"Yes, aren't you?"

"No, I'm seventeen. It's none of their business. We've already had more sex than my parents in their whole life."

"Maybe…but it is their house."

Allison abruptly yanked off the covers. "Okay, scaredy cat, let's get dressed and join the rest of the dysfunctionals."

Rolling off the side of the bed, Allison shook loose her tussled copper-colored hair, finger-combing it to reasonable straightness. Reaching down, she gathered her black lace bra and panties, slipped them on, and then moved with languid feline ease toward a full-length mirror propped beside the window. She stood before it, approvingly checking out her fully-formed body, primping her hair, flashing her brilliant eggshell blue eyes while striking seductive poses. Smiling to herself, she mouthed the words "coo coo," winked at the mirror, then flicked her tongue against her upper lip, holding it there like the spring of a trap. Todd sat up on the side of the bed. He grabbed his jeans, and lifted his legs, grappling to put them on. He caught himself staring dumbly at Allison, admiring her perfect figure, and the coiled sultry sexuality of a woman ten years her senior. "My God, you're beautiful."

"You don't think my hips are a little big?" she asked, angling toward him, pushing her hair up with one hand and placing the other on her left hip.

"You're perfect, Allison. "What can I say?"

Jimmy walked briskly to meet his mother Cynthia and brother Michael who were sitting at a table beneath a red, white and blue "Happy Birthday Allison" banner. The aftermath of a party was on display; the table was strewn with crushed paper plates, plastic cups and silverware, open containers of food, a jug of ice tea, and a half-eaten birthday cake.

Jimmy gave his mother a gentle hug, pulled up a chair, and placed the gift on the table.

"How is the party going?"

"You're late son," said Cynthia.

"Sorry, I had some unexpected business."

"Have you eaten yet?"

"I had a sandwich at the bar," said Jimmy, eyeing the birthday cake. "You save a piece for me?"

"Of course," said Cynthia.

Jimmy reached over, sliced a piece of cake, wolfing down a big bite. "Hey Michael, what's up?" he asked, flecks of hot pink frosting rimming his mouth.

"Not much," said Michael, "Still working in the West salt mine."

"The napkins are over there," interjected Cynthia, followed by a slight exasperated head shake.

"You're not letting mother drive you too hard are you?" asked Jimmy, wrapping the piece of cake in a napkin, and then grabbing a can of Coke from a cooler.

"Of course not," said Michael. "She even gave me a ten-minute break the other day—with water.

"How kind of her!" exclaimed Jimmy, flashing his mother a smile, a wink, and a nod.

"Actually," said Michael, "We were talking about that asshole Grisham."

"What's he up to now?"

"The guy is a greedy fucking virus, buying up more and more independents, hostile or otherwise."

"But, we're safe," said Jimmy. "He can't possibly get over fifty-percent ownership."

"I know, but he's been contacting some stockholders."

"Come on, Michael! He'll never get enough to replace the current board members—which, by the way, I see are all here."

"Well," said Cynthia, "We're not going to be caught napping. Our percentage of the market is holding steady, but he beat us for the first time last quarter."

"What's his market share now?" asked Jimmy."

"We don't know yet," said Michael. "We'll know on Tuesday."

"Don't worry, Jimmy," said Cynthia, "If he tries anything, we'll crush him like a bug."

"Mother, I can believe that!" cried Jimmy. "I'm glad you're on my side!"

"How's the team doing?" asked Michael.

"Oh great...except for bad pitching, shoddy defense, and weak hitting."

"What about attendance?" asked Cynthia.

"Fans?" asked Jimmy, eyeballing the playground as if there might be some fans loitering in the backyard. "Oh yeah...we had one last game. His car broke down outside the stadium, and he watched us until the tow truck came."

"That's pitiful, said Michael, grinning.

"Maybe you should give it up," said Cynthia.

"It's not that bad," said Jimmy, looking around the patio. "Hey, where is everybody?"

"Inside, watching the races," said Cynthia.

Jimmy glanced through a glass partition exposing the rec room. His father, a middle-aged couple, and three children were huddled around the TV, their eyes glued to a NASCAR race.

"What's the race?" asked Jimmy.

"Coke Zero 500," said Michael.

"How's Kyle Busch doing?"

"I don't know," said Michael. "Dad hasn't given us an update."

"What's her present?" asked Cynthia.

"It's a book. A Willie Mays biography...plus a card."

"Very nice," said Cynthia. "She is such a huge fan."

"I'll be right back," said Jimmy, standing up and grabbing the gift.

Jimmy entered the rec room, instantly greeted by a flurry of excitable shouts and waving hands. He saw his father Tyler sitting upright in his favorite La-Z-Boy recliner. He went over, leaned over the chair, glancing at the TV. "Hey dad, how's Kyle doing?"

"Not too bad," he responded. "Second place and surging."

On the screen, Jimmy spotted Kyle Busch's number 18 car emblazoned with the yellow, red, green, and blue colors of M &Ms trailing Dale Earnhardt, Jr. by half a car length. Suddenly, Busch got around him in a turn as the cars bumped each other, igniting sparks. Then, out of nowhere Jeff Gordon materialized in the frame to make it a three-way race going down the front stretch. Everyone in the room jumped up and down, screaming and hollering for Kyle Busch, "Pull away, Kyle! "Step on it, Kyle! "Make 'em eat your dust, Kyle!"

Jimmy yelled in his father's ear, "How many laps to go?"

Tyler held up three fingers as Busch got inside Earnhardt, Jr., just past the start/finish line, but Earnhardt, Jr. regained it going into a turn. Busch got inside Earnhardt, Jr. then Earnhardt, Jr. got him back at the end of the backstretch by driving hard into another turn. Running furiously, Earnhardt, Jr. came in low, drove up and almost touched the fence, and then cut sharply off the corner. Busch jerked the wheel hard, practically making a left turn, driving in the middle beneath Earnhardt, Jr., and Gordon before and miraculously racing full-out to the finish line.

"Holy shit! Did you see that!" exclaimed Tyler. "Have you ever seen that many passes in such a short time!"

"That's the most exciting finish I've ever seen," cried Tyler's friend Homer Wilson.

Michael's wife Katy came running in from the kitchen. "What happened!?"

"Busch just kicked Earnhardt's ass," cried Tyler, triumphantly lifting a bottle of beer in the air. "Here's to Kyle! The best damn driver who ever lived!"

Everyone raised their drinks in the air shouting words of praise for Kyle Busch. In the midst of the mayhem, Jimmy leaned in toward Tyler. "Where's Allison?"

"Upstairs, I think," said Tyler, not looking back.

Jimmy headed for the stairs passing two high school girls with faces of wax sitting stiffly on a divan, separated from the others, on the sidelines bored with their heads bowed texting. Jimmy assumed they were friends of Allison's. He was about to ask them about Allison, but one of the girls raised her head, and diffidently pointed her index finger toward the stairs, flipping it up as if gesturing for a waiter.

Allison went over to a dresser and grabbed a pair of Guess jeans with the knees torn out. As she was slipping on a blue halter top, there was a sudden knock at the door. Todd lunged swiftly to a wingback chair on the side of the bed. Allison turned off the stereo and calmly opened the door.

"Uncle Jimmy! What a nice surprise! Come in."

Jimmy entered. Todd stood up from the chair, rubbing the front of his jeans with both palms

"Oh, this is Todd. We were just listening to music."

Jimmy shook his hand. "Nice to meet you." Then he handed the gift to Allison. "Happy birthday."

Allison unwrapped the package, revealing the book.

"Uncle Jimmy! This is awesome!"

"It's also got a bookmark."

Allison lifted a baseball card from the pages and checked it out. "Omygod! His rookie year! Thank you so much!"

Todd leaned over her shoulder. "Can I see that?"

Todd looked at the card. "Wait a second! His name is misspelled."

"What?" asked Allison.

"It says, 'Willie May.' This must be worth..."

"It's just a baseball card," said Jimmy.

"Uncle Jimmy, you shouldn't have."

Jimmy grinned. "Try not to lose it. Are you a baseball fan Todd."

"Yes, a big one. I made the varsity team this year."

"What position?"

"Third base."

"Keep practicing. The Red Hawks could use another good infielder."

"Are you the manager?"

"No, I own the team."

Following a slight pause, Jimmy said, "Well, I'll let you get back to your music."

Jimmy walked back down the hall, spotting a door cracked open. He peeked in and saw Stuart sitting up in bed reading, surrounded by posters and memorabilia of black athletes. The entire side of one wall was devoted to old black and white photos of the Negro League players.

"Hey Stuart, what are you doing?" asked Jimmy.

"Just reading."

"What?"

"1984."

"That's a good one...maybe a little depressing. Hey, you should join the party!"

"Stuart smiled thinly. "And watch a bunch of cars go around in a circle? Did you see Allison?"

"Yes, just now. I brought her a gift."

"She with some dork?"

"I guess so."

"What did you get her?"

"The Willie Mays biography...and a card."

Stuart set the book on his lap. "Lucky her. Are you going to give away your whole collection?"

"No, just a few to my favorite fans."

As Jimmy opened the door to leave, Stuart asked, "How are the Red Hawks doing?"

"Not so good. We're in last place."

Stuart laughing. Well, it must be the owner's fault!"

"Right you are! You want me to fire myself?"

"Hell no, your players suck."

Jimmy noticing a photo on the wall of Satchel Paige in a Kansas City Monarchs uniform rearing back to throw a pitch. "I could use Satchel in his prime."

"Uncle Jimmy, he wouldn't even have to be in his prime. You know he pitched three scoreless innings for the Kansas City A's when he was 59 years old?"

"No kidding."

Jimmy and Michael sat at the bar in the Grand Slam Tavern drinking Coors draft beer, Jerry Lee Lewis' version of "You're Cheating Heart" playing low in the background. The two men were surrounded by a colorful collage of sports memorabilia dominated by baseball photos, prints, pennants, and artifacts. Three big screen TV's lined the upper walls showing baseball games with the sound muted.

"Go on," said Jimmy. "Have another one. I'm buying."

"Okay," said Michael.

Jimmy raised his arm and waved his hand, attracting the attention of Harriet Johnson, the bar's principal owner. "Hey, Harriet! How about two more!"

"Coming right up!" exclaimed Harriet, cheerfully.

Michael drained the last of his beer and looked at his brother. "Are you sure the team can turn a profit?"

"I think so," said Jimmy. "We've got some good prospects."

"That doesn't bring out the fans."

"No, winning does, said Jimmy, finishing off his beer. "By the way, did you know Jerry Lee Lewis and his dad had to sell a few dozen eggs so they could get gas money to travel to the Sun studio?"

"No, I didn't, said Michael. "But it doesn't surprise me. Every one of those rockabilly guys was just poor white trash nobody took seriously."

"Sam Phillips was a genius."

"I know," said Michael, glancing up at a Red Sox/Yankee game on TV. "How about cutting payroll?"

"I'm down to bare bones," said Jimmy. "Three coaches, one secretary, and one scout.

What about promotions? Giveaways...that sort of thing."

"Christ, we've tried .. giveaways ... fireworks ... rock and country bands. Last month we even brought in strippers dressed like cheerleaders."

"What?"

Jimmy took a pull of his beer. "It wasn't my idea."

Harriet placed two beers in front of them. "Here you are, my sons."

"Thanks, Harriet," muttered Jimmy. "You're the best... Say, Harriet, who was the bigger pain in the ass growing up? Me or Michael?"

Smiling ruefully, Harriet responded, "You were both lovely boys."

"Come on, Harriet!" cried Jimmy. "Are you running for office?"

Harriet turned, walked a few feet, and leaned her elbow on the bar, her thoughts drifting back to her days as a housekeeper for the West family...

I can still see them playing in the backyard. Jimmy gleefully riding his cherished Schwinn bicycle, weaving in and out of the swing sets, see-saws and monkey bars. Michael, more subdued and serious, sitting quietly n the grass assembling a dog house made out of wood. Their mother Cynthia opening the back door, eyes brightening, walking past me toward her boys. Jimmy spotting her and immediately picking up speed, riding faster, weaving in between playground equipment, laughing uproar- iously. Michael jumping up and running to his mother, leaping into his mother's arms at the precise moment Jimmy crashes into a swing set, tumbling to the ground. Cynthia, flashing a look of concern, quickly puts Michael down, runs over to see about Jimmy.

"So, how much do you need?" asked Michael.

"Two-hundred thousand would get me through the year."

"Is this throwing good money after bad?"

"Probably."

"Okay, but don't tell mother. She's---"

"I know," said Jimmy looking up at the Red Sox/Yankees game. "Do you remember when baseball players were normal size? Now, they all look like the Incredible Hulk."

"It's the steroids."

"You're right," said Jimmy. "My players tell me it makes the baseball look like a grapefruit coming in there."

"Have you heard from Troy?"

"Not lately. I hear he's staying out at the old farm—probably cooking up meth with his crack head girlfriend."

"He's not going to college?"

"He dropped out again. I have the only son in the known universe who's flunked out of seven colleges."

"Maybe he's still trying to find himself."

"The only thing he's trying to find is his next high—at my expense."

"Maybe you're being too tough on him."

"Are you serious?"

"No...that's not what I mean. I guess...what do you want? For him to be like you?"

"No, I don't want him to be like me. I know what you're implying."

"What?"

"Me being a drunk—a bad role model. Addict- ed to alcohol and driving like a manic...running from the cops. No fucking driver's license."

"That's not what I meant Jimmy... I mean there are some good traits he got from you."

"Like what?"

"Troy is a smart kid. I know he takes a lot of risks—but he's got...something special."

"What? Special irresponsibility?"

"No, I guess I would say he's interesting...he's got your personality. People...they want to be around you."

"You're losing me."

"Jimmy, let's face it. I am very successful, and you're not. But I am a nerd and you are cool. Maybe it's as simple as that."

"You're not a nerd."

"Do you see anybody else in here wearing kha- kis and a Polo shirt?"

Jimmy laughed, and then hugged his brother, wrapping his arms around his shoulders and pulling him closer to him. "Okay, Mr. Nerdo, I see your point. But, Michael, being cool is not worth much on the open market---"

Suddenly, a blustery red-faced man with a rud- dy beard broke in between Michael and Jimmy, holding a bottle of beer in the air.

"Hey barkeep!" he shouted. "How about putting on the Quaker State 400? I wanna see my man Jeff Gordon!"

Harriet looked up from reading a newspaper and stared impassively at the intruder.

"What gives around here?" he asked. "Nobody cares about this baseball shit."

"Actually," said Jimmy, "We were watching it."

"Bunch of pussies," hissed the man. "What's their biggest risk? Getting their uniform dirty?"

"You think NASCAR is a sport?" asked Michael."

"Damn right! Damn right! These drivers got two balls! They got muscle, endurance, hand-eye coordination---"

"Yeah, sitting down in a seat," interjected Jimmy.

"You don't know what the fuck you are talking about!" He hollered.

Jimmy shrugged. "Last time I checked they had a woman competing. I don't see any women up there playing for the Yankees."

"Oh yeah, asshole. That woman could kick your ass!"

"Okay pal," said Jimmy. "Have it your way. Hey Harriet! Can you put on the race for this gentleman here?"

Harriet nodded, visibly sighing before grabbing the remote and changing the channel. "That's more like it," said the man rudely, puffing out his chest, and lumbering down the other end of the bar.

"The world will never run out of assholes," said Michael.

"How about another one?" asked Jimmy.

"No, I gotta split. Katy is preparing a special vegan dinner for us—some kind of tofu or coconut shit."

"Is that what she's into now?"

"This week, anyway," said Michael. The world is not going to run out of fads for bored housewives either."

"Michael," said Jimmy. "Thanks for the loan. I really appreciate it."

Michael stood up to leave. "Don't mention it—but I expect a front row box seat in the playoffs."

"You got it."

About the Author:

John David Wells has written numerous articles on popular culture, two academic books on American studies, and three novels. He lives in Virginia with his fox terrier "Mickey."

A MEETING WITH THE PIG
by Carolyn Soyars

Give not that which is holy unto the dogs, neither cast ye your pearls before swine, lest they trample them under their feet, and turn again and rend you. - Matthew 7:6

"You made a mistake," I heard my mom say from the kitchen as she prepared dinner.

I was irritated that my mom, who could barely plunk out a slow, clumsy boogie-woogie tune on the piano, felt she had to call attention to my musical error. It was especially distracting while I was trying to concentrate on my playing. I didn't need a critic from the other room interfering with the process. Since I was only eight years old, though, and not yet an acerbic teenager, I couldn't quite put my annoyance into words.

That was Tuesday night. The next night, Mr. Marquez would arrive for my piano lesson at 7:30 sharp.

I was always a nervous wreck on Wednesday nights. In anxious anticipation of my piano teacher's arrival, I would be too sick to my stomach to eat much dinner. My nerves tightened, and my heart pounded each minute before his arrival. Even the familiar, comforting voice of Mister Rogers, whose show came on just before my piano lesson, didn't help. I would watch as Mister Rogers calmly, cheerfully arrived home from his job (we never knew what he did for a living), take off his tie, exchange his suit jacket for a casual cardigan, remove his stiff black dress shoes, and lace up his sneakers. I wanted to crawl inside the television, hang out with Mister Rogers, and follow the magic trolley into the Neighborhood of

Make Believe, to visit King Friday XVIII and Henrietta Pussycat. Mister Rogers would have spoken kindly and soothingly to me. He would have told me everything would be okay.

Mr. Marquez did not speak soothingly.

Mr. Marquez was short, serious man, who always wore a suit. In the winter, he would wear a long, black overcoat, black leather gloves, and a fedora. His stern face was somewhat lizard-like, with bulging eyes and thick lips. He had stubby fingers, which flew effortlessly and deftly across the piano keys.

Approximately five minutes to his arrival, I would walk slowly into the living room over to the piano, as if I were about to face an executioner. Our living room was formal, with dark green, velvet drapes tied back with gold and green tassels, and white sheer curtain panels underneath. Since the other family members were rarely in this room, it was always immaculate. Nothing ever happened in the living room, except piano lessons and Christmas.

I would peer through the drapes and await the piano teacher's arrival. As soon as I saw him getting out of the car, I'd quickly move away from the curtain and take my place at the piano.

My mom would answer the door, greeting him enthusiastically. She adored Mr. Marquez, and later in the evening, after he had left, would affectionately imitate his accent. "Play three more may-zures. May-zure. Tray-zure. Lay-zure. I just love his accent!"

Every night, I practiced my Herz and Hanon finger exercises. Mr. Marquez scrawled instructions at the top of the sheet music: "5 measures. Repeat 30 X." I would hold down C and G with the thumb and pinky, while playing D and F with the second and fourth fingers and would repeat thirty times – or until my fingers ached. Then came the scales, followed by the arpeggios. Only after doing the exercises did I get to practice Bach and Beethoven--like a kid on a baseball team made to do tedious, repetitive exercise before getting to have fun and play ball.

The piano lessons lasted an hour. I was grilled on the usual pieces children learned at the time: Beethoven's Fur Elise and Moonlight Sonata, the Chopin waltzes, the Bach Inventions, Scott Joplin's "The Entertainer."

Mr. Marquez did not hesitate to interrupt and admonish me if I wasn't playing something correctly. He often sat down and demonstrated how the piece should be played, his short fingers flying across the keys, beads of sweat forming on his forehead.

When he played piano, I temporarily forgot my anxiety and his strictness, and was carried away by the sheer skill and emotion of his virtuosity. He brought life to the pieces of music that, to my young eyes, appeared as a confusing jumble of notes on a piece of paper.

During one of my lessons, I was struggling with a Brahams sonata. He asked me brusquely if I liked the piece. Being incredibly shy, not quick to voice my opinion either way, I hesitated before answering. Too impatient to wait for my reply, he angrily scrawled at the top of the music: "DID NOT LIKE IT." I wanted to protest, "Wait! You didn't even give me a chance to respond. You just decided for me I didn't like it!" I remained silent, and never learned the sonata.

If I made a mistake, he would rap my knuckles with a ruler. Nowadays, there would be horrified parents and lawsuits and negative online reviews and videos gone viral. But this was 1973, and no one really cared.

Ultimately, neither did I. It wasn't the fear of any knuckle-rapping that made me nervous; it didn't really hurt, not physically, at least. It was the constant scrutiny and the arduous work, the demands and the expectation of perfection – from both Mr. Marquez - and my mother,

who listened to me as she chopped carrots in the kitchen.

I loved playing piano, but it was almost like they were conspiring to take the fun out of it.

#

I was really excited about my new doll.

I'd been gazing at her in the Sears Wish Book ever since September. She was a Madame Alexander baby doll and was perfect--she had deep brown hair, long eyelashes, red cheeks, and, except for little white socks, was dressed entirely in pink--pink bonnet, coat, dress and shoes. I liked some of the modern baby dolls of the day, like Baby Tender Love (who cried and wet)--and my life revolved around my Barbies and their many adventures--but the Madame Alexander doll was exquisite. She was a queen among dolls.

Grandpa Simons was visiting from California. He had difficulty hearing. His friends and family tried to convince him to get a hearing aid, but he refused, making up some excuse that hearing aids picked up every little distracting noise.

"Oh, pooh. He just doesn't want to hear. There's a reason he doesn't buy a hearing aid: it's so he doesn't have to listen to Meli yack all day," grumbled Mom, referring to his talkative, gregarious second wife.

One afternoon during his visit, Grandpa Simons was seated in a recliner in the den. I placed the Madame Alexander doll on the back of Grandpa's chair and spoke loudly. We all had to speak loudly to Grandpa so he could hear us.

"Grandpa, this is my new doll, Victoria," I yelled, lifting her up off the armchair for his perusal. "She doesn't cry and wet like all the new dolls, but she's old-fashioned and she's pretty. I picked her out of the Sears Wish Book and told Mommy I wanted her for Christmas. I take her everywhere. Sometimes, I have to put her back in her crib when Kathy and I are playing Barbies, when their boyfriends come to visit, and sometimes our Barbies have to go to their stewardess jobs on the Barbie Friendship, and then Kathy and I make them go back to the 1800's and wear old-fashioned bustles, and . . . and . . . Mommy likes to make mermaid tails for them out of aluminum foil and then so they're mermaids and that takes up a lot of time--we spend hours and hours with our Barbies--but mostly, I take Victoria everywhere. I like to take put her in the stroller when Mary Ellen and I walk our dolls down to the field. Then we stand at the front of the field and hold up our babies, and show them how pretty the meadow is, all green and wide and open. Mary Ellen's brother, Chrissy, said that he . . . "

"That's nice," Grandpa interrupted gruffly. "She's a pretty doll. That's a nice gift. Every little girl should have a pretty doll like yours. But, very soon, you know you're going to have to set her aside, maybe put her up on a shelf. You'll need to practice piano more, if you want to get into any competitions, if you want to become a concert pianist. Toys are fun, dolls are nice, but those are for children. You're going to have to set her aside, and you're going to have to get serious about the piano. And you're going to have to grow up someday real soon."

I frowned, bowed my head, lifted Victoria off the back of the chair, and stormed out of the room.

"Don't worry, Victoria," I whispered to my doll. "It will never happen."

#

Mr. Marquez lived on a small farm, in a rural part of New Jersey. He told me that he got up at 2:00 A.M. each morning to feed the chickens and the pigs.

The piano recital was coming up. I'd chosen my two pieces – "Fur Elise" and "The Entertainer." More importantly, I'd also chosen my outfit --a red and white gingham dress, with ruffled sleeves, and a large red satin sash around the waist, tied into a big bow in the back. After a night of sleeping in sponge rollers, my hair would fall into Shirley Temple ringlets, and I'd wear red satin ribbons in my hair to match my sash.

The piano recital was going to be held in the living room of Mr. Marquez's house. I wasn't looking forward to the recital. The only thing I was looking forward to was seeing the farm and the animals.

"I want to see the pig," I told him, in an unusual burst of assertiveness.

"Sure, sure. I'll bring you out to the yard, to show you the pig," he replied, with his usual seriousness.

#

Hanging over the couch in our formal dining room was a painting of a lion. My father had brought it home from Korea during the war, and his mother had promptly placed it in a 1950's gold gilded frame. The frame was embarrassingly gaudy, clashing hideously with the stark, minimalist Korean painting.

There was nothing showy about this lion. Painted with thick, bright, angry strokes, he stood on top of a rock, his right foot thrust in front, glaring furiously at the viewer. Behind him, beyond the rock, seemed to be a limitless black void.

From the stairs in our house, I had a view of the entire living room: the lion painting, the couch, the piano to the right, the antique chair and table to the left in front of the green velvet drapes.

Every night, I played a game: I had five seconds to get to the top of the stairs, or else the lion would come flying out of the frame and devour me.

Standing on the bottom step, I would meet the malevolent glare of the lion's, take a deep breath, and begin counting. I ran up the stairs, two steps at a time.

I always made it up the stairs in five seconds; my life depended on it.

#

The night before I saw the pig, I dreamt I didn't make it up the stairs in time.

In my dream, I waited on the bottom of the stairs, and began to count.

This time, the lion bounded out of the canvas before I'd finished counting.

"Wait!" I yelled. "I haven't counted to five yet! You're supposed to wait! That's cheating!"

The lion didn't attack me, but ran past me and up the stairs, where my parents, brother, and sister were asleep.

"I need to go save them!" I thought, and tried to run after him, but my legs were suddenly heavy, as if I were wading through syrup in slow motion.

Mr. Marquez appeared at the top of the stairs, ruler in hand, scowling.

I stopped, terrified.

I began to feel angry, and started running, fists clenched, towards him. But my legs were still slow-motion heavy.

The lion stood next to him, and the two of them remained at the top of the stairs in a bizarre show of unity. I felt furious and annoyed, though I wasn't sure why, and had an urge to pummel the both of them with my little fists.

I woke up before I reached the top of the stairs.

#

Mr. Marquez lived in a part of New Jersey that was older than the modern, state-of-the art 1968 suburb where my family and I lived. His living room was small and stuffy, with faded upholstery and the smell of old books and sheet music. It was a claustrophobic setting for a recital, with approximately 25 guests crowded onto folding chairs.

Surprisingly, there was enough room for a Steinway baby grand. As I played my recital pieces, I found the keys less responsive than our piano console at home. The keys were cold, hard, and made of genuine ivory, unlike the plastic keys of my own piano. I had to stomp down hard on the sustain pedal with my little foot to get it to respond, but I remember getting through the recital well enough.

Afterwards, while another student was playing Mozart, Mr. Marquez tugged gently on my sleeve. "Come on; I'll show you the pig."

The room was dark and we slipped away unnoticed. I put on my heavy winter coat, and the piano teacher donned his long black winter overcoat and hat. Even at that age, I wondered at Mr. Marquez skipping out on another student's performance, and how that student would feel if she'd known. Would she be offended?

It was bitterly cold outside, but it felt good to get out of the stuffy, crowded room and into the night air. Mr. Marquez walked quickly, his expression stern as always, hands in his pockets. I had to jog slightly to keep up with him. We walked down a rural dirt road, my shiny patent leather shoes quickly becoming dusty.

The pig was not what I'd expected. It wasn't what I was used to seeing in cartoons or children's books--small, perfectly pink little animals, with long lashes and curly tails, and ridiculous smiles. The swine, even from behind the safety of its fence, seemed enormous and intimidating. He was not pink, but sort of a grey-brown color, filthy, snorting, loud, and did not seem to welcome my presence. I thought of Dorothy in The Wizard of Oz during an early scene in the movie, still in dreary, black-and-white Kansas, when she balances herself precariously on a fence in the barnyard and falls into a sty of squealing hogs. Screaming, she's rescued by one of the farmhands (who chastises her for "not having any sense" – he later emerges as The Scarecrow). As I gazed at the threatening beast, I wondered why Dorothy would have done something so stupid.

As I peered over the fence and watched the pig at a safe distance, Mr. Marquez stood by, hands in pockets, never smiling. Although his stern, aloof manner was intimidating, it was also a welcome relief from the cloying, saccharine tone of the adults who were around me that night. "Oh my! Don't you look pretty, with your curls and your dress and shiny shoes? And what a good little pianist you are! Your parents must be so proud!"

I think he enjoyed taking a break from the recital, from the crowded, stuffy room, and into the winter air; from the stifling atmosphere of the recital, into the barnyard.

As for me, I felt honored that he'd chosen me, and not any of his other students, to be his ditching buddy, to cut class and sneak out to the barnyard, like a couple of rebels – to escape the claustrophobic atmosphere of the recital, the formality, the polite applause, having to patiently listen to the classics being torn apart by young hands. Was I his favorite? Did he like me more than the rest of them? Did he think I was the best?

It only occurred to me years later, when I was an adult, that Mr. Marquez probably had the pig slaughtered for meat.

#

The day my mom informed Mr. Marquez we were moving out to California, he seemed distressed. It meant he would no longer have any control over me.

"You need to make sure she continues with her piano lessons," he lectured her, "or everything I've taught her will just to garbage. Make sure she does her Hertz and Hanon daily, and to keep up with the pieces she's learned! As soon as you're settled in California, you need to find a quality piano teacher. Don't just choose anyone! Get recommendations! All these lessons are for naught, if she doesn't continue!" My mom nodded obediently.

I felt elated. I was free.

I imagined my Wednesday nights now – somewhere in California, maybe with a horse in the backyard, like Mom promised – a backyard with palm trees and desert shrubs and cacti and lizards. Maybe I would be playing outside on the beach or running across a sunny hill during dusk. Or maybe I would be inside our new house, fussing over Victoria, changing her outfits, and still maintaining my Barbies' high standard of living and thirst for adventure. No more waiting for Mr. Marquez, no more anxiously peering out from behind the white sheer panel curtain, no more ruler rapping my knuckles

We moved to southern California – there was no sunny beach nearby, and of course no horse in our backyard--but there were layers of brown smog that made my throat constrict and my eyes water--and there were mean, tan, athletic pretty girls who made fun of my pale skin and sudden allergies.

I would never be free from Mr. Marquez and his ruler. He would still dominate every musical piece I played, everything I said or thought, every decision I made in life, whether minor or

major. He would always be there waiting at the top of the stairs, ready to admonish me, to rap my knuckles with a ruler the second I screwed up.

"Repeat that measure 20 more times," I'd hear him say.

And I would obey.

About the Author:

Carolyn Soyars is a musician and writer, who lives in Ventura County with her husband, Dave, and their neurotic tuxedo cat, Roscoe. She is a regular contributor to The Los Angeles Beat, and has written film, concert, and CD reviews. You may read more of her writing at www.carolynsoyars.com

KAZANTZAKIS AT HOME

by Larry Smith

He was so old that some of the kids said he took the very first shit that ever made the olives grow. Many of the people on the block believed that he was over one-hundred, although he himself wasn't sure. His people may have come from Africa originally, or at least that's what he remembers his grandmother saying, or perhaps it was a dear friend of his grandmother whose family also transported over that said it. Somewhere in his mind he still saw sand so white that, when the sun struck it, the light bounced back up again, like a burning mirror in the thick hot air. But he could recall no strange animals, only the familiar ones of this country. And while he was the darkest person they'd ever seen, he wasn't dark like the jet black people who lived over there.

This land had its own deep white gleam every spring when the people repainted their houses. The heavy lacquer mixed sweetly with the orchids and gave April a gummy distinctive smell. For a long time now he's been sitting on the front stoop watching and not saying too much. He's a tall man, almost bald, with a wispy grayish beard that falls down straight along his cheeks and chin.

Perhaps the family had to fight for its life when they first came to Crete. Their enemies could have been anyone. He let his mind wander back to those days. If he closed his eyes tight enough, could he hear the world as he had heard it from inside his mother's womb: musket sounds, cries in the night, whispers of insurrection? He remembers as much as he can. He figures they all probably landed in Heraklion off some rude skiff, beneficiaries of a week's calm wind on the sea. Maybe the Turks had already subdued the forlorn island, if not

the enduring rage of its inhabitants, raped his grandmother as she wandered about, herself darker than the Turks, darting between alcoves in the dusty city. Or, who knows, maybe they chose instead to throw in their lot with the usurpers: themselves grim invaders spying on the townsfolk and peeking out from behind blood-spattered walls when the soldiers cut down the day's conspirators. But no one had condemned him, and of course the people here, who find out everything, never forgive or forget. Someone would have known about grandmother's furtive visits to the police had she been a teller of deadly tales.

It wasn't much of a trek from the city to what would be their home for the next century or so. Due south through the city past the ramparts built by earlier invaders, then past the Turks' new office buildings, to the lamb and fish shops full of life where crones even more ancient than grandmother bargained for the day's catch. Then to the magnificent fountain older than all the crones those crones ever knew. Past old walls and ditches still full of goats grazing on scattered patches of grass. Plenty of space, finally, to build a house or rout a beggar from another house abandoned by some other family in flight, maybe, from the Turks and heading for the sea. Later they built the great wall against the invaders and, when he was already old, he watched them bury the famous writer. How sullen the priests who followed him up, how uncomfortable they seemed carrying this strange dead child of theirs. Surrounded by the winding walls, they laid him on top of the Martinengo Bastion and put many beautiful flowers there.

He had never learned to read, and he spoke very little. Only to his sister would he relate those of the day's events he saw that seemed worth relating. Over the course of his many years he did indeed see a few worth the telling. For example, he'd seen adultery once, which he knew they'd find out about and kill someone for. From the very beginning he watched as John Tzortzis started hating his wife; there was a flicker in Tzortzis' face one day, and for the next ten years the old man saw it harden and become a shadow growing darker and darker. He mentioned what he saw to his sister, who nodded and kept her silence. Tzortzis finally met a young girl living over by the Church of St. Catherine, and they disappeared together. His wife went screeching along the road and through the big ditch, scattering the goats, who raised their own cacophony. Her brother and the young girl's father went out after the elopers and when they brought back the girl some weeks later no one asked where Tzortzis was.

As time went by he saw more and more. Many strangers came, most of them fair-skinned and with pleasant manners. They would hike along the ditch, amused by the goats, and head for the Martinengo Bastion. Often the kids followed them up on bicycles. Sometimes as he lay down on his bed against the wall, he'd hear the footsteps heading in that direction. One night he doubted it was a stranger's walk.

The next day as he sat on the stoop, George, a local policeman, came by to see his niece. George's heavy eyes were unblinking, their lids held back as if propped by little sticks. They spoke awhile, then his niece's husband strolled along. The niece and her husband nodded and shrugged as George spoke. He heard all three of them grunt quietly and cluck their tongues.

George walked past him, moving on toward the city. But before he had gone thirty paces the old man spoke up. "It was a light step I heard last night," he shouted over to the policeman. "A young man's. But his shoes were heavy, and struck up some dust, and echoed in my ear for a count of ten before it settled."

The policeman, taciturn child of a race of perfect detectives, nodded thank you and continued his way.

They saw the old man sitting on the stoop just off the road as they skirted the goats on Evans St. By what Connery could read of the map in the old guidebook, Kazantzakis was buried on a kind of high rampart, or perhaps a natural plateau, which was called the Martinengo Bastion. "Somebody here might have heard of this 'bastion,'" he said to Thalia.

"I'll try that," she said, and approached the old man. He looked up with a blank expression as she spoke to him in Greek. The early sunset was taking the bite out of the day's heat, and there was a slight breeze. Connery had drunk some Domestica but not even half the bottle. If he felt settled inside himself at that moment, satisfied while not quite serene, oblivious at least to the usual torments, it was apparently some natural gladness. It was perhaps these last few pleasant weeks in Greece that had given him surcease.

He'd been told Kazantzakis' grave was worth a look, that it would be especially restful after the torturous intellectual-seeming Knossos. This, unlike most of Greece, was a place where history could be recollected in tranquility. Not that Greece agitated him; quite to the contrary, he had driven around Thessalonica like a native and, in Athens, even enjoyed the sooty outdoor cafes. The other tourists hadn't bothered him. And, when he got off the ferry from Kavalla and saw Thasos' rugged beauty, he decided to stay a week. For a day or two, he enjoyed being alone; then, when he met Thalia Voutas, he was delighted to stay the extra time with her. They continued traveling on together when the week was over.

"Sit with me, of course," she said at the tavern. Although he seldom hungered for women, Connery attracted them easily. His pocked and homely face was a gentle one. He was, in fact, a gentle man, when not too drunk, or set upon by the obscure and at times only half-articulated demands of a parent or cousin or brother. Women like Thalia, also of upper class origins, raised in Paris by her mother and a succession of stepfathers, naturally gravitated his way without much effort.

There was no pretense of love, yet he may never have loved a naked body this much, not just the sculptured breasts and butt which were easy to admire along conventionally aesthetic lines, but also the ungainly dash of moist hair winding around from her crotch to the crack in her ass. Of course he couldn't put his mouth between her legs--he could never do that--but she was kind enough not to ask, which he appreciated.

"You like American men?" he asked her in bed.

"I've only got you to go by," she said, teasing. "It's funny, though. I don't think of you as an American. I think of you as an Irishman."

"And you give allowances to the Irish that you don't to others?

"Yes, very simpatico--but not because of the poets you've made. It's because of the church..."

"That unmade us?" he interrupted with a wink.

"Just so!"

Hers was a sympathy given lightheartedly, without condescension, so he accepted it without shame. Besides which, she seemed to enjoy him so much, even love him a little after a fashion. Next day she put her mouth on him, it happened on the beach, and that he was willing to allow.

Something in all of this he loved. Himself a poet, that evening he wrote

No one ever recovers,

but I will soothe your ancient wound

and lave your sand-encrusted skin,

like death laves its phantoms.

He stopped writing and took a walk over to the little museum, but you couldn't get into it even during the day unless you found the caretaker. So he went back to the inn, and worked by the window as Thalia was falling asleep:

Wait for me,

wail for me,

finish, read me

the monologue

you pass as dream

and, lapped in my ear,

I'll cradle you

like earth's first tulip

bellied with dew,

peeking toward the sun,

proudly, astonishingly black.

Purge the verbs,

fire each new word to world,

thick as night,

echoing like day--

the truth of you

your endless whispered

reverie holds!

My part is old hunger

lined in sawdust,

a rhythm seeking embrace:

O Thasos, Thasos,

yours is the music

all worlds dance to.

The family claims were stupendous. The great-grandfather came from Ireland, though no one knew for sure which part. Somewhere he had stolen a horse and sold it for a pot of porridge then sold two portions of porridge which left him enough to buy more porridge and a few potatoes as well, which, once sold, was enough to book passage to America. When he landed in New York, he began the horse and porridge cycle all over again, except now instead of more porridge he bought a seat on the New York Stock Exchange and, from there, through conspicuous international vistas, diamond mines, canals, and the ear of kings.

His children were feeble. One was kicked off the Exchange, another committed suicide. The grandchildren were only slightly better. One raised horses and subsidized anti-communist paramilitary groups. His brother, Connery's father, took over one of the world's largest typewriter companies and within a decade had turned it into one of the smallest. Sometimes he'd forget his son's first name, which was William. All his affections, such as they were, were tied up in his daughters, while Connery's mother followed her husband about in a haze of gin and bitters.

The family branched. Some of William's cousins went back to Ireland and rested there. Nieces and nephews materialized at parties in New York. During visits to the family estate in Westchester, or throughout long summers at the house in Canada, the eyes of others fastened hard upon him. They were as drunk as he was, as feckless, and, for all their pride in pedigree, just as rootless. But, equating impotence with privilege, they utterly despised Connery, who was too honest not to know himself a sad shambles of a man. And he showed them he knew it, if only in the way he'd avert his eyes or lower his head. Although he really loved only poetry, in the last analysis the redoubtable lineage thrilled him too. Poor Connery, he hated himself for not rising to the fabled family aureole even as he saw through it.

He wrote:

Our child is monster;

he has perfumed the once-strong satraps,

and now Persia is sweet meat

strung for the Northern tribes.

Scenes booze helped erase. The worst, of course, was the boarding school his father had picked out for him. Having gone there himself in the 1930s, he'd remained piously loyal, as well as philanthropic. When the seniors, tacitly approved by the winking priests, buggered the freshmen, Connery shivered to see the callous and disembodied face of the father at each window, peering fiercely. No one came to the rescue. Fear soon obscured those memories; they grew so indistinct, he saw upperclassmen, all smirks and puckered jowls, without really remembering if they were ones who laid him or roughly used his face, or only made him watch as they set upon the weakest of the newer boys. Yet he didn't grow up to hate homosexuality. Just Catholicism.

College, a hotbed of European intellectualism, was a great haven for awhile, and the professors there refugees in their own right. Connery felt the world well lost but for the passion in ideas they'd salvaged from the flames. Even Keats they recast; the clerical hacks who raised him wouldn't recognize their old world now! At home, though, his own unkempt old world awaited, the gothic tableaux unchanged albeit a little worse for alcoholic wear. One day, after visiting with a Jewish friend from school, his mother slurped, "Watch what he wants from you!"

"I don't understand," he said. "We have nothing he could possibly want."

"William!" barked the old man from the other side of the room, rebuking the perceived insolence.

"But we haven't," he said, more confused than defiant.

"If you don't learn what we have to teach you, then--" at once Connery saw his father was drunk and probably didn't know what the conversation was about--"then it's something only long and hard experience will lead to, and a learning experience that you'll have to learn without the help of experience."

Connery mumbled in defense of his friend. "His father just acquired the -- Corp."

"But with only the narrowest majority of stockholders approving!" exclaimed mother.

When finally he went out into the world, it was as a clerk in an antiques store. Half the people he waited on also came from great families and the other half were nouveau riche, but, once they found out who he was, everyone sought his acquaintanceship. It was, he wearily realized, the saving grace of his class that, while success, enterprise, all the predatory graces came naturally to some of his own, others like himself were sufficiently picturesque to be exempt from such expectations.

He watched Thalia approach the dark old man as the goats scampered up the side of the ditch. They tore at the small clumps of grass and meandered back down again. He did love her somehow; he did not want to part from her! The waning sun shone through the light green dress against her buttocks. "Martinengo Bastion," he called out to remind her what to ask for. Thalia, her Greek a flat nasal whine, begged the old man's pardon and inquired about the locale. But "Martinengo Bastion" didn't seem to mean much to him, or at least he didn't respond to the name. She started to walk away.

"Kazantzakis!" he called out abruptly. His long spindly arm pointed up toward the road to their right.

They looked out past his grave across the hill. It was an open structure, the wall against the Turks winding down as far as they could see. And it was beautiful, just as Connery was promised. The grave itself was a simple stone sculpture bedecked with a half-dozen bouquets. One shrub with blue flowers seemed to grow out of the grave itself, Kazantzakis' flesh feeding the roots. Not like that other flower, he thought, the single daisy plopped mockingly amid the unspeakable ooze. Little Sheehey, was it? A flower, alone and upright and absurd, which someone stuck in him as he lay there after the seniors finished with him...He drove away the image, as he always had. Not like that, these flowers here for blessed remembrance.

"You know I'm a cold bitch," she whispered to him suddenly, incongruously. "Always been."

"You?" he said. "Never."

"It was my upbringing." She lifted an eyebrow. "Just like you, I was taught to despise everything around me, but we had no illusions about ourselves either. My mother told me that nothing was genuine, everything is for sale. Grace and style and breeding are commodities on a market." She nodded toward the grave. "My mother would say this too is a commodity. A great writer buried in a beautiful spot, that's something the Cretans can sell us, and, even more important, it's something we can sell ourselves. A beautiful experience to sell ourselves, so we'll believe it was, after all, worthwhile to wake up and live through this day. A dreary way of looking at life, no?"

"Was your mother's cynicism as eloquent as yours?"

"Perhaps not," Thalia smiled, "but she made me a democrat in a snide way. We were so full of contempt, it made us respectful. My mother would say, `Don't look down on the merchants because of their manners or because you despise whatever it is they're selling. The rest of us aren't very different. We're all mercantile under the skin.'"

"Did you always believe her?"

"Once I argued with her when I was very young. It was during my first period and I was very emotional. I was bleeding so heavy, I couldn't believe then that everything wasn't real, so real!" Thalia curled her lips and smiled narrowly. "`You'll get over it,' my mother said, and she wouldn't argue with me. She never argued."

Flowers always made Thalia think of sex. She often imagined orchids between her legs, and when she bent over a bouquet it was her own cunt, or another woman's, she was savoring. Sometimes the sight of a rose reminded her of the first time, and, if she closed her eyes tight enough, she could hear the soft hissing sound of herself being deflowered. Sex at least seemed real, and she had had many lovers. Her intentions were always indisputably heartfelt. The first dinner with Connery at the tavern, for example, her legs were spread under the table. How that thrilled her, his not knowing she had already opened wide. And she liked his poems so much, after she read them she asked him to recite a few.

> O my woman,
>
> > purge the verb to love;
> >
> > > score from old thunder
>
> the new moon song.
>
> > Sing, I am no wayfarer.
> >
> > Sing, I am here to die.

The early evening breeze over Kazantzakis' grave. They'd been holding hands. "At least you're not pitiful," he said to her.

"Oh William," she said, full of compassion. Still arm in arm, they descended the steps on the opposite side of the grave. Walking up toward them was the policeman, George. His jet black eyebrows cast an almost glowering shadow but he smiled at them pleasantly. Thalia said hello and, pausing on a step, he asked her in Greek if they were enjoying their visit.

"It's a beautiful monument the people gave this man," she said. He agreed, commenting that Kazantzakis was a great poet. He started up past them but then stopped short and turned back to speak again. He spoke somberly, his voice lowering to a near whisper as he finished.

When they reached the bottom of the stairs, Connery saw that Thalia's eyes were alive-- startled, aroused, yet a little amused as well. "What was that all about?" he asked.

"The policeman said that a few days ago someone smeared shit on Kazantzakis' grave."

"No kidding," said Connery.

"He said they were going to find whoever did it."

"I don't doubt they will," he said.

"And when they find him," said Thalia, her eyes wide and her voice vibrant with the inescapable reality of the matter, "when they find him, he says they'll kill him."

About the Author:

Larry Smith's novella, Patrick Fitzmike and Mike Fitzpatrick, was published by Outpost 19. His stories have appeared in McSweeney's Quarterly Concern, Low Rent(nominated for a Pushcart Prize), Exquisite Corpse, The Collagist, Curbside Splendor, Sequetrum, and [PANK], among numerous others. Smith's poetry has appeared in Descant (Canada) and Elimae, among others; his articles and essays in Modern Fiction Studies, Social Text, The Boston Phoenix, and others. Visit Larrysmithfiction.com.

SOMEPLACE WARM
by Paul-John Ramos

1

About every 20 to 30 minutes, I put my hand on the radiators and pipes. It was usually bedroom radiator on the far right, pipe running down through the bathroom, then kitchen pipe, then living room radiator on the left. They were all cold and I could keep my hand on them forever.

It was something with the boiler, the building people admitted. They were working on it. I got acquainted with a variety of draughts that I didn't know were coming through the window trim. I also found out what it's like to be distracted every so often and confuse a passing bus outside for the sound of air beginning to pulse out of the valves.

2

Sunday afternoon was cloudy and around 15 Fahrenheit. The entire winter seemed to be like this. I was fully dressed and felt an urge to shudder.

Bedroom radiator, bathroom pipe, kitchen pipe, living room. The bedroom radiator felt vaguely warm. Was it warm or was I imagining that it was, since it's always the first to come on?

I looked outside at the gray sky, salt-stained highway, and flags of a Goodyear dealer that were tattered in the wind. The phone then went to my ear. Super's number: no answer, no voicemail. Building company's number: answering machine. I didn't really feel like speaking to them. The chicken breast and rice that I made hadn't tasted very good and I couldn't read in peace.

3

My alarm went off at six on Monday. I slept, but not well. I dragged myself from underneath the blanket and stretched in the cool air. The Sun hadn't come up yet and the highway lights still shone over tractor-trailers in the dark. Snow from three days before lay alongside the roads and streaks of frost zigzagged across the bedroom window.

I got ready for work, slipped on my coat, and locked the front door. The hallway tiles were coated with salt, dirty snow, and dust. I walked one flight down before footsteps came racing up. I stopped when the super was in front of me.

>   - Hi.
>   - Hello.
>   - I need to look at your toilet. Are you here today?
>   - No, I'm going to work.
>   - I need you to leave me your keys. We need to do some work on the pipes in your bathroom.
>   - How would I get them back?
>   - You know where my apartment is? 1C?
>   - Yeah.
>   - I'll leave them under the stairs in an envelope. You can just look under the stairs when you come back.
>   I reached into my pants pocket and handed him the keys. He thanked me.
>   - If I haven't come back, you can call me.
>   - The boiler hasn't been working right.
>   - Yeah, they know about it. They're working on it.

-Okay.

- Thanks for your help.

He turned to hustle back downstairs.

- Okay.

I stood on the landing for a moment, my bag dangling over my shoulder.

4

Helping others is an art. Most people can't be relied on and the few who can aren't very good at being relied on. Usually, all they can do is try.

My mother and father kept giving me advice from 300 miles away. They told me over the phone to use my space heater, turn on my oven, and dress in layers. Nothing worked, but I didn't complain very much. I was supposed to be a man. A man with some-where to go. I needed to be on my own.

Gretta popped into the office around ten. Her look at the time of entrance was usu-al: upright, shoulders squared, a noticeable smile, and alert, brown eyes behind oval, white-framed glasses. She had to walk past my cubi-cle each morning and almost always said hello.

I had to get up and speak with one of our directors on the opposite side of the room. Then I ended up at the copy machine, next to her desk. Her dark brown hair was tied back and her eyes were clinging to a proofsheet on the monitor. She glanced over and noticed me. I didn't care to be noticed that day.

- Good morning.

- Hey.

- How are things?

I shrugged my shoulders.

- My apartment is cold.

- Oh. You don't have any heat?

Not much, I told her. Some in the morning, some from 5 to 10 in the evening, and nothing overnight. I hadn't slept well for four days, my throat was raspy, and I wanted to punch someone.

- It's terrible to be cold at home. I know, I've been through it.

I said Yeah.

- How long has this been going on?

- Since the beginning of December.

She asked me what they were doing about it, how large my apartment is, where it is. I told her.

- There are always people staying at our place. Would you want to come out to Brooklyn? We have a big living room where you can stretch out.

- Oh, thanks, but you don't have to offer something like that.

- You sure?

- Positive. You and your roommate don't need me taking up the place, anyway.

She insisted it wouldn't be a big deal for one or two nights. I said I would see what happens.

5

Things stopped working altogether on Thurs-day night. It dropped to 8 degrees outside, with no heat or hot water on the inside. My space heater in the bedroom kept me from freezing to death. I stood at my bathroom sink the next morning, shaving with ice-cold water next to my new toilet they installed the other day.

6

I met up with Gretta in the elevator at lunchtime. I could go over that night.

7

It was an older building like mine, on a street near the main drag in Bensonhurst. They lived on the third floor. I rang the bell and Gretta answered.

She said hello at their door and wel-comed me in. I stood in the foyer with my bag. Then she offered to take my coat. I took my coat off and leaned my bag against the foyer's wall like I do at home.

- Did you find it easy to get here?

- Yeah. A bit of a walk from the train, that's all.

She pointed with her arm as she hung my coat in a closet. There was a big couch in the living room. She told me to make myself comfortable. It was a brown imitation leather couch that I didn't like the idea of sitting on.

Someone's brown hair and red sweater were visible along the door frame after I sat.
- He's here?
- Yes, this is my friend from work.

She must've felt safe to face into the room. Antoinette was her roommate's name. She was tall, maybe 25, with short hair and narrow, pouty lips. Antoinette looked very bemused about me.

- Hi.
    - Hi.
    - No heat in his apartment.
    - That sucks.
    - Yeah.
I shrugged my shoulders. Antoinette gave no expression. Gretta looked back over to me.
    - Do you like chopped steak?
    - Yeah. Why?
    - We're making it.
    - Oh. For what?
    - For us.
    - Oh, you don't have to do that. I can eat out.
    - No, no. It's alright.
Marie Antoinette kept looking to Gretta and to me as we took turns speaking. She still had that neutral look on her pale face. The lips didn't move, just stayed straight and together.

So I agreed to dinner. I sat on the couch with my hands folded, wanting to touch as little imitation leather as possible.

8

They went on with their lives. I got up to look out the window as an excuse for raising my ass off the thing.

Apparently, Antoinette liked to absorb a guest into her routine. Either that or they had too many guests over through Gretta's kindness and she was tired of adjusting her lifestyle. Or she didn't like me. Or she didn't like Gretta but liked the apartment and put up with her. Or something else completely.

I was still sitting in the middle of the couch. I dreaded the idea of my arm atop the cool ruffles of an armrest. Antoinette strutted in and picked up the TV remote from their coffee table. She turned on the set and lumped against the armrest to my right. Channel 360-something was put on. A show was starting.
    - Do you watch this?
    - No, can't say I do.
    - It's a good show.

She sat with the remote in her hand as if ready to switch the channel again.

After five minutes of the program, I wished she'd had.

9

Gretta was making dinner while we sat in the living room. The apartment was getting stuffy, but I didn't care. The television was too loud. That I did care about. A smell of steak, mashed potatoes, and something else was easing in from the kitchen. An alien feeling came over me when it entered my nose.

Antoinette smiled at the program a couple of times and I couldn't quite figure out what induced that. The first time was when two of the main characters were in the front seat of a car, arguing while going somewhere. The second time was when one of them poured a glass of something from their liquor cabinet.

We sat there for about 20 minutes without speaking to each other. Then Gretta said quietly from the kitchen, "We're ready."

Antoinette got up from the couch, stopped before the threshold, and switched off the television. I looked at a blank screen for a moment before going into the kitchen. Antoinette was sitting down when I arrived.

10

There were platters of steak, mashed potatoes, and boiled string beans. Gretta sat on one side of the table, Antoinette took up the other side, and I was at the head. I guess Gretta tried to make me feel important. The food wasn't what I was used to.

- You always do this?
- Often, yeah.

I looked at Antoinette. She glanced at me and kept to her string beans.

- I hear the rents aren't too bad out here.
- Yeah, well...We pay 1,200 for this.
- Yeah?
- Yeah...It's alright...It's in a good area.

Antoinette spoke up.

- Where do you live?

I told her. Antoinette said Oh and crawled back under her rock for a while longer.

There was no dessert. Not that I had a right to expect it, but there wasn't any. I offered to help clean up but Gretta held her position. I pulled out a newspaper bought on the way and sat back on the imitation leather. They stayed behind in the kitchen to wash. One of them turned on a radio atop the refrigerator and music started belching out. I tried to read the first paragraph of an article six or seven times.

11

I pretended to read the paper. Antoinette came into the living room and I prayed that she wouldn't turn on the TV again. Instead, she walked past me and opened a window. It was apparently getting too warm for them after dinner. The cold air flowed under the pane and I tried to ignore it as each blast jetstreamed over my body.

12

The music kept playing as they cleaned the kitchen and other places in the apartment. Gretta asked if I needed anything. Antoinette, it appeared, couldn't give a shit less if I were breathing or not. It came about nine when the music stopped and they announced getting ready for bed. They both had places to go in the morning.

13

They turned in across the hallway and I stayed in the living room to read my paper. In case you're wondering, they slept in separate beds. It got very quiet inside and outside the building, I began to think I was happy.

14

I started to doze off an hour later. I pulled a quilt out of my bag and lay down on the wheat-colored rug. The floor was a bit hard, but nothing I hadn't dealt with before.

15

I fell off to sleep and woke up after what felt a short period of time. The side of my head was smarting from hardness of the floor. The room had turned cold; I got up and shut the window almost completely, then lay back down again. My spine ached from the sheer rigidity. It was oak boards underneath. I doubted I would fall asleep again. Then I looked up to judge the couch. Ruffles could be picked out in the streetlight that shone through the blinds and I thought No...just...no. So then came the old college try: I turned over on the rug, pulled the quilt over my head, and tried to think about something else.

16

I was wide awake for another hour or so when a baby or some young kid began crying next door. It could be heard right through the wall. I wanted to move into another room but it wasn't my place. Gretta and Antoinette appeared to sleep right through it, I heard no stirring behind their door.

17

It went on for about an hour. Then it stopped and I tried to calm myself down. It got too hot in the room and I reopened the window a few inches. The neighboring houses looked sad and a dog was barking in the distance. A police siren sounded closer. My body felt inflamed but not particularly exhausted.

Just a place, I thought. Just a place somewhere, anywhere, that could give me inner peace without fail. Outside of your family's home and mother's womb, there seem very few places worth discovering and trying to remain in. Your friends are only your friends and owe you nothing. The hotels put on their fake smiles that readily turn to frowns when they don't understand your problem or you can't pay anymore. The churches nowadays are bolted shut at night and cops move everyone off the park benches at dusk.

18

I dozed off again and came to with the sound of floppy footsteps in the hallway. I looked up from the rug and saw Antoinette in a white robe and fluffy blue slippers with a bottle of pills in her hand. We looked into each other's eyes as she walked towards the bathroom. We said nothing. She had that expression on her face, except this time while half-asleep, and I sensed nothing in it. I turned to my opposite side and tried to go back under. The bathroom light went on, water ran into the sink, and the light went out. Then she flopped back to their room and closed the door.

19

My shoulders and the small of my back ached when I woke up next morning. They had gotten up around 7:30 and the commotion stirred me. Both dressed for the day: Gretta in a teal blazer and Antoinette in a gray pullover.

They both looked nice. I could've tried to become Gretta's boyfriend, I suppose, but I already had my fill of disappointment.

- How did it go?
- Not bad.
- We tried to keep quiet.
- You were. Don't worry about it.
- We're heading out, but we can leave you a key-
- No, no, it's alright. I have to go, anyway.

Antoinette stepped to the hall closet and took out her coat and scarf.

- Are you sure? It's not a problem.
- Nah, I need to go back to my area. I have some things to do. But thanks – for everything.

I beckoned to Antoinette.
- Thanks.
- You're welcome.

20

Upon returning, I ran into a tenant who said that a repairman and people from the oil company were there in the morning. We were delivered a bad load of oil and it jammed up the pipes running from the boiler.

They must've gotten some hot air in the morning. It felt kind of warm when I arrived, but not for long. It was the afternoon hours when nothing would come up, the timer or whatever part still needed an adjustment.

In watching cars, trucks, vans, and buses stream over a highway, you wonder where on Earth there's room for all of them to be kept. It might explain why no one seems to have enough room or time or attention for anyone else. You wonder if anyone will ever truly have space in their lives for you and when that day might come.

An hour after arriving, I thought I'd heard the bathroom pipe ping. I put my hand on it and felt nothing, just its age-worn roughness. They said that spring was only five weeks away. And at least it was quiet. I felt calm, I felt aware of myself, and it was ever so quiet.

21

My phone rang later that day. I heard a familiar voice on the other end that didn't readily
come to mind.

    - It's Antoinette. Gretta's roommate.
    - ...Hi.
And for what?
    - How's everything?
    - ...Alright.
    - Are things okay over there?
    - Yeah, they're alright.
    - I'm just calling because you're more
than welcome to stay with us if you need to.
We didn't want you to feel rushed out this
morning.
    - ...It was nothing, really.
    - Feel free to come. Anytime.
    - Gretta's okay with it?
    - Yeah. And me, too. Both of us.
I sighed jokingly.
    - ...What a couple of pals.
She laughed. Never thought it would
happen in my lifetime.
    - You're good company. We don't get
that often.
    - Well...Thanks. Maybe I'll come by
again. Hopefully I won't need to, though.
    - How is it over there?
I glanced at the dead pipe in my kitch-
en and out at the gray sky.
    - Alright, I guess.
We paused.
    - Let us know, okay?
    - I will.

    All they can do is try. I hung up and
the Sun began to faintly gaze out from the
clouds.

About the Author:

Paul-John Ramos is a short story writer, poet,
and essayist whose work has recently appeared
in Workers Write, Romance Maga-
zine, Cahoots, and Trajectory. He lives in Yon-
kers, New York, and is employed as a dean's
assistant at City University of New York.

BLISTERING EYES

by Bettina Rotenberg

She woke up and carefully climbed down from the large bed which seemed like a vast sea of pillows, sheets, and quilt, rumpled now, as she tried to organize her covers into a semblance of comfort from her place on the floor, so that she'd be able to fall asleep again; as though the memory of never having been alone had kept her from experiencing the bliss of unconsciousness, even in this solitary retreat of her bedroom. So she walked uncertainly across the wood floor in her bare feet, and her white cotton nightgown, which fell down to her ankles, was creased in places where she'd hiked it up above her waist while lying in bed, for any pressure but the soft smooth pale blue sheet bothered her skin.

"I must go quietly," Anna said to herself, "for Sam is asleep."

She pushed the door to the kitchen open, exerting a little force, for it had been jammed shut with a wine-colored cloth with ridges on it, since the other rooms must be closed off for the night, or she didn't feel safe enough to fall asleep. The two bedrooms faced each other at opposite ends of a hallway that opened on to a bathroom where the light from the neighbor's night lamp streamed into the hallway and allowed her to see without turning on a light when she left the circumference of her bed. Sam, her husband, slept in the adjoining library when he came in late at night from working and then drinking at the Albatross, a local pub down on San Pablo Avenue where homeless men panhandled, sitting or lying down on the sidewalk.

He'd constructed bookshelves, floor to ceiling, to house the myriad books in his library. Frequently he'd organize them alphabetically, lovingly handling them as he shelved and re-shelved them. He didn't like to disturb Anna when he showed up after midnight, so he'd flop down on an easy chair and immediately fall asleep.

He was a handsome man with a good deal of charm, and worked in a book distribution business, writing the catalogues every season. Each catalogue summarized essential aspects of hundreds of small press books which he learned to describe by digesting publishers' comments on each title. He was deft at this work and was respected in the community of writers as someone who had a finger in every book published in that world of literature and criticism.

Though relatively unemotional, he could be compassionate, and was popular among their friends for this quality; but he could also be mean, and this fluctuation was exaggerated by his bouts of drinking followed by periods of abstinence. He inflicted his cruelty primarily upon Anna, but kept her tied to him by his intermittent kindness.

Anna entered the kitchen, a large room in comparison to the close quarters of her bedroom. It seemed particularly vast this night for she was so tiny, so unbalanced on her small unsteady feet. She reached for a cup half-filled with milk and drank it. Her mouth felt dry; her feet were cold.

When she reached her room again, she scanned its contents: the paintings, her tiny sculpture, the large dark mahogany wooden dresser, the orange enclosed light that beamed gently from a small table beside the bed, and a long rug pinned to the wall woven into a complex pattern of colored stitches with no rhyme or reason, so that it made her eyes somewhat cross-eyed when she tried to follow its zigzagging paths while lying in bed. Why the weaver of this old Moroccan rug hadn't composed a sane repeating motif of colors, why he had chosen to confuse the eye by never leading its observer into a harmonious, peaceful resting point, she failed to question. So her attention would not deviate from this particular wall where the rug hung, and she found she couldn't leave her side of the bed, arrested as she was by this visual quandary.

And if she tried to abandon this sight upon which her gaze fixed before a reasonable hour and climb out of bed, Sam's voice, suffused with fear and anger, would exclaim, "Don't get up! It's much too early. Go back to sleep!"

It seemed to her that this panic about her night-time movements had followed her all her life and culminated in this particular voice that became furious at her disruption of his sleep. She wondered, was it fear for her safety? or was it outrage at her departure from normal sleep behavior? Was it the rug hanging the length of the wall that drove sleep from her eyes or an unhealthy animation of the mind? She learned she had to limit her clandestine movements to those times when no one was watching her. But if she went outside the bounds of her usual day time activities – if those expecting her to keep appointments missed her and she strayed beyond the predictable temporal and spatial bounds, then all the forces circumscribing her burst into calamitous activity – to locate and restrain her and bring her back. All this activity was unleashed under the heading of "safety", and certainly, once she was encumbered by nurses and doctors in the confines of a healthful setting, and she happened to listen to a message from a loved one from far away, she heard such heart-rending tones of entreaty for her to return the call that she became very contrite.

But this contrition didn't last. Anything to break the constraints that bound her! And these bonds took multiple forms, appearing most frequently, it seemed to her, in the form of those relations who depended upon her finite resources: a lame and ailing mother, a sister shackled by a domineering husband, a brother who'd disappeared at the age of thirty

when she remarried, a friend who'd cut her name into her forearm with a knife, a sister who'd slept with her lover...This parade of figures encumbered her mind and appeared during the hours that passed between the time of retiring to bed and the moment that sleep overcame her. She had strategies for eclipsing this mental theatre before it got too late. But instead of commanding her mental arsenal to fight this onslaught before sleep, she'd entertain them nightly with as much aplomb as a hostess, decked in fine clothes, presides at a dinner party during the hours accorded for polite society.

"Mommy, Mommy, Mommy, Mommy!" she intoned, sending her voice into her pillow in a piercing whisper. She felt as though she was breaking in two, and her only comfort would come from this figure that was completely absent. She was the only one who could mend what was broken.

In her mind, Anna supplicated her mother:

"Come back, Mommy; don't be sad. I've hurt you, and you're a wreck. You're never here when I call. You can't speak? You won't talk to me? What's so important? Don't you need me too? You do? So where are you? If I call you now, you might answer and speak to me. But you might not. Perhaps I'll call you when you say you can't talk, just to check, to see if this time you'll speak to me, because I'm important to you.

But I won't call – just to hurt you. You'll see what it's like not to talk to me. Then perhaps you'll want to talk, just to hear my voice. Perhaps I'll call you today, just to feel you close to me again. But that's all over. We won't talk like that anymore.

I'm so mad at you. You don't deserve to hear from me. I won't call now. I'm too angry. My anger maddens me. I teeter on a precipice when I tell how you've hurt me. I won't go near you; I'll refuse to see you. You take control of me, abuse me, enrage me. I beg you not to wreck the writing I sent you. 'I can't stand colloquial language,' you say. 'It's perfect as it is,' I tell you. 'Don't change it,' I beg. 'I won't come to see you if you change any of it.' You laugh like a hyena at the thought that you can't change it. Your impervious voice sends me over the edge. You obliterate your daughter.

I see you. You're a bee in my garden and you multiply. The azaleas, the camellias, the rhododendrons, the roses – all ensure there will be bees galore in the clover in the grass. You're the baby I'm going to give birth to. My little puppy. You're manageable – such a tiny one – the size of a fly on the place where my dog defecated. I put my face next to your blue wings, and you barely smell."

*   *   *
*   *   *

Anna arranged the sheets and the quilt on her bed and lay down so she could easily slip into slumber. Scenarios from her nightly array of images tumbled into her mind:

She was in the restaurant downstairs and was looking for her dog in every possible hiding place. She put him in her lap and he peed on her skirt. Then she shut him outside the door and lost him. The restaurant owner who was the waiter locked him in his car. She was so mad she threatened to report him for cruelty to animals.

She drove to the marina where she followed her dog's tail that glowed blond in the dark and kept them both safe. They climbed over rocks, careful not to slip, completely alone on the island. Her father appeared briefly as Hitler, so she abandoned her dog, who she knew was not a murderer, though he was no longer protecting her, and drove like a madwoman to Mills College campus in Oakland.

She left her car and walked to a clearing where tall deciduous trees surrounded her. She lay down in the spikey grass and held her husband's hand, though he was invisible. She talked to him in whispers and sang to him, and as morning came, she rose and made her way among the sprinklers, refraining from drinking the cool water for she could feel that her sister, Dinah, who managed this campus, was gassing her out of there. She'd usurped the college administration with the intent of getting rid of her.

Anna retraced her steps to her car, found the key, climbed in, and drove towards the exit. Perhaps her sister had forgotten about her.

Dinah had a lot to take care of on the college grounds and she must have seen how weak Anna was. She didn't even have a husband, for where was he as she drove slowly through west Oakland in the early morning traffic on route 80, headed towards Berkeley?

Anna stirred in her sleep, her mind struggling to hold all the images together in the half-light of early morning, and then submerged once again in a scene from her nocturnal adventures:

Sam was in the jeans she bought at the thrift store on 5th street. The label said 'designer jeans' and they reminded her of him because of the bulge at the crotch. She imagined she could double as him, and no one would recognize her. Or she could walk the streets in a sixteen-year old party dress with beige sandals and the idea that he made up half of her body; so still they were indissolubly united.

It was a boiling hot day and she didn't have any water with her as she marched past the groups of kids, the army contingents, and the drunks lingering at the corner bar. It was all dangerous, all frightening, but she was safe because she was disguised as a teenage love-sick girl, and was with a man who put his arms protectively around her when she needed him.

Anna woke up to discover that her dog was outside in the yard and her husband wasn't with her after all. Where was he? She'd called him three days before and told him she was writing again; and, as usual, he sounded pleased to hear from her; but, as the phone call dragged on, he seemed only minimally interested.

She tried to reach him in a hurry a few days later when her landlord threatened her with eviction after she showed up without a car, having braved the Sunday crowds, only stopping for a soda, and asked to spend the night with him and his wife. She thought she'd lost the keys to her apartment and her car, but they were in her purse all the time.

She begged Sam in a fraught voice to come to the landlord's flat; and then there he was, standing at the door, in his usual brown coat, in his usual way, and she tore past him into the street, and her landlord cornered her after she hit him with a karate chop, and he forced her into his car.

The landlord drove Anna and his wife to emergency, and she sat on a cot, facing his wife, making faces at her until the doctor showed up and the wife nervously tried to explain why she'd brought Anna there. But Anna convinced the resident that it was the landlord's wife who was confused and should be admitted, and the doctor let her go.

But Sam didn't lift a finger in her defense on that occasion, and she soon forgot his treachery. After all, he was only her husband in name. She'd driven him out, and when she asked him to return, he'd understandably refused.

He'd cemented her need for him soon after they got together by showing up at a hospital and sitting at the head of her cot when she thought she was dying. By the end, however, she got the impression he couldn't stand her, and if it hadn't been for the tender way he'd clean her eyes out in the morning, she should have wondered what made him want to stick around. He disapproved of her so thoroughly. She remembered what must seem like minor incidents: the way he dismissed the "wimpy voice" she'd use to command the dog to "come," "wait," " sit." Clearly, she had little impact on the creature at those times, but she and the dog had an understanding, and if he didn't want to budge when she softly commanded him to move, then she just yanked him, and he came; or he came, from time to time, when she spoke more urgently; but they weren't unhappy with their arrangement, and her husband clearly was. Years later, his criticism came back to her, as she'd hear her voice from his point of view, and feel like the worst effects of their union would haunt her on her daily walks with the dog whose companionship she eventually relied upon.

At times she imagined he was beside her as she rode the subway, pointing out the men and women he happened to find fault with in one way or another, and she couldn't help feeling as though she was a part of this assemblage of unfortunates. She thought that perhaps she

conjured up this impersonation of his consciousness as an alternative to the absence of the actual man.

If she wished for a reprieve from the memory of his criticism of her, she longed, at other times, to run into him or just drop by his apartment and hang out for hours as he played CD's for her. For on one or another occasion, he might show concern for some hurt or injury she suffered, and in that moment, make her feel completely enveloped by his attention. She couldn't shake the feeling that the criticism he visited upon her, even in his absence, was overshadowed by a general intention to watch out for her and keep her person presentable to the outside world. She assumed that her well-being was fostered in this way because he believed she was hopelessly wanting without his overseeing eye. Ironically, it was her paranoid version of this view that she needed most protection from after he left.

If her subsequent visits to his apartment were punctuated by jabs at her appearance or if some anecdote she told him made him wince, she'd ignore it or simply brush it aside. But afterwards, the sensation of the pleasure of seeing him disappeared and she was left with plaguing memories of the distant coldness in his look when he said goodbye that always implied for her that her personal appearance gave him such pause that he was forced involuntarily to withdraw all warmth from her.

She kept a photo of his image in her pocket like a toy that she took out to examine now and then. But its cracks didn't worry her at any particular moment of study and she clearly saw the blue eyes, the blond hair with hints of grey, the glasses that seemed to cave in at the temple. But the intoxication of his cold unwavering eyes blistered her like hot coals. The burn left marks on her eyes, but when she tried to tend them, she forgot how painful they were.

She'd recall that his hands and feet were shapely, as though the Creator had thought to bestow upon him some beauty to make her forget the ways he hurt her.

To be fair to the guy, he always met her when she called him, and if she needed him, he'd come early that day to meet her for breakfast. So she couldn't shake the idea that the criticism he leveled at her was part of his general intention to care for her..

About the Author:

Bettina Rotenberg grew up in Toronto and studied History and Literature at Radcliffe College, expressive therapies at Leslie College, and got a PhD in Comparative Literature from University of California Berkeley. She taught literature at various colleges in the Bay Area. Bettina founded an organization called VALAL (Visual Arts/Language Arts) which sent all different kinds of artists and poets into public schools in the East Bay. She is currently writing, teaching, and taking care of her dogs in Toronto.

NUMBER SIX

by Leslie Kain

Having spent two hours testifying in court on behalf of one of her patients, Dr. Samena Burns headed to her office. It was a brilliant spring morning, with daffodils nodding their golden heads, robins poking at greening lawns to find breakfast and sparrows busily gathering bits for their nests. A light breeze carried intoxicating scents of warm earth, lifting Samena's imagination to faraway unknown destinations. But she resisted the siren call of nature's seduction, even though it would have been excusable to play hooky that morning.

She entered her drab gray office building and took the stairs to Walden Therapeutic Services on the fourth floor. When she came to the suite, she thought it odd that the door was still locked at 10:30. Most of the therapists and other professionals in her group were always in the office by 8 a.m. for appointments. As she fished out keys from her purse she saw no one through the glass door – not even the receptionist – although all the lights were on.

Aside from there being no one visible, nothing else seemed amiss. Telephones were ringing and going to voicemail. She thought she heard someone's voice from the large group therapy room at the end of the hall. As she walked toward her office, she saw that each office she passed was open and empty, paperwork strewn on desks, lights on.

Samena's office was the last before the group room. She deposited her briefcase beside her desk and turned on the computer. She opened the window blinds, watered her plants on the sill, and settled down in her chair to compose the report from her morning in court.

She didn't recognize the male voice coming from the group room across the hall. Despite the soundproofing built into the room, she could nevertheless hear the man's angry barking, but not his specific words. The practice always posted reservations for the room to avoid double-booking, but she hadn't seen anything on the schedule.

Group sessions were sacrosanct. It was critical to never interrupt; momentum and dynamics are often precarious and can easily be thrown off. So she continued working.

But then she heard a long terrified scream from a woman, coming from the group room. And then even louder angry shouts from the same unknown man. The session seemed to be veering out of control. It was the responsibility of the supervising therapist to ensure the physical and psychological safety of the patients, but that clearly wasn't happening. She waited to hear an intervention from one of the group's therapists, but only heard more shouting and crying. She didn't know what was going on in there, but finally felt she had to intervene.

Samena crossed the hall and knocked lightly on the door of the room. No response, although she did hear muffled sobs. She tried to turn the doorknob; it was locked. She pounded on the door. It burst open suddenly, and she was greeted by a man with what looked like an assault rifle. He was one of her patients, Jacob Fisher.

"Well, well," he growled. "If it isn't Doctor Burns," he sneered, drawing out her title with dripping sarcasm. "Just who I was looking for."

Jacob grabbed her arm and threw her up against the wall, then leaned into her ear. "Go lock the front door, Bitch, then get your ass back here. We need to talk. And if you try anything, I'll kill everyone in this room," he spat, waving his gun in the direction of a large group of people lined up on the floor.

He stood with one foot in the hallway and one foot in the room, holding his weapon pointed toward his hostages. The hall was a straight line to the front door, so he could see everything she did. Samena walked slowly to the door, her mind spinning, trying to think how she could manage to send for help without endangering the group. She hoped an incoming patient might be standing at the door at that moment, whom she could signal, but no such luck.

He saw her lock the door then snapped, "Get back here now, bitch." She walked slowly back down the hall; the lack of haste clearly agitated Jacob, who barked "Step on it!" and waved his weapon toward her. When she finally returned, he threw her onto the floor of the room and slammed the door closed.

She looked up from the tweed carpeted floor. All twelve of the group's therapists and staff, plus two of their regular patients, were sitting on the floor at one end of the room away from the windows. The chairs had been stacked at the other end, up against the windows. There was a pile of cell phones under one of the chairs. Wires of the sole landline in the room had been ripped out of the wall and the useless device with trailing cords sat pathetically in the middle of the room. One of the therapists had blood streaming down the side of his head. Isabella the receptionist was crying. Shireka the part-time bookkeeper was shaking visibly. Old Dr. Gordon's Tourette's tic was going haywire. The rest of the group were sitting rigidly, with fear creasing their faces.

Jacob walked over and kicked Dr. Burns. "Sit up, cunt." He was a large man, over six feet and beefy. His long blond hair was tangled and disheveled. He was wearing dirty camouflage clothing and what seemed to be a hunting vest with multiple flapped pockets. He hadn't shaved, and he smelled like he hadn't bathed in several days.

Samena struggled to regain the breath he'd knocked out of her. "How can we help you, Mr. Fisher?" she coughed out.

"Help?" he laughed, derision contorting his snarling mouth. "You think you were helping by telling the judge that my kids should be put into protective custody?" He pounded the butt of his weapon into her ribs. She lost her breath again. No one in the room made a move; they may not even have breathed.

"I'm sorry, Jacob," Samena said, her voice weakened to a whisper. "You know it's not permanent. Only until you can get treatment, so your children can feel safe with you."

"Well, aren't you just the perfect bitch." He drilled his words, searing into her. "You think you know what's best for everyone else? Well, not having my kids is killing me. They're my life. So I tell you what. I'm gonna kill one of these people, one every fifteen minutes, while you watch. So you can feel the guilt, roll in it, taste the pain. So you can feel what I feel."

Jacob pulled a cylinder from one of his pockets and fastened it onto the muzzle of his gun. He swaggered around the room, seeming to revel in his power. He began circling, considering each person, waving his weapon in each face.

I've passed out three times in my life, which occurs to me as odd. I'm certainly not a weak or timid person. But after minor incidents in childhood I checked out for more than half an hour each time. Once when I fell backwards off a six-foot ramp. Another time a dog jumped up and bit me on my face. And the time my cousin pretended to swing my baton at me but the rubber end flew off and hit me on my glasses, gouging the frame into my eyebrow. It's almost like I wanted to stay wherever it was that I went, like I didn't want to come back.

She was being kicked again. Harder. "Well, bitch, how does that make you feel?" Jacob yelled, pointing to Isabella lying on the floor in a dark pool of blood spreading in an irregular pattern on the carpet, like a living Rorschach test. "You killed her. It's your fault!"

Dr. Burns almost passed out, seeing what he'd done to Isabella. "Jacob, stop," she pleaded. "I understand. And yes, you've succeeded in making me feel what you feel. I'm sorry. But I don't think this is the way to get your kids back. You have to stop now."

"There you go again, telling me what I have to do." He hit her upside the head with the butt of his gun. Gongs reverberated in her head, distorting her hearing.

One of the other doctors began to speak …

I often used to travel through a long spiral tunnel into a daydream where I wasn't present in West Virginia with my Aunt. Instead I'd find myself in a coma in California, where my mother and father were lovingly standing over me, anxiously waiting for me to awaken. I'd escape into a different reality, away from the hateful monster who beat me and frequently reminded me that no one wanted me, not even my father, that she took me because she had three boys and no girls to help around the house, so I'd better get to work …

"Well, Doctor," Jacob strutted and taunted. "How does it feel?" Puffing up his chest, elbows out like a prizefighter showing off, lifting each leg and planting his feet hard like some badass paratrooper. He kicked the lifeless body of Dr. Rothstein, one of her most beloved colleagues. Her mentor.

She almost threw up. "Jacob, please stop," she begged him. "You should just kill me. Wouldn't that resolve things for you?"

"Not a chance, bitch," he shouted, pacing back and forth, swinging his weapon, almost in a frenzy. "I want you to suffer. Over and over again."

He walked over to a side wall and smashed a framed inspirational poster imprinted with graceful script against a mountainous background: 'Difficult roads often lead to beautiful destinations'.

As glass shattered to the floor, Jacob shouted, "So you think this here is a beautiful destination? I sure traveled a lot of difficult roads, and where did it all get me?"

Dissociation. So cool. I always wished those episodes could last forever. Auditory amplification. The slightest brush against soft cloth, light tiptoe across the floor, a breeze ruffling a

window curtain, … sounds booming and echoing like from a deep cavernous well, bouncing off the walls, miles separate from me, slowing my movements as if I were floating in the stratosphere, disconnected from my miserable reality … Those 'trips' ended after childhood; then I began using alcohol to escape …*

Crack! The dull silenced shot pulled her back. Her head whipped around and she saw Dr. Avenir, the group's newest psychiatrist, lying on his back. At least she thought that was him. His face was pretty much gone. A wrenching eruption from her gut exploded onto her lap and splattered onto the doctor.

Jacob smirked. "Gotcha, huh? How's it feel?" He roared with incongruous laughter, then kicked her again and resumed his pacing, taunting his captives. Acrid smoke hung in the air, apparently not enough to set off the smoke alarm.

"So, you all think you can fix people like me?" he challenged, waving his weapon at the group. "After all these months of Dr. Burns' therapy, and pills that screwed with my head, you think I'm doin' just fine now?" He stomped over to another poster with bold block letters: **'Ask yourself if what you're doing today is getting you any closer to where you want to be tomorrow'.**

"I did everything the good doctor told me to, and look where it got me!" Jacob shouted, swinging his arms and his weapon around the room, then smashed the offending poster.

I was there. I was two and a half the day she did it. Or someone did it to her. That final part always eluded me. The violent multisensory nightmare would interrupt my memory dream and take over, year after year, all throughout my childhood. So I never managed to recapture the last piece of the story of how my mother died. I kept checking out when it mattered, going somewhere else. Pattern of my life.

Another dull Crack! This time it was Duane, the IT guy. That made four.

Jacob's captives – those remaining – were slumped, eyes glassy. They weren't talking or even whispering among themselves; they had witnessed how that set off Jacob's rage. But

Jacob seemed to be gaining more energy, increasing his resolve. He was on a mission as he walked around considering each person, choosing his next victim.

"So who's next, cunt?" Jacob goaded her.

She glowered at him. "Why not you, Jacob? Can you turn that gun on yourself?"

Something magical happened the day my aunt finally crossed the terminal line, the day I first fought back, the day I decided to leave. From the moment it clicked, the minute the switch turned, I floated through my days, my feet barely touching earth. I knew what I would do, intoxicated by the vision of freedom I would gain. Coin by stolen coin, it took me six months to squirrel away enough money for the long bus ride to California. On that final day, at the age of fifteen, never having traveled alone, I just … left.

Samena doubled under the weight of guilt. Jacob was achieving his objective. It was as if each time her mind slipped away to some other place, another person died. She didn't purposely drift off; it was as if something was pulling her. The victim this time was Harriet, the intern. Sweet young Harriet. Five people now.

Jacob's smug satisfaction with each kill seemed to be waning. He was becoming more agitated. His breathing was rapid and shallow. His eyes were darting all around, from one person to another. Unlike earlier, he now seemed to be warily looking for indications that one of them might retaliate.

She wondered whether there would be an uprising, whether there was anyone in the group who might decide to rush him when his back was turned. She would, but she was half his size. It would require more than one person, and since he had isolated her in the middle of the room, she could exert little strength lacking numbers.

"Jacob, please stop," she begged him once again. "If you would just kill me, you could finally settle the score, achieve real satisfaction."

"You'd like that too much, Doctor," he snarled. "Then you wouldn't have to feel guilty anymore."

"And you won't feel guilty?" she challenged him. She turned to look over her shoulder, past the chairs, out the windows. The sun had clouded over. The skies were dark and threatening.

When I knocked on my father's door after that long confusing bus trip, he didn't recognize me. Decades later, a former classmate from West Virginia found me. He told me my friends had felt abandoned by my abrupt disappearance without a goodbye.

Samena stood. Jacob raised his weapon. "Sit down, cunt!"

She threw herself at him. She felt the blast through her abdomen as she fell onto him.

Now there are many arms lifting me up, helping me leave.

About the Author:

Leslie Kain has a B.A. in Psychology from Wellesley College, an MBA from Boston University, and currently resides in Maryland. Leslie has written much nonfiction throughout her various professions and began writing fiction in 2016. She draws from her careers in psychology, business, high tech, Intelligence and nonprofits to create stories steeped in psychological complexity with multilayered plots and typically dark character arcs. Although occasionally dabbling in memoir, she usually prefers to repurpose those memories into works of fiction. She has completed her first novel (looking for an agent!) and has begun a new novel.

DOG'S LOVE

by Dave Gregory

Sheila often said: "I love animals more than most people. Maybe all people." She meant it. Though utterly devastating, her father's sudden death and her mother's drawn out demise never reached the same soul shattering level of annihilation as the passing of Winston, her rescued black greyhound with a grey face.

"He taught me how to love," she said of the former racer who was her constant companion for six years. Despite his almost deer-sized frame, he slept with her on the bed and woke her each day with a lick. Always, he followed her like a shadow; not only from room to room but even from bed to closet, or from kitchen table to refrigerator. She was heartbroken each time she left for work and heard him bark and whimper, with the sadness of abandonment, from as many as four houses away. But his unbounded joy when she returned – wags, zoomies, wet kisses and a delighted howl of pure relief and exhilaration – completely erased this despair.

Sadly, their time together was marred by a dispiriting amount of suffering and hardship for Sheila yet Winston's support never wavered. He was there through three abysmally ill-equipped bosses. One too demanding, one too demeaning, while the other sexually assaulted a co-worker on a day Sheila called in sick, leaving her to wonder what would have happened if, instead, she had been the one at work instead of her colleague.

There was also a neighbour, some college kid in a rented, rotting, heritage house, who hosted rowdy fraternity parties Sheila suffered through only with the help of ear plugs. Yet the same neighbour never hesitated to call the Humane Society any time Winston so much as barked at a squirrel during his morning walk.

Still more stress was caused by a landlord who failed to deliver on promises and, worse, a difficult breakup descended to a painful, petty and argumentative division of nearly a decade worth of assets.

And through it all Winston remained a silent, supportive presence, who instinctively knew, without a word, how to exude serenity and inspiration. Just seeing his face filled her with warmth and gratitude but, when life was at its most harrowing – and Sheila found herself sobbing uncontrollably, curled in a ball on the bathroom floor, legs drawn up to her chin and hands clasping her elbows beneath her knees – Winston immediately took action. He stood behind her, sniffed the air, nuzzled in, then rested the bottom of his chin on the back of her neck. Letting her absorb his warmth and compassion, Winston remained until the job was done and her tears had dried.

Sheila knew this was Winston's way of hugging her and saying: I'm here, mum.

Then he started limping. An initial X-ray of Winston's right, front foreleg found nothing. She requested a second X-ray when the limp worsened; a prognosis of osteosarcoma followed. Subsequent tests determined the cancer had already spread to Winston's kidneys and lungs. Only three days later he was gone.

Without the dog, the neighbourhood – and life overall – was dreary and the healing process glacially slow. Grief placed an additional weight on her shoulders that she was even less

equipped to handle with a massive hole piercing her heart and continuing through her soul.

It was too soon to think about getting another dog. That seemed disloyal; plus, she didn't want to burden any creature by unfairly comparing it to a being who had taken on saintly attributes following his departure for the Rainbow Bridge, where all dogs ultimately go.

Her only respite came from the many neighbourhood dogs. Some owners knew Sheila's situation and stopped longer than they normally had the patience for, in order to let her kneel and say a special, lingering, hello. Gratefully, Sheila hugged any canine she could get her arms around, talked to them in that sweet, soothing voice she used and let them kiss her open mouth – all while her neighbours struggled to avoid checking their watches. Many felt pity, even magnanimity, toward the bereaved woman but the kinder ones also felt compassion and empathy: they would likely all outlive their pets and it made them happy to witness this almost holy connection that left all parties – Sheila, the owners and their dogs – feeling enriched.

Often, Sheila encountered new dogs leading people she didn't recognize. Being respectful,

she let pass anyone who seemed in a hurry or upset with the weather but, if they appeared receptive, she politely asked to say hello to their pooch. Almost always, the humans happily obliged.

Six months after Winston's passing, Sheila spotted a stranger walking toward her, accompanied by an energetic golden retriever. Constrained by his leash, he tried to take in everything – the movement of traffic on the road, squirrels on overhead power lines, butterflies bouncing on the air. Even stationary objects – trees and fence posts – caught his attention, so did smells – whether in the air or on the ground. Strutting along, the hound eagerly trounced from one edge of the sidewalk to the other, nose downward, conscientiously seeking out differences of scent.

Her heart filled with joy at the sight of this hankering creature, bearing that carefree, open-mouthed smile only big, happy dogs could pull off.

Never doubting her ability to communicate with animals, she inevitably heard the voiceover that was, she knew, an echo of the dog's inner thoughts: Hey, I'm out for a walk. This is my favourite thing!

The retriever's human seemed unhurried and approachable. True, moments earlier, he had tossed the butt of a burning cigarette into the middle of the street but Sheila decided not to let that reflect poorly on the dog.

Only steps away, Sheila paused, steadied herself for a surge of boundless love, while a smile rushed up, unimpeded, straight from the warmest spot in her soul.

Ever alert, the dog sensed her attraction. Eagerly, he raised his head, craned his neck and unabashedly wagged his tail.

Hey, I get to meet a new human. You need to pet me and give me scritches behind my ears. That's my favourite thing!

Since the dog was clearly keyed up for a loving interaction, Sheila looked at the man on the opposite end of the leash and effused: "Oh, he's such a good boy. Can I please say hello to your dog?" Her voice sang, her knees bent with anticipation.

But the human simply said: "No," and kept walking.

No pause, no smile and no acknowledgement of the feelings of either the canine or the woman. Defensively, the man positioned himself between the two would-be friends and walked rigidly past, tugging firmly on the leash and barking: "Come on, Ryland," when the dog tried to circle back to the receptive human.

Sheila was stunned, frozen, her spirit crushed. Never had a single word sounded so devastating, so out of place and uncalled for. Maybe the man also had an inconsiderate neighbour, a bad boss, a poor marriage – a life of disappointment – or maybe he was just running late but Sheila had been slapped by that one word. Her face hurt, her heart had stopped.

Noticing the voiceover had gone silent, Sheila straightened, put her hand on her chest and waited for her heartbeat to return.

Ryland obediently kept up with his human but looked back, twice. He might have been too far to witness tears in Sheila's eyes but he instinctively knew they were falling.

About the Author:

Dave Gregory was a young writer in search of the world when he inadvertently ended up with a career in the cruise industry. Two decades later, he has retired from life at sea and returned to his first love – writing. His work has recently appeared in the Eunoia Review, Soft Cartel & The Short Humour Site.

THE POET LAUREATE OF MALCOLM'S DINER

by C. Billingsley Adams

Someone tapped on my shoulder today when I was feeling all bluesy as my long-time friend had just recently died. The last of my real friends, I guessed, as good friends are mighty hard to come by and at my age of sixty five, I'll probably never meet another. Other friends had been in and out of my life over the years, but they had all been forgotten, died, or moved away to be near their offspring in their golden years. But not me, nor Selma. We had decided that we weren't gonna die and we weren't gonna move anywhere to be near our kids as we both had the idea that if our kids had cared that much about us, then they wouldn't have moved away so far to start with. My own lives about three states away but Selma's son had moved clean across the country and hardly ever came to see her. That was all okay though, as long as we had each other, Selma and I. But, Selma did die and I was feeling so alone. Until someone tapped on my shoulder.

The funny thing about this tapping is that when I looked up, there was no one there. Just my imagination playing a trick on me, I thought, and I tried real hard to believe that. Better than thinking that it was Selma, come back to haunt me. She and I had sometimes talked about such things, about haunting each other after death.

"I'm gonna do all those traditional things that ghosts do," she once told me. "I'm gonna knock things over and slam doors shut. I'm gonna pull old Jessie's tail and make her yowl and run away with her hair standing on end."

"You better not!" I said, "Cause that would make you one of those poltergeist ghosts. They're all mischievous like that. And, I don't want you to be a ghost. I want you to be an angel."

"Spirits gotta have some fun, don't they?" she asked. "I can be your angel and a ghost too, can't I?"

"And, what about you, Ruth?" she continued her queries. "What you gonna be if you go first? You gonna be a ghost or an angel?"

"I don't know yet," I replied. "Guess I'll just have to wait and see what it's like on the other side. I just may be so busy reuniting with all my relations gone before that I just might not have any time for either of those things."

But none of that speculating seemed to matter much now that Selma had gone. Now that I was feeling so lonely already, even though it had only been a week or so since she was buried at Magnolia Park Cemetery next to her long deceased husband, Sam.

"Selma, is that you?" I asked into the air around me. Air that didn't turn chilly like you always hear from those ghost hunter people that you see on the TV. No. The air around me was warm. Warm and soothing, like an opened oven on a cold winter's morning with the scent of a pan full of baking biscuits waffling out to calm me. And that's when I knew, I think, that Selma was not a ghost, but an angel. A sweet angel come back to comfort me.

After that I felt Selma real close to me for a few days, just being near and offering a soft touch when I needed it, until I had reached that place where I could laugh again at some antic that Jessie, my aging Golden Retriever, would do, and which I did when I saw old Sally Sue coming down the road on her bicycle that didn't have any brakes and almost run into a privet shrub before she could stop it.

"When you gonna get those brakes fixed?" I hollered out at her. "You needs to get 'em fixed before you go and kill yourself, running out into traffic or sumpthin'."

"I can always drag my feet when I wanna stop. Ain't been hurt yet!"

I never had felt too close to Sally Sue. She lived up on the hill above me and she was a bit of a weird one. Some folks thought she was just a little batty, like her belfry was full of vermin and all that bat fluttering about and mice scurrying around and chewing on her brain cells that what they did up there kept her from thinking real clear. Not to mention, too, that she had a way of talking to herself all the time. I tried to eavesdrop one day when I was out trimming my roses and she was coming by. I was just curious as to just what she might be saying to herself but all I could make out was that she had a plumbing problem in her kitchen and was on the way to the store to buy some of that stuff that you pour down your drain and hope that it will dissolve the grease-ball down there that was stopping the thing up. Not very interesting so I never tried again to hear what she had to say to herself. Like folks were saying, she was a bit touched but she wasn't real creative in the skill of conversation like a touched person ought to be. Why couldn't she talk to herself about little green men from Mars or burglars that come in the night to steal her cats? Real 'cat burglars', ya know. Geez, I suddenly think to myself. I'm the crazy one.

Selma was the creative person in my life and one time she did something real good. She wrote a poem and sent it off to one of those journal magazines. And they printed it too and even sent her a free copy of the publication. And Maggie, a waitress down at Malcolm's Diner, where most all the working stiffs in town have their breakfasts and coffees, made a copy of it and taped it up there on the back side of the cash register for everybody to see. Then the whole town was bragging about Selma being a published poet and saying how she put our little village on the map.

To Walk In Fear

By Selma Thomas

To walk in fear, is to walk in courage

Otherwise we'd never walk at all

We must tread among the rocks and sand

to reach our destinations,

our realizations of hopes and dreams

Else, we'd never walk at all

but stand stagnate here, and never know

the courage to be found in fear.

Maggie wasn't just a waitress. She was an actress too. Most of her stage work had been for community theater, but she was forever auditioning for roles in our one professional theater, over at the county seat. It was called The Florence Theater and sometimes shows featured famous actors that were on hiatus from Broadway or Hollywood.

Soon after posting Selma's poem, a show was coming through that featured a performance by a well-known star named Zumar. His leading lady had fallen ill and, due to the rush of it all, the company was looking for a someone 'with experience' to step into the part for the three day local run.

"I was real scared to be auditioned for that show with Zumar in it," she confessed later but she did and she was awarded the role. "It was reading Selma's poem every day that gave me the courage," she said.

And a customer named Rebecca, stopped by the diner on her way out of town one day as Selma and I were having our coffee there, saying that she just wanted to give Selma a hug. She had finally found courage in her fear, she continued, and it was the poem that inspired her to pack everything she could in her old station wagon and leave. She had taken violence from her abusive husband for six years, being too scared to leave him before as he might come after her. But she was leaving now. She was ready to stand up to him and follow her own dreams for a good life, with a good job, a good man, and a houseful of children.

Another resident, Michael Gates, whose wife Norma had recently passed, shed an open tear after reading the poem. She had suffered a long illness and he, after caring for her for months, realized that it was fear that kept him from fully rejoining the everyday world of living, until he read the poem.

"I had watched Norma fighting for her life," he said, "and then she just gave up. And, I gave up a little too. What else could I do? But the poem, Selma's poem, made me realize that it was courage that kept me going all that time. I am proud that when Norma needed me, I was there."

All this attention embarrassed Selma but she was proud of it all too. Proud of being able to help people but for also being recognized for accomplishing something. She spent the better part of the next year writing more poems and sending them off to publishers. No more was ever wanted by the magazines though and she finally just gave up and quit. I felt right bad for her and begged her to keep writing and she did. Just never did try to get any more of them published.

When I was sitting with Sally Sue and enjoying a cup of coffee one morning at the diner, a few weeks after Selma's death, the local handyman for hire, Pete, came in and joined us. He had gone over to her house to help her son to move out her furniture and haul it over to the consignment store, he reported, and told me that the son had found a manila folder full of Selma's poems. He didn't want them for himself so he threw them into a big dumpster that he had the trash people haul right up into the front yard.

Other stuff that the son didn't think was worth selling, like her little chairside table with the wobbly leg, old family photographs, and memorabilia stuff was thrown out too. Like the Australian lorikeet feather she had picked up after one of the winged creatures had escaped his cage at a wild animal park nearby and spent a few days perched in her front yard chinaberry tree. She was just thankful, Selma had said, that it was only a bird that had escaped and

not one of those big animals. Said she just couldn't imagine the scare if she woke up some night with a giraffe having his neck all bent over and poking his head through her open bedroom window, like they do the car windows when the tourists drive through, looking for a food handout. Sometimes she would place the feather in the band of her old brimmed hat that she liked to wear whenever we went out shopping the yard sales. We didn't much like yard sales because each of us already had enough junk in our houses that we didn't think we needed to be buying more but it was something fun to do and a way to get a curious glimpse into other people's lives.

I went by that afternoon, feeling Selma by my side, just as her son was leaving in his rental economy car, and explained that his mother was my very best friend and asked his permission to retrieve the folder from the trash. He didn't care, of course, seeing no value in an old woman's rants and raves, even if they were set in her thoughtful and laborious form of poetic prose.

"Hope you'll help me to get out of here," I spoke out loud to Selma as I lowered myself down into the depths of that metal dump.

"You're getting more like me, everyday," a voice spoke aloud, echoing against the sides of the vacant top walls of the container. "Talking to yourself, like that."

Didn't sound like Selma, I thought as I looked up and saw a head, darkened by the back light of a setting sun.

"That you, Sally Sue?" I asked, shading my eyes against the horizon's glare.

"Yep!" she responded. "What you doing down in there, Ruth? A little dumpster divin'?"

"Well, first off, I ain't talking to myself. I'm talking to Selma!" I said.

"She down in there with you?"

"Why yes, she is! And we're looking for that folder Pete told me and you about. The one with her poems. Son told me that he didn't care if I took it, right before he left town. He was pulling out when I got here. Said everything in here was garbage, as far as he was concerned, and I could take anything I wanted."

"And folks think I'm the crazy one," Sally Sue said. "Looks like you're on track to give me a little competition!"

"But, I was talking to Selma!" I exclaimed. "Not to myself!"

"You, and all those others, only think I talk to myself," she replied. "I'm talking to Buddy Boy! Just like you're talking to Selma!"

"Oh!" I replied, a little taken back by this revelation and feeling a little ashamed of myself.

"Yes. I talk to Buddy Boy, my husband of forty-five years. And if I didn't feel him beside me, since he died, if I didn't know he was here for me to talk to, well, I don't think I would make it."

"Well, get in here then," I demanded with a false firm. A flood of emotional understanding had passed over us and Sally Sue and I had grown, within only moments into two women who understood each other. Two women who could be friends. "You and Buddy Boy both. Y'all come on in and help me and Selma find her poems."

Sitting at my kitchen table that evening, a glass of chardonnay in my hand, I read through many of the hundreds of poems and creative musings of my good friend. Such an insight she had into the human experience. More in-depth thoughts than I even known existed. Thoughts to be shared on the register of Malcolm's Diner.

Seeking relief from thirsty palates at the diner, Sally Sue and I had enjoyed a good morning of yard sale adventures. She had never done much of this shopping before because, as I previously mentioned, folks around just took her as being a little touched so most weren't too welcoming to her at their homes. And even before Buddy Boy died, he wasn't much for visiting neighborhood sales of what he termed as 'other people's throw-aways' so Sally Sue, who might have been welcomed back then, didn't want to be dragging him to places that she already knew that he wouldn't enjoy. He didn't seem to be minding too much now though as he was seeing how much joy these

outings were bringing to his widowed wife as she was becoming more accepted. And he was probably enjoying the break of not having to converse with his widow for a while as we girls, Sally Sue, Selma, and myself traveled from yard to yard, me donning Selma's old straw hat with the lorikeet feather, the one other thing in that dumpster that I had retrieved.

"Hey, it's 'Besties' night at the movie theater. We'd get in at half price."

Did Sally Sue just call me her 'Bestie'? I looked over in her direction and she was grinning ear to ear. 'Besties' with Sally Sue? Wonder what Selma would think of this? Sure, she and I had enjoyed visiting the sales together, and she sometimes parked her bike in my yard and accompanied me on walking Jessie around the block, but 'best friends'?

"I'll ask Selma 'bout it!" I said. "See what she thinks?"

"Okay. I already talked to Buddy Boy and he thinks it would be a fine idea. The two pairs of us 'Besties' going together." She seemed a little embarrassed about the forwardness of her previous statement and wanted to clear up any misconception that I may have but, regardless, I knew what she had meant.

"Course Selma and Buddy Boy won't have to pay at all," she added with a laugh. "Nobody'd know they were there 'cept you and me!"

"Is this okay with you, Selma? My being friends with Sally Sue?" I asked later. "I haven't been feeling so lonely lately, since she'd been stopping by."

"Of course," said Selma in her non-physical way. "You need a friend that is there with you, a friend to go on outings with you, to walk Jessie with you, whose tail, by the way, I have refrained from pulling!"

And so it was decided. Sally Sue and I were now to be earthly 'Besties' with Selma and Buddy Boy staying around as our angels. Or were they our ghosts?

Every now and then, Selma would go away for a few hours or so. It frightened me at first, as I could feel the emptiness when she was gone, until I figured out why. When I questioned her about it, she confirmed that it was true so, sometimes, when she wasn't around, I'd take a little stroll over to her house. It was kind of nostalgic to look in the windows and relive the memories, even if the house sat bare and chilled, I could still envision the way it used to be, all cluttered up with yard sale finds but still a cozy living place too. And, well, every now and then, I'd see some real estate person taking in prospective buyers to look it over and soon I'd see them almost running out the door. I'd know then that Selma had decided she didn't like them much and she was pulling some of her poltergeist tricks on 'em. Turning lights on and off. Opening and closing doors and windows, that kind of thing. Wouldn't take much to scare most folks off and she and I would have a good laugh about it later.

"So, just what are you, Selma?" I'd ask. "A ghost, an angel? Or the Poet Laureate of Malcolm's Diner?"

"Think I'm all three," she would exclaim. "Whatever I'm needed to be at any given time, I guess."

One day, after Selma had been missing for a long while, I walked over to her house just as three young kids came running out. But they weren't running out of fear as they were laughing and buzzing around the yard. They were happy. And as I slowly sauntered by, Mom and Dad and someone who appeared to be an agent came out too. With a lot of smiling and handshaking going on, the agent was holding some papers in her hand that looked like they could be signed offers to the owner.

"What's going on? Did you like this family?" I hollered out to Selma after I got on down the street.

"Yes," she said. "I think I did. The parents seemed nice and the children were pretty polite. For children. And I really believe that they loved the house and will take good care of it. House needs a good family."

"They make a good offer? You think your son will take it?"

"Yeah. He'll take it. Probably getting pretty anxious. Been waitin' for his money for a while."

"Well, you can just live with me forever. I don't got any house buyers to scare but you can run off all the burglars and those grabbers taking packages from people's front porches like you see on the news. And any attic squirrels and mice that might come around."

Selma fell quiet even though I could feel her presence. I could sense that something was wrong, something she didn't want to have to say.

"This means you'll be leaving soon, doesn't it?" I finally asked.

"Yes, I'm afraid it does," she silently replied. "I must be passing on. My essence for hanging around this old earth is getting weak, Ruth. Because you don't need me anymore."

"No, Selma," I cried out even though I had known that this moment was coming with Selma being willing to give up her house. "You can't leave me. What would I do? You're my best friend."

"Yes, I am, but I'm not your only friend. You have a new friend, an earthly friend, and that's how it should be. 'Sides that, I need to be hooking up with that fellow I used to be married to. He's gonna start thinkin' that I don't love him anymore, if I don't."

I'd been having a particularly hard week. Maybe it was a couple weeks. I was just all wrapped up in the idea of Selma's leaving that I wasn't allowing myself to enjoy her company while I still had it. Didn't even feel like getting up and putting on real clothes most days, just been sitting around in my jamas being a nag and fussing at my departed friend about my woes of impending loneliness.

"And will you tell Buddy Boy to tell Sally Sue to quit comin' 'round all the time. She's driving me to be just as nutty as herself. I don't wanna be her 'Bestie'. I just want you, Selma."

"I don't need for nobody to tell me anything. I'm standin' right here and I already been told."

I turned and was startled to see Sally Sue standing just inside my open doorway.

"I had thought you might want to go down to the diner with me. Hang up one of Selma's poems seeing as to how you haven't put a new one up all week. But, I guess not. And I'm sorry that I've become such a burden to you lately. Sure didn't mean to. Buddy Boy thinks you're too angry for me to be hangin' 'round with anyway. Thinks it may rub off on me someday when I'm missing him an extra lot."

"I'm sorry, Sally Sue," I said. "I didn't see you there and I was just having a conversation with Selma. I didn't mean it, really! I was just talking!"

She turned and walked back out the door without saying another word though I was sure that she'd be having a bunch to say as soon as she and Buddy Boy got back on the road. I immediately felt shame for what I had done. Sally Sue was turning out to be a really sweet woman, now that I was getting to know her, and I have to go and hurt her like that.

Blame

By Selma Thomas

For things I've said, things I've done

I feel much sadness, feel much shame

Without ill intent, for those I've hurt

With a beg of pardon, I own the blame.

I was feeling really bad over Sally Sue overhearing me like that. But I was feeling a little angry too. Why should I have to lose my friend to the afterlife when Sally Sue still had her Buddy Boy? Just wasn't fair, it didn't seem.

"Go and make up with her," I heard Selma saying as if she was my own conscious. "She's your friend."

"Who? Sally Sue?" I replied. "She's not my friend! She's only a nuisance, bein' around all the time! She could never understand me like you do! 'Sides, she's got Buddy Boy."

"No. She doesn't," I could hear Selma reply. "Buddy Boy crossed to the next dimension soon after I died and when Sally Sue had you. She didn't need him so much then."

I was a little startled over learning this. "Does Sally Sue know that?"

"Yes."

"Then why does she still talk to him all the time?"

"Habit mostly. But also because she didn't want you to know. Didn't want you feeling sorry for her and goin' 'round with her just because she was all alone."

In a day or two, I looked out just as Sally Sue came flying down the street on her old bicycle. She must have got distracted by something, maybe a bird flying over as she loved birds, and she forgot to be draggin' her feet to slow herself down and was soon out in the middle of traffic down past the intersection with another street. Tires were screeching and a horn was blowing, and I thought for sure that she had ended up under some big SUV or something. That she was gonna be laid out in the road dead.

I took off running down the hill and was joined by a couple of other neighbors but before we could get there, we could see Sally Sue, sitting up in a ditch. She had managed to turn out of the road and not get herself killed. Had a little trouble standing up but I think that was from the fear of her near painful death with lots of potentially broken bones. Before we got to her, she had already jumped on her bicycle and was gone. Don't think she would have minded the passing away so much, but not that way. Everyone wants to go peacefully in their sleep, don't they? Not all flattened and broken like gettin' run over by a car would do.

"We have to do something," I said to an agreeable Maggie that next day over a cup of morning coffee. "Let's have a sale, right here at the cafe! A yard sale of our own! With all proceeds going to purchase Sally Sue, a new bicycle. One with brakes. Think Malcolm will let us take over his parking lot one weekend?"

"How 'bout it, Malcolm?" Maggie called out to the proprietor through the open service window.

"Of course it's okay!" Malcolm replied, seeing an opportunity for increased food sales as well as an chance to help out one of the town's most colorful characters and a loyal customer.

Michael Gates, who had been privy to the hearing of this conversation and the beginning of the planning between Maggie, Malcolm, and myself, stood and left, just as we were discussing how to prevent Sally Sue from knowing that the event was to be for her benefit as she was a woman of pride which might cause her to reject the effort. And getting the townspeople to donate items and to come to shop might be difficult as most still believed that she should have been locked away, long ago, for her own well being. But, while being so often spoken, such opinions were usually said with sheepish grins, with ill-disguised compassion, and we thought that many would gladly support the cause.

Michael, in short time, returned, wheeling in a shiny new bicycle. Seems that his wife, Norma, before losing her battle with cancer, had always been inspired by Sally Sue's spirit and at one time, decided that she, too, wanted to ride a bike around town. Wanted to live her remaining days on her own terms, so Michael had bought one for her, shiny with embellishments, with all the bells and tassels, and had parked the two-wheeler in their bedroom as an incentive for Norma to regain her strength. But she never did, was never able to ride.

"What do you want for it?" Malcolm asked.

"Well, tell ya what, I'll take whatever you all manage to raise at your yard sale. I wouldn't even do that if I wasn't still paying off Norma's funeral bills because I know that she would be so pleased for Sally Sue to have it."

A conspiracy was then born. It was decided that the sale would be promoted as a fund raiser to help with Norma's final expenses and Sally Sue, our secretly designated recipient, would never know that it was also for her benefit. And when word got out, Malcolm's outback storage building, which normally held only excess paper napkins, plastic straws, and professional grade floor polishing cleaners, was soon jammed packed with donations and promises of more to come.

The bicycle was kept on full display in the diner and Sally Sue would come by and look it over dreamily each day, buying herself a raffle ticket whenever she could scrape together an extra dollar. Tickets were being sold for it but only to buyers who were privately made aware that they were not real and their cost was only a contribution. All slips added to the drawing jar had only one name, Sally Sue's. Pride or no, she was going to have this bike, and if deceiving her was the only way to put it in her possession, then, we all decided, so be it.

The event was a success with a big dent put into Michael Gates debt for which he was mighty thankful and Sally Sue cried tears of joy when her name was drawn. Went hugging everybody around, including me, before taking off down the road on her new bicycle. An hour later, a newly arriving customer reported seeing her down by the water works, clear on the other side of town.

Neighbors

By Selma Thomas

Neighbors, with open and outstretched hands

Like music flowing from gazebo bands,

Bestowed songs between themselves, and you

Like rhythmic rides at a village fair revue.

"Do you think that Sally Sue has forgiven me?" I asked Selma that evening as I was laying down for bed.

"Oh, yes," she replied with a voice that had lately been sounding a little weak.

"It's time, isn't it?"

"Yes, my dear," she replied.

"Okay, my friend," I said as I was drifting off to sleep "Goodbye, Selma. For a little while."

"Goodbye, my dear Ruth," she whispered.

About the Author:

C. Billingsley Adams is a playwright, a novelist, and a writer of short stories. A resident of rural Georgia, Ms. Adams has authored three novels and numerous stage pieces. Her short stories have been included in such literary publications as "Edify Fiction", "One Person's Trash", the "Morsels From the Chef" Anthology by Zimbell House Publishing, "The Charles Carter Anthology" of the University of North Carolina, "Beneath the Rainbow", "Voices From the Unknown" published by Maïa Veruca Books of Norway, and "Savannah Anthology 2016", in which she has received both Honorable and Notable Recognitions.

WHAT WE TALK ABOUT WHEN WE TALK ABOUT TURKEY
by E. P. Tuazon

My colleague, Faruk Irgulu, was talking. Faruk was the head of our English Department at the school we taught at and sometimes that gave him the right.

The four of us were sitting around his backyard drinking tea. Sunlight colored the grass a golden green while the half that remained in the shadow of his home took on a cool, brittle blue. There were Lusin and I and his wife, Ayla, sitting on the dark side of the grass, while Faruk sat in the sun.

Somehow, we had fallen on the topic of Turkey because Faruk and Ayla and Lusin's parents had come from there. Faruk loved the country just as much as he loved America, he said, but, if he had to choose between the two, he would've chosen Turkey, the one from his childhood. He tried to explain it to us, the tea spilling in his hand. He poured half a cup with tea from the pot and filled the rest with the water from the kettle. He said that they did that to make it easier to drink, less intense on the palette. It couldn't be too strong, he said, or else you wouldn't be able to taste anything.

All of it had come from the samovar that still steamed in the shade beside us. I had seen nothing like it before; a coal kettle that both heated water inside and heated a pot of tea outside, on top, simultaneously. It had three chimneys: one on the left for the water, one on the right to heat the pot of tea, and one in the middle for the coal.

I watched Faruk get it started. He took the coals from the grill he used for our lunch and dropped them in one of the samovar's chimneys. He had picked the coals out of the ash with a pair of tongs; they glowed a faint orange when he blew on them to bring them back to life. I thought of his past making the same glow, his talking about it just the same as his blowing.

"I would read a book in one hand," Faruk was saying now, holding up a cup of tea like it was Anna Karenina, "and, with the other, I'd steer my bicycle up and down the road, to and from school. My village is a beautiful place with the lake and the trees and the fresh air. I read everything riding my bike by the water; Tolstoy and Chekov, Updike and Cheever—they were my riding buddies. That's what I love about my country. The rest, I guess, is in my blood. I learned to love the rest of the country like I learned to love everything else."

His wife smirked at this. She didn't touch any of her tea. It sat in her lap as she sat with her legs open, her long, red hair nearly touching the mouth of her cup. "Yes, where he's from, it's such an easy life. He used to borrow his father's bike when he was a child. You know Faruk still rides all the time?"

I nodded as I held Lusin's hand in her lap. By then, both of our cups were empty and at our feet. I thought of the time when Faruk asked me if it was worth it to spend a grand on a bicycle part. I told him that it was asking a lot for only a part of something.

"Yeah, I still ride," Faruk said, looking down at our hands, "but, you know, not with the book in one hand anymore."

We all laughed. Faruks eyes went back to his wife.

"He rides his bike all the time," Ayla continued, "just like his father."

"Yes," he said, "My love for my country is just like my love for my bike."

"Like what," Ayla interjected, "borrowed from your father?"

We laughed again. Faruk gave his wife a look.

"Ayla doesn't think well of him."

"Now," she said with mock surprise, "I never said that."

"You meant to," he said and then added, "You always say he's lazy and wasteful."

"He is. Like you. How much money do we spend on your bikes? How much money do we send your father every other month?"

"Not now," he said to her and then turned to us, "Ayla doesn't understand. He was someone who fixed things in our village, but everyone just buys new things now and don't care for fixing things anymore. He needs the money."

"Ok, I can understand that, but that doesn't explain why we spend so much money on your bikes. I just don't know," Ayla sighed, "the more I allow this the more I feel like I'm encouraging you to waste more and more. You just do what you want and don't think of the people suffering, like your daughter or me, our family. And look at your Turkey now."

"What about it?"

"Exactly! You always have your head in the clouds, that's why you're fine with what Erdoğan's doing to it."

"That's a different issue. I'm not fine with it. It's just that the politics of it is useless to think about."

"Useless?" Ayla lashed out, "Is it useless to think about all the religious persecution? The sexism? The censorship? The writers in prison?"

"You're blowing it all out of proportion." He said and exhaled. He drank his tea and looked at Lusin and I, "I'm sorry you're seeing us fight."

Ayla relaxed and picked up her tea but didn't drink it. She looked at her husband. "We aren't fighting, we are having a discussion."

Faruk rolled his eyes. "Oh, I'm sorry, Balım, I spoke incorrectly." He looked at us. "I'm sorry you're seeing us 'have a discussion.'"

We laughed. Ayla eyed him.

"OK," she said, "Well, you may not like the president but you condone him like you do."

Faruk spoke with his cup to his mouth before he sipped his tea. "Yeah, I condone him like I condone my wife not wearing a hijab."

"Oh, Tatlım," Ayla scoffed, "it reminds me of when we first met, you were so enamored with my hair."

Faruk looked fondly at it. I wondered what the red looked like in the sun. "Where I was from, every woman wore a hijab. Imagine my surprise when I left to go to school in Istanbul. I was like, 'wow, these women are beautiful!'"

"He was like a little boy who had never eaten ice cream before."

The two of them shared a look with each other, as if they were holding each other in their eyes.

Ayla drank her tea and continued, "I was never one for the hijabs. It's an unnecessary burden, especially here. People automatically judge you for it and you end up standing or not standing for something because of it. Don't get me wrong, I love my faith and being a Muslim woman, but I don't think I need to wear anything to empower me or showboat my faith. I'm too lazy for that."

She looked at her husband again and they smiled at each other. "Lazy like you, Tatlım."

"Speaking of lazy," Ayla said, stretching her legs up, her tea going up with her arms, "did Faruk tell you that he did some time in the military in Turkey?"

"No," I turned to Faruk. I tried to picture him in a uniform but I couldn't, "you never mentioned that. For how long?"

Faruk finished off his tea and put the cup down under his chair as he began to speak. "If you went to college, you only had to do six months. Every man in Turkey has to do service."

"And he did it so late! He waited until after college and right before he married me." Ayla laughed.

Faruk laughed as well. "I wanted to get it out of the way before anything else."

"By then, he'd put it off for so long. He was already thirty and mostly everyone else was nineteen or twenty!"

"Yes, I was the oldest soldier. I was the oldest lowest ranking soldier there was, I think."

Ayla smiled and put down her tea, the rest of its contents spilling into the grass. "He became the torpilli of his higher ranking officers just because they were all the same age!"

"What's a torpilli?" I asked.

Faruk thought of an answer but Lusin beat him to it.

"It means he was like their favorite. You know, like how teachers or parents have favorites." Lusin said. She said it close to me and squeezed my hand.

"Yes!" Ayla said, her eyes shining at Lusin. "Like a child. So spoiled!"

"I was!" Faruk chuckled, "I can't deny that!"

Ayla stayed on Lusin. "I didn't know you spoke Turkish, Lusin."

"I don't. I just know a little." She said, her right shoulder rubbing with mine, "My parents never taught me, but I picked it up. I can understand it just fine, I just don't speak it. Same with Armenian."

"You're Armenian, too?" Ayla leaned forward. Her hair touched her knees. "A lot of my friends in Istanbul were Armenian!"

Faruk got up and walked to the samovar as he talked. "Oh, here we go."

Ayla shushed him, "Tatlım, sus!"

Faruk shook his head at her and picked up the pot from off the top of the samovar. He turned back to us. "Would you all like more tea?"

"Yes, please." I said. Lusin nodded.

"Great!" Faruk said, he took the pot inside the door to the kitchen while he talked. We could hear him from inside. "That's why we get along. You love to drink tea!"

Ayla looked at me and smiled. "In Turkey, everybody's crazy about tea. I think our country spends the most on tea in all of the world!"

"And guess what's his favorite, Balım?" Faruk said from the kitchen. I could hear the water run from his sink. "Earl Grey! I'm making some!"

"Masallah!" Ayla exclaimed in mock enthusiasm and looked at me. "You're a bergamot lover like him and his father?"

I smiled. "I'm pretty attached to it."

Faruk came out with a pot of water and poured it into the samovar, then he returned to the kitchen.

"Are you sure you aren't brothers?" Ayla asked and then turned toward the house and yelled after her husband. The water ran again. "Tatlım, are you sure your father never left your village? Are you sure he didn't visit the Philippines?"

We could hear Faruk guffawed from the kitchen. "We are brothers in tea, not in blood."

We all laughed. Ayla picked up her cup and spilled the rest in the grass. "I was not a fan of bergamot until I met Faruk. It's something I've had to get used to."

Lusin moved her arm away from me and bent down to pick up her own cup. "Same here. Actually, I never really drank tea at all until we started dating."

"Yeah," I said, reaching down for my own cup, the cold grass tickling my fingers, "imagine my surprise when I took her to a tea place in Pasadena."

"It was cute!" Lusin laughed. "To be fair, he had told me where we were going and I just didn't mention it."

Ayla smiled at me. "She must have liked you a lot then!" She winked.

Lusin leaned into me, her cup in her lap. "Well, I'm still thinking about it." She said, grinning.

Ayla turned her gaze back at Lusin. "You two remind me of Faruk and I when we were younger," She turned to the house, "isn't that right, Tatlım?"

Inside, it was quiet. Ayla shrugged. "Must have put the pot on the stove and gone to check on Sumayya. She's taking a nap."

"How old is she now?" Lusin asked.

Ayla continued to look at the house. She smiled. "She just turned two now! Oh, she's a lot of energy."

Lusin gave me a look. She put her cup in one hand and reached for my hand with the other. I did the same and took hers in mine.

I turned from Lusin to Ayla and caught her watching us. She didn't look away. "So, Lusin. Your parents were Armenians living in Turkey?"

"Yes," Lusin said, "several generations, but they moved before they had me."

"Have you been back?"

"No," Lusin said uneasily, "only my mother goes back for my grandmother, but, other than that, there hasn't been any reason to."

Ayla tapped her cup with her index fingers. "I haven't been there very much since I left, myself. Most of my family and friends have moved here anyway. I wasn't very partial to how things were going over there, if you could tell by the way I am."

"I have to admit, you're not what I expected." Lusin said and looked at Ayla's red hair.

Ayla smiled. "Yes, well, my husband is very conservative, but I am the exact opposite. You should have seen his father! Oh, he was not very happy!"

Lusin and I laughed. Ayla kept going. "You should have seen me when I was in college. Rally after rally. Most of my friends: Armenian women. Everyone in Istanbul protesting for Turkey to acknowledge the Armenian Genocide!"

Midway through Ayla's last two words, Faruk groaned from the doorway of the kitchen. He came out with a pot of Earl Grey in one hand while the other secured their daughter slung across his chest, her chin resting on his shoulder. "Basima agrilar girdi senin yuzunden!" He said and put their child in Ayla's arms. Ayla took her with annoyance. The little girl was still asleep.

Faruk moved to the Samovar and put the pot on it. "You give me a headache with that kind of talk!" He said and walked over to his seat. He bent down to pick up his cup but did not sit down.

Ayla rubbed her daughter's back and ignored her husband. "Sum-Sum, my anoush!" Ayla kissed her head and smelled her hair. It was short and black and soft. "I picked that up from an old Armenian friend of mine. She used to call me Anoush, and now we call our daughter Anoush."

"Does it mean anything?" I asked.

Faruk chuckled and put a hand on his chair. "It means 'sweet' like Americans call others 'sweetie'."

"Yes," Lusin said. She squeezed my hand and looked at me, "maybe I'll start calling you Anoush."

"Oh they're sweet, Tatlım." Ayla said to her husband then turned back to us. "Tatlım means 'sweet' too, 'my sweet'."

Faruk smiled, "Yes, I'm your sweet, like you're my honey. Balım. That's what I call her, Balım. Can I take your cups?"

Lusin and I extended our cups and Faruk took them, putting his and mine together, mine inside his. He then went to Ayla and he put Lusin's in hers and took it out of his wife's hand.

"Thank you." We said and Faruk went back into the kitchen and started the water again to rinse them.

Ayla gently ran the back of her hand up and down her daughter's back. "So how do you feel about it?"

"What?" I asked but I noticed she was looking at Lusin.

"The Armenian Genocide. How do you feel about America and Turkey not acknowledging it?"

I expected to hear another groan from the kitchen but all I could hear was the water running.

"Well," Lusin started, "I definitely had a lot of Armenian friends in college who were pretty vocal about it. They would be in the Armenian Club and try to get me to come to events and things. But, sometimes, I thought they were just fighting just to fight, you know? They put down Turkey because of it and it turned into a general hate for all Turkish people. I couldn't get behind that. Being both Armenian and Turkish always put me in the middle about it."

Ayla looked like she was about to respond but Faruk emerged from the kitchen with our cups. "Yes, I totally agree with you." He took the cups to the samovar and put them down except for one. He picked up the pot and began to pour tea into the cup, and then the water. "I've never been a part of any of it, and, all of a sudden, I have strangers blaming me for what others have decided." He said, and, after pouring a second cup, he picked them up and walked them to Lusin and I. "On top of that, I never had any issue with it until I came to America. Armenians seem to only hate us here in America!" He handed Lusin hers first. Ayla looked at this in surprise. "It is supposed to be the oldest who drinks first, but I like you, so let's make an exception." He said and winked.

The two laughed at this and Lusin took her cup. Faruk handed the other one to me and returned to the samovar.

Ayla looked back at her. I couldn't see her face. "That's because we were in Turkey! You can't hate Turkish people there! Here, in America, you can hate whoever you want as long as its justified."

Faruk poured two more cups and carried them over to his seat. "Justified? Now, come on." He handed his wife her tea and she took it and put it down in the grass, her daughter dangling from her like hanging fruit. I watched her tea tip a little, half of it spilling in the grass.

"More than a million lives, Tatlım. A million. There are pictures, witnesses, victims! The genocide did exist!"

"Balım." He said, calm, unlike his wife. He took a sip of his tea and smacked his lips before he continued. "I'm not saying that it didn't exist. No one's saying that. It's just very political. The word 'genocide' is being thrown around too easily. It was war. It was not genocide. People are just using that word because they want to use it as a platform to hurt Turkey for selfish reasons."

"So justice is selfish?"

"Balım." Faruk said, pointing his cup at their daughter.

Ayla repeated herself with a softer voice. "So justice is selfish?"

"There is no justice if there was no injustice in the first place. This has all been manufactured for years by people trying to ruin Turkey's way of life. People who are for dissent rather than disagreement. They don't want to change things. There is nothing that really needs changing. They only want to hurt Turkey, hurt our home."

Ayla's lips grew smaller. They tightened more and more into a frown. "Then why are there so many people like me there? Why is there so much outrage against the president and against the government?"

I felt Lusin's grasp tighten. She stared at the samovar behind them. It steamed.

Faruk drank more of his tea. "Like I said before, it's because all the problems people are saying about Turkey are all exaggerated. People are allowed to say and believe whatever they want. The government is merely trying to keep the peace. They are not trying to oppress or censor the people. On the contrary, Balım, they are trying to keep everyone's freedom intact, everyone's way of life, everyone's peace. They are merely protecting Turkey."

We all waited for Ayla to respond but she remained quiet. She looked at the grass, the light of the day almost upon us.

Faruk drank more of his tea and then continued. "To use the word "genocide" so lightly is diminishing its actual weight. When we think of the word, we think of something unforgivable. We think of Hitler, and the Nazis, and an evil plaguing the world with a demented ideology. Turkey would be comparing themselves to the Nazis if they ever used the word. I wouldn't disgrace our entire country by calling all us Nazis just like I wouldn't disgrace all Muslims by calling all of us terrorists."

I felt my throat dry. I drank all of my tea and there weren't any words in me I could say.

Lusin continued to look at the samovar. Her face looked relaxed but there was something in her face. In her hands her tea had gone untouched.

Ayla continued to look down at the sun, and, before anyone else could speak again, she exhaled and finally spoke. "You know, it's easy for you to say this because you're not a victim. You're so far removed from everything and everyone."

Faruk laughed. "We're all removed! All of this, it really has nothing to do with us, these are all somebody else's problem. We look like fools thinking we know what we talk about when we talk about Genocide."

Ayla looked to Lusin. "And you, what do you think about this? Do you think it's not your problem as well?"

Lusin's eyes went from the samovar and back to her tea. She looked into the black liquid. "I've never really thought about it. My parents are from Turkey and their parents were from Armenia, but they never really concerned themselves with the politics there. And it wasn't like they left because of political reasons either. My father worked in film doing set design and he jumped at the very first opportunity he got to live out his dream of working in Hollywood. He dragged my mother here, they had me, and that was it. My parents were never really political until 9/11, actually. No one here really was until then, not about things like this."

Ayla looked at her husband again. "And that's another thing."

Faruk drank his tea and sighed. "Can we talk about something else, something lighter? I don't want to disturb Sumayya with our talk."

Ayla looked at her daughter still asleep in her arms. She caressed her little feet. "She's asleep, Tatlım. Besides, it's not wrong to talk about 9/11. She needs to know about it. You can't hide it and things like this from her."

Faruk then said something to his wife in Turkish I did not catch. It was quick but I could tell it wasn't anything nice. Ayla responded in kind

and the two narrowed their eyes at each other. Faruk got up and tossed the rest of his tea in the grass beside him. He turned to the samovar.

"The coals were not enough. The heat is dying." He said.

Ayla rocked their daughter in her arms. "Let it, nobody's going to drink anymore tea."

Faruk ignored his wife and poured himself more tea. He took a sip. "It's still warm for now. Anybody want more tea?"

I looked at my empty cup. "I will." I said and got up. I started walking over to him and the samovar.

Faruk walked towards me. "No, sit. I can get it for you."

"Oh no, that's alright." I said, walking passed him and in front of the samovar. "I want to try doing it myself."

"You know how?"

"Yeah, from watching you." I said and picked up the pot and poured half of my cup. Then I put it under the spout for the water. I pushed down the tab and filled the rest.

"You're making real tea now!" He laughed and sat back at his seat.

I took my tea back to mine. Lusin smiled at me and took back my hand. I drank my tea.

Their daughter made a sound and woke up. Ayla smiled at her. "Hello Anoush! Did you have a good nap. Do you want to say hello to our friends?"

Sumayya did not lift her head. She groaned, gripping at her mother's shirt.

Ayla kissed her head. "She's shy! Aren't you, Sum-Sum?" She said and kissed her head again. The little girl giggled.

Faruk shifted his seat closer to his wife and daughter. He rubbed his daughters back. "Anoush, do you want to hear daddy's story about how he lived in a castle?"

Ayla put on a face of annoyance. "Fine, tell your story, Balım."

Faruk looked at his daughter. "Huh? You want

to hear the story about how your father lived in a castle and called mommy every day?" Faruk winked at Ayla. Ayla frowned, unaffected by his crooning and looked away from him.

Their daughter didn't respond. She only laughed at his touch.

Faruk turned to us and drank his tea. He smiled as he talked. "When I was in the military, I was stationed at a castle near Ardahan, this small farming village close to the boarder of Armenia. It was the castle of Suleiman the Magnificent. It was built when Suleiman owned most of Africa and Asia. The soldiers stationed there were more like tour guides. There wasn't any fighting there so all they had to do was tell visitors about the history of the castle. Besides that, it was very carefree and relaxing. And, because my captains and commanders liked me, they let me have my own phone, keep books for me to read, and use my own samovar."

Ayla jeered and brushed her husband's arm with her hand very quickly. "So spoiled, Tatlım!"

. "Like I said before, I agree. I was," Faruk scoffed, "but the higher ranking officers were always trying to give us soldiers something to do. One of those things was Ot Yolmak. Every solider hated it. It was everyone's least favorite thing to do at the castle."

"What's 'Ot Yolmak'?" I asked. I drank my tea and it was then that I noticed the sun on my hand, its reflection in my cup.

"Ot Yolmak," Faruk explained, "is pulling grass. There was a lot of tall grass around the castle and the officers would have us pull it out and burn it. It was an annoying, useless job. But I only had to do it once after I figured something out. I had made friends with some of the farmers in Ardahan and they often fed their cows the grass, so it gave me a really good idea. I went to my captains and commanders and said, hey, why don't we invite the farmers to collect the grass and sell it to them. We wouldn't have to pay them for the work, in fact they would pay us!

"The higher-ups were so happy! I mean, this was money for them. So they said yes and I told my friends and the whole village came with their trucks and pulled all the grass. The villagers were so happy as well; we sold it to them for cheap! It was a win-win situation.

"After that, everyone saw me as a hero and no one ever asked me to do work. The rest of my days were peaceful. That was happiness. Of course, I have happiness now, here, but the happiness there, still,"

Faruk didn't continue. He looked at his wife and daughter and what was behind them, but I could tell he was looking at something else, something moving further in the distance. In the sun, it was glowing.

Lusin and I, in turn, looked at each other. We were all completely in the sun now, but it was hard to adjust our sights to the brightness of everything before us. What else could we do, I thought, but to shade our view from the sun?

About the Author:

E. P. Tuazon is a writer from Los Angeles. His fiction and poetry have been published in several publications. He is the author of several books, including two poetry collections, ANIMALS and LOVE WILL TEAR US APART, and a short story collection, THE SUPERLATIVE HORSE AND THE LAST OF THE LUPINS: NINE STORIES. For more information, visit https://ericptuazon.wixsite.com/happybivouac

EASY WAY

by Alexa Findlay

He sits at his spotless wooden desk reviewing the patient's dental history. Perfect teeth and no cavities.

His stomach drops to his knees, as he sees the name Veronica Reeve printed at the top of the page, along with her personal information. Is it the woman he had a one-night stand with before he married his current wife? It can't be! But she has the exact same name. It must be a coincidence.

"Dr. Moss, your patient is ready to be examined," one of his office assistants, Debra, says peeking into his office. He smiles at Debra and gestures for her to go back to work. He gets up out of his leather chair and puts on his white lab coat.

He strolls into one of the nearest dental rooms. Lying calmly on the beige dental chair is a young woman with straight blonde hair, wearing a solid white T-shirt, blue jeans, and white converse tennis shoes. Just before approaching her, he grabs a mouth mirror, a sickle probe, and a scaler from the cabinet located behind her chair, ready to examine her mouth.

He lays out the unused tools on the tray connected to her chair. He turns around. It's the same woman he slept with five months ago, days before his wedding. He takes a deep breath. In order to keep the peace between them, he decides to be as cordial as can be.

"Veronica, nice to see you again. How is everything?"

"Hi Stephen. Everything is going great. How about you? How are the wife and step-kids?"

"Wonderful. Thanks for asking. Now let's take a look at your teeth," he says trying to put an end to their conversation.

Stephen grabs a new pair of protective blue gloves from the box sitting on the countertop and slips them on. Stephen's heart starts to race, as the memories from that night flood his mind.

***

5 months ago…

Stephen, a thirty-five year old handsome man, took a seat at one of the barstools at his favorite bar, Chuckie's, located on the outskirts of San Diego, California. His wedding was just two days away. He needed to take a breather from all the wedding planning.

"Sir, what can I get you?" the bartender asked.

"Rum and Coke, please."

"Of course, sir."

Stephen swiped his thumb over his phone's touchscreen, as his drink was being prepared. He checked his emails. Nothing. His text messages. Nothing.

"Here you go, Sir." The bartender handed him the drink. Stephen slowly took individual sips, savoring it.

Suddenly, a slim blonde woman took a seat beside him, wearing a black sequined dress and black stilettos. Stephen tried to ignore her, but couldn't. She was exhilarating. Her perfectly slim body, perky breasts, and flawless skin astounded him.

Stephen sat there observing the blonde woman call out to the bartender, but the bartender never heard her. He was preparing drinks for a group of ladies at the end of the wooden table.

"Ma'am, I don't mean to sound creepy, but you are beautiful."

"My, oh my. Well, thank you. You are not so bad looking yourself."

"Thanks. So may I ask what your name is?"

"I'm Veronica Reeve. And you are?"

"I'm Stephen Moss."

"Nice to meet you," Veronica said holding her hand out, indicating she wanted to shake. Stephen made sure to return the favor.

The bartender eventually made his way back down the long table and asked Veronica what she wanted.

"A shot of tequila, please."

"Of course, Ma'am."

Stephen admired her alcoholic taste. Most women ordered the fruity drinks.

"Oh, and one for my friend as well," she pitched to the bartender.

"No, you don't have to do that," Stephen quarreled back.

"It's no problem at all."

Before Stephen could say any more, the bartender handed them their shots of tequila. They clinked their glasses and chugged their drinks. Veronica commanded the bartender to prepare several more shots. As the alcohol got to his head, Stephen craved her body more and more. She was voluptuous. Before he knew it, he had five shots. He couldn't think clearly. His vision became distorted. He couldn't grasp what they were talking about. He was no longer coherent.

He woke up the next morning in an unfamiliar bed, lying next to Veronica. The room was elegantly decorated with string lights, candles, and flowers. Nothing was out of place. A flat screen TV rested high on the wall.

Somehow, he made it to her home, but he couldn't remember how he got there. Everything was such a blur.

As he took a peek under the silky white sheets, his nude body said it all. They had sex, and there was nothing he could do to change that. If his fiancé found out, she would kill him. He decided to steadily inch his way off the bed, in hopes of not waking her up. He found his white button up shirt, his black dress pants, and black leather loafers sprawled across the wooden floor. Veronica's black sequined dress, pink lacey bra, and underwear were lying just beside his.

As he stepped into his pants, his phone began to beep. It rested on the white painted nightstand beside Veronica's queen-sized bed. It was probably Janet, his fiancé. He restlessly tried to make his way to the nightstand, but tripped and plummeted onto the hardwood floor. Luckily, he put his hands out in front of him, which saved him from seriously injuring himself. His loud fall immediately woke up Veronica. Stephen pulled himself together and got up from the floor.

"Baby, where are you going?"

"I have to get back home to my fiancé and my kids." Stephen grabbed his phone off the nightstand and noticed that Janet had texted him. She wanted to know where he was. He replied back letting her know that he went to the bar and had a few drinks, so he decided to stay the night at his friend Jason's house, since he lived close to Chuckie's.

"You are engaged?! You have kids?!"

"Yes and yes. They are my fiancé's kids, but I consider them my own. Listen, I'm so sorry. I drank too much. I didn't even know what I was doing. This shouldn't have happened." Stephen continued to dress himself and buttoned up his shirt.

"What are you saying? I thought we were going to be together forever?"

"No, Veronica. This was ALL a mistake."

"No, it wasn't! I refuse to believe it. We are meant to be together, baby," Veronica said crawling across the bed, seductively. When she finally reached him, she wrapped her arms around his neck, trying to pull him back into bed.

"VERONICA, STOP! This is insanity," Stephen hollered. Veronica untangled her arms from his neck, startled. He slipped his feet into his loafers.

"What does your fiancé have that I don't have? I'm perfect for you. I can give you everything you've ever wanted. You don't need her!"

"Veronica you are perfect, but not perfect for me."

"Of course, I am. You just don't see it now. You will someday."

"There isn't ever going to be a someday! You need to get that through your head! We are not meant to be together, EVER! I have a woman for me. That's my fiancé. NOT YOU. Got it?"

Veronica screeched like a barn owl. She grabbed the pillows off her bed and threw them at him. "LEAVE! NOW!" she screamed. Stephen slipped his phone into his pocket, grabbed his keys, and bolted out of her room, exiting her apartment.

***

Stephen stands beside the dental chair, positioning it with several buttons until it's perfect. He grabs the set of tools from the tray and tells Veronica to open her mouth wide. He examines her teeth with the dental mirror. Other than the plaque clinging to her teeth like glue, everything looks perfect. As he begins scraping the plaque off of her teeth, Veronica mumbles unfamiliar words.

"Yes, Ms. Reeve?" Stephen says removing the tools from her mouth.

"Stephen, I miss you. I need you. It's been too long without you. I'm sorry I threw the pillows at you. I was just angry."

"Ms. Reeve, I accept your apology. But I think it's best after this visit, that you don't come back. I can refer you to several other dentists. I apologize for any trouble that I have caused you. I wish you the best," Stephen says firmly.

"You are going to regret this!"

"Listen Ms. Reeve, I need to clean your teeth, so if you could please stop talking, that would be great."

"Fine," Veronica says pouting like a child.

As Stephen cleans the remainder of Veronica's teeth, he notices that tears are falling from her eyes. He ignores them, hoping that maybe his sternness will make her stop. Once complete, he shakes her hand and exits before she can say anything else.

***

One week later...

Stephen sits at his spotless desk, with only a picture frame of his wife resting near the edge, his laptop, a business phone, and a desk plant. He contemplates whether he should reiterate to his office assistants that Veronica Reeve will not be scheduling any more appointments with them. He wanted nothing to do with her, especially around his practice.

Janet sometimes came to visit, out of the blue. She would prepare him his favorite meal: a peanut butter and jelly sandwich, an apple, and several of her famous oatmeal cookies. The last thing he wants is to have Janet and Veronica cross paths. He never told Janet about "them." It would have ended their marriage. He made a dumb mistake and doesn't want Janet or her kids to suffer from it.

He packs what he needs into his briefcase and locks up his office as well as the remainder of the building. He saunters to his car, just feet away from the building's front door. He steps into his 2015 Cadillac Escalade, placing his brief case in the passenger seat beside him. He starts his car, relieved after a long day taking care of patient's teeth and makes his way back home.

As Stephen walks through the door of his home, he notices that no one is anywhere to be found. He calls for Janet, his step-daughter Rebecca, and his step-son Tyler. Finally, Janet yells for Stephen to come into the kitchen.

As Stephen walks into the kitchen, he notices Janet sitting beside Veronica at the dinner table. How did this happen? How did they meet? What is she doing here? Stephen's heart begins to thump. His body starts to quiver as they lock eyes.

"So, sweetheart. You know how I'm going to be working full time as an Accountant?"

"Yes."

"Well someone is going to need to take care of the kids while you and I both work."

"So, my parents or your parents could watch the kids."

"No, honey. I don't think that's a good idea. Our parents are too old to watch the kids. They need someone younger. So, I think Veronica is perfect for the job."

"Excuse me, who?"

"Stephen, this is Veronica. She is going to be our new nanny."

"Our what? We don't need a nanny."

"Yes we do."

"No we don't. And may I ask how you two met?" Veronica smirks at him as he tries to get to the bottom of their unnecessary meeting.

"Well honey, I was taking a jog at the park earlier today. As I was changing to a new song on my playlist, I wasn't looking where I was going, so then I literally bumped into Veronica. After we did plenty of talking, I came to find out that she is a nanny. She has watched over ten kids in the last few years."

"And you know this how? Do you have any proof that she is an actual nanny?"

"Stephen, how dare you be so rude," Janet says infuriated.

"I'm sorry, where are my manners? It's been a pleasure meeting you Veronica, but I think it's best you go."

"Stephen, may I have a word with you in the living room, please?" Janet says livid.

Stephen follows Janet into the living room, bewildered by Veronica's presence.

"Stephen, what is wrong with you? How dare you be rude to the poor girl. She wants to watch our children while we are working. What more could we ask for? You go in there and apologize to the poor girl."

"Fine. Your wish is my command," Stephen says sarcastically. Unable to deny Janet, he does as she asks. He saunters into the kitchen, ready to apologize to his ex-lover.

"Veronica, I apologize for my behavior. We are thrilled to have you work for us," Stephen says trying to be nice.

"Oh, thank you so much, Mr. Moss. I can't tell you how much this means to me. When do I start?" Veronica says putting on an act.

"Tomorrow would be great," Janet pitches in.

"Perfect. Is that okay with you Mr. Moss?"

"It's fine. Now if you will both excuse me, I'm going to be heading upstairs."

"Okay, sweetheart. Me and Veronica will just be down here chatting."

Stephen leaves them to talk while he climbs the stairs to take a long nap.

***

2 weeks later...

Since his last two appointments cancel for the day, Stephen decides he is going to come home early for a change.

He pulls into the driveway, but instead of using the front entrance, he decides to use the back door that leads to the kitchen, to avoid seeing Veronica. He steps in, setting his briefcase on the kitchen table. Veronica is no where to be found. He breathes a sigh of relief and pours himself a cup of coffee from the carafe that Janet made earlier that day. Just as he is about to place his coffee mug in the microwave, he hears Veronica's voice. He places the coffee mug on the granite table and follows the voice. It's coming from the living room. He rests his ear against the door and overhears Veronica asking Rebecca about her new step-dad.

"Becca, do you like your new step-dad?"

"You mean my daddy? Of course, I do," Rebecca says cheerfully.

"That's good. But can I tell you a secret?"

"Sure," Rebecca says jumping up and down like a kangaroo.

"Okay, can you promise not to tell anyone?"

"Of course. Pinky swear!" Becca says holding out her pinkie. Veronica returns the favor.

"So, your daddy doesn't like you," Veronica says mimicking the child's tone.

"He doesn't?" Becca says heartbroken.

"No, he..."

Before Veronica can say another word, Stephen bursts through the kitchen door into the living room.

"Veronica, may I have a word with you, please?" Stephen says enraged. He notices Rebecca discreetly crying.

"Of course, Mr. Moss." Veronica follows him into the kitchen with a smirk on her face. Stephen closes the kitchen door shut, so Rebecca can't hear.

"Veronica, what in the hell are you doing? How dare you tell Rebecca I don't like her."

"I told you, you were going to regret this."

"Veronica, you need help. This isn't normal behavior. You need to tell Rebecca what you said isn't true."

"I can't do that."

"And why not?"

"You hurt me, so you are going to pay."

Before Stephen can say any more, Veronica bolts out of the room. Stephen takes a seat at the kitchen table, appalled by her behavior. He places his head in his hands, uncertain about what to do.

***

1 month later...

Stephen awakes from a deep sleep when he hears Veronica and Janet laughing uncontrollably in the kitchen. It's 3:15 P.M on a Sunday. Just when he questions Veronica's presence, he reminds himself that this is the usual time that his wife and ex-lover "hang out." It has been going on for the past month now. This friendship of theirs started immediately after they hired her as their nanny. Janet seemed to just adore Veronica, and Stephen couldn't figure out why.

He forces himself off the couch and just as he is about to open the kitchen door, he hears his name.

"So tell me. How's your sex life with Stephen?"

"I don't really feel comfortable talking about this," Janet says nervously.

"Oh, come on, Jan. We are good friends, aren't we?"

"Yeah of course."

"So, then you should feel comfortable telling me anything."

"Alright, alright. Well honestly, not that great, because of our busy lifestyle."

"Jan, have you ever considered the fact that Stephen may be cheating on you?"

"Cheating on me? No way!"

"Are you sure?"

"Didn't you say that he comes home late, even though the office closes at six?"

"Yes, but that doesn't mean he is cheating."

"Well Jan, you don't know that. He could be going to a bar after work, having some drinks, and banging a woman, while you stay at home taking care of Rebecca and Tyler."

Within a matter of seconds, he can hear Janet whimpering.

"Oh Jan. Don't worry. How inconsiderate of me. I'm sure everything is fine."

Stephen steams with anger. How dare she convince Janet that he may be cheating? Veronica has crossed the line, but he can't just storm in there and start yelling. Veronica and Janet will team up and start accusing him of cheating. He takes a deep breath and decides to let them be. Hopefully Janet will calm down and Veronica will leave.

***

Stephen sits at his desk, skimming through several of his patients' file folders preparing himself for the remainder of the day. As he goes to grab his lunch that he prepared for himself earlier that morning, he realizes that he left it in the fridge at home.

He places his head in his hands, frustrated with his life. He can hear a knock on his office door. He looks up and notices it's Debra.

"Dr. Moss, your wife is here to see you."

"Oh, bring her in." Debra disappears to get his wife.

Before he knows it, Janet walks in.

"Janet! How are you?"

"Hi Stephen. I've brought your lunch."

"Oh, thank you. For some reason, I left it in the fridge. I must have not been thinking."

Janet smiles and looks about the room, as if searching for cheating clues.

"It's fine, dear."

"So how are you, honey?"

"I'm fine."

"Honey, take a seat. Just relax. It's my lunch break."

"Okay." Janet takes a seat and glares at her husband as if doing so, will make him confess to his cheating habits.

"What Janet? What's wrong?"

"Have you been cheating on me?"

"What in God's name are you talking about? Why would you say that?"

Janet starts to sob.

"Janet, why would you say such a thing? Who did you hear that from? Veronica?"

"Oh, so now you are blaming the nanny for your mistakes, because it's just easier. You are a piece of work." Janet storms out of his office, before he can get any words in. Stephen places his head into his hands once again.

***

After a long day at work, Stephen decides to stop at the grocery store to grab a few items. He needs to prepare himself before he confronts Janet about what happened earlier that day. He grabs a grocery cart, and strolls along the dairy aisle, looking for non-fat milk, because Rebecca drank the whole bottle.

As he strolls along the aisle, his eyes fixate on all the sliding doors that contain the various products. All of a sudden, his cart smashes into another individual's cart. It's Veronica.

"What the hell was that for?"

"I told you before, you are going to pay."

"For what? What the hell are you trying to do to me?"

"If you don't tell your wife about us, I'm going to make your life a living hell. Worse than it already is. Got it? You can either play this the easy way or the hard way. Which do you choose?"

"You are fucking insane."

"Which do you choose?"

"The hard way. I'm not going to let you get away with this."

"You already have," Veronica says chuckling. She waves goodbye, leaving him to wallow in his own lonesome.

***

1 hour later...

Stephen pulls into the driveway, feeling drained from his unpleasant day with his wife and Veronica. As he grabs the grocery bags from the backseat of his car, he decides that he is just going to tell his wife the truth about that night. He can't let this go on any longer than it has. He walks up to the front door, unlocking the door with his key. As he switches the lights on with his index finger, he stumbles. The groceries plummet onto the tile floor, making a mess. He gathers the food, placing them back into their bags. He stands up, the bags dangling like ornaments from his arms. As he walks into the kitchen, he notices splatters of red like juice all over the light tile floor, creating what seems to be a line. He drops the grocery bags onto the tile floor and follows the splatters of red. As he turns around the corner of the butcherblock, he witnesses Janet's bloody body lying lifeless on the floor. He drops down beside Janet's body, yelping. He places his ear on top of her chest, in hopes of hearing a heartbeat, but there is none. He wails at the thought of never hearing her voice again.

He lets go of Janet's body and considers the lives of Rebecca and Tyler. As he moves away from Janet's body, he continues to follow the trail of blood, which leads into the backyard. He notices Rebecca and Tyler's bloody bodies lying beside each other. He shrieks at the sight of their innocent lifeless bodies.

In complete shock and full of rage, Stephen races around the side of his house, until he reaches his car in the driveway. He hops in, and heads straight for Veronica's apartment.

Once he finally reaches Veronica's apartment complex, he parks his car and races up the stairs. He finally reaches the second floor. He violently knocks on Veronica's red apartment door with the #302 mounted in gold.

The door opens. As Stephen takes one step in, he gets a strong whiff of a chemical like substance and then everything turns black.

***

Stephen slowly opens his eyes. As he adjusts his eyes to the brightness in the room, he realizes he is back in Veronica's bedroom. He tries to get off the bed, but realizes he can't. His hands have been handcuffed to the bed's headboard. What in the hell? He squirms, but is unable to break free.

Suddenly Veronica walks in.

"Stephen. Stephen. Stephen. You've been a bad boy. Didn't I tell you, you could play this the easy way?"

About the Author:

Alexa Findlay is an Undergraduate Creative Writing Major. She has an Associate of Arts Degree in English from El Camino College. She spends most of her time writing fiction and poetry. She aspires to receive her Master's Degree in Creative Writing with a Specialization in Poetry. She hopes to one day become a Professor, and write books in the process. She is the Founder and Editor-in-Chief of The Mystic Blue Review and Cadaverous Magazine. Her work has appeared in El Camino College's Literary Arts Journal: Myriad, See Beyond Magazine, Pomona Valley Review, Better than Starbucks Magazine, Adelaide Literary Magazine, Halcyon Days and forthcoming in Sick Lit Magazine and Quail Bell Magazine.

NEVER TOO LATE
by Jose Recio

From her last alcohol binge, instinctively, she ended up at his door. They had been drinking buddies, and later, lovers—a long time ago.

With whatever remained of her, and her seventy years of age weighing on her shoulders, she sat down at his kitchen table across from him.

"What's left of you besides bones and a flicker of spirit in your eyes?" he asked, fearful of smothering her last breath of hope.

"Habits we develop over the years. Some bring happiness and others tears," she said in a shaky voice.

"You're consumed by alcohol. But you won't admit it, will you?" His confrontational approach softened as he viewed her pathetic appearance.

"Perhaps this is my last port. I drop anchor."

She had a coughing spell; then, she lit a cigarette.

"Sure," he said. "I guess next you're going to make smoke rings and tell me stories of years gone by."

"Why should I?" she said and exhaled halos of smoke through her protruded lips. "You know them all. Alcohol, nicotine, gambling—"

"Indeed, I know all your habits, your joys, and hurts."

Through ringlets of smoke, she threw him an avid look.

"Maybe we pray to break these bad habits," she said.

I doubt praying alone will do it. I also struggle to stay sober."

She offered him a cigarette. He shook his head; then, he got up and brought two glasses and a bottle of water.

"Please," she said and pushed a glass toward him. So he poured a glass of water for her. "I guess you're happy," she added. "Spring is here. You made it through winter."

He poured water into the other glass for himself. "I'm listening," he said.

She drained her glass.

"I want to quit my drinking," she said. Now her voice didn't sound shaky.

He became aware of her return to life.

"You took off on your own," he said, trying to dissipate any tone of reproach in his voice, "and now you return to my door, wasted and in need of compassion."

She dropped the cigarette butt inside the empty water glass. "Without alcohol, I fear my life will turn dull," she said.

He rapped his fingers on the table. "I fear alcohol will soon kill you."

She raised her eyes toward him, and now her facial features softened, and tears ran down her cheeks. "I don't want to face life, stripped bare."

"Nobody's completely alone with life."

A silence followed. She tried to recompose herself. "I need help," she said, dabbing her tears. "I need your guidance."

"Not so," he said. "Alcoholic Anonymous ought to be your guide. I can only support your initiative."

"I'll start tomorrow," she said.

"Why not next month?" he replied ironically.

She hesitated. "Today," she said.

"Now."

She nodded. They got up and left together.

About the Author:

Jose L Recio was born and raised in Spain. He studied medicine in Spain and later left for California on a Scholarship. He currently lives with his wife, Deborah, in Los Angeles. While in practice, he published several papers in specialized journals. Over the last few years, interest in creative writing keeps him busy. Having grown to become bicultural, he writes both in Spanish and English, and sometimes he translates his texts.

BLUE WATER

by Andrew Mitin

I The Home

Twilight moon through now-falling snow. The quiet flakes embrace over asphalt fissures of street bed. The world has changed since last the sun. Benevolent spirits have been decorating and not for any special Day. For this one. He rouses to the new world, deciphers alarm's bleat. Hair pulls from beneath the silver wristband. Not always so painful this: consciousness of father's time. Women: one now; two, though not for some a long time. Silence after difficult press why the button has to be so damn her unquiet churn. Outside the window is dawn and she will be up shortly. Slowly for a moment allow her supine warmth. One moment more for her body's needful rest, before the demands of new desire's pristine pulse. Remove soft coverings carefully. Duvet, now valance; rise, come and see. His toes wave then press into the carpet, sturdy now. Winter mornings were made for small families. Huddle together in the chill to bask in the groggy mood: of time-brewed coffee, the warming skillet; the tiny sprawl atop her soft blanket asleep is, yet in peaceful fullness. Awe. Red fists clutched and holding air beneath her chin tight jaw and sore, clenching still the wonder in home's secret pleasure. The click of the furnace and mark the scent of heated dust day's second coming a moment's fragrance. Alone with the sizzle and pop until she emerges, tired eyed sleepwalker. Good-morning-buries her face in man-smell t-shirt. He rubs her back. Kisses hair mess, her lips tender offer for this baby notices mother's closeness, somehow. Good-morning cries for girlfriend to tend too simple she harkens to unpleasant memory the small bedroom filled now with muted cooing.

She speaks to the child's now insistent cries, rising in true revelry that mother is, after all. He pours one cup, a second can't remember caffeine while breastfeeding newly wet lips thrust beneath lid-crushed eyes why a worried look always upon its face unable yet to separate reality from dream and this, dreamlike he kisses warm, soft and quiet now. These small moments: a blip in a day a year, ever rapid flutters still substantial, building one upon the other a loving world in miniature. His lips release against warm smelling head, lingers there not vanilla, not talcum neither pleasant. It's baby, she says in sleepy content costs the same, more his lips upon her now-turned check diaper mess more like checks the bacon. Flips curling fat, watches daughter lowering toward her matt. Anxious at approaching pink blur, her sign signifying very soon Momma's hand will release squirming torso. The final slip from between bare flailing legs. Bottom-patted she strains weak neck. One final glance to her must be all departures final toward love and care; now stands, hands hip-sigh. He shuffles the strips, scoot and press. Little head overcome into the matt laid upon lately revealed hardwood labor-loved for home sobbing from will's futility doesn't know we know the squiggles succeeds only in chafing cheeks. Small nose twist, red fists succumb to disappointment, says. She's wet, says. The indicted crying like mother like back turns to bacon tend. Charred strips go limp across the spatula and sweat onto paper towel. Shell-cracked eggs slip into bowl salt and pepper stirred some tabasco. Harried screams during changing why do they something about the skin the shackled ankles increase with heavy foot falls, says We're out of diapers again with this You said you would etcetera yes blah blah blankly disrobes before his morning ceremony is consummated would the other stripping hadn't been would be sleeping now changing to greet the charge that night not her likely someone inevitable suppose smitten with the cold and those oh so dark outside the engine turns with considerable convincing. In the hard-won roar the interior sings aglow with blue dials red numbers, a benediction gas pump yellow. Hail, wipers. He sits in the chill eyes to believe she once so breathing hard now and I too exhausted over miserable balled hands. A spasm against the frozen windshield then nothing. His lungs filled with the car's silent cold fills the car with caustic cloud-breath that dissipates into ice slick boughs bared and still in lunar light shining upon pried loosening. The snap of malleable rubber and one fell swoop of an arm clears the hood of snow. Ice scraper stabs at hoarfrost. The pleasant grip should be comfortable the weapon-feel natural in the window now she scowling probably watches him chop at the windshield, reaching across too far and shaking her head at What? hands red-fingered tips splitting his whimsical way of charging without foresight the unintended consequences nobody tells life without, she often says, too literal my house filled now with unintended contributions to the well-being clear-minded and breakaway clear-glassed and humming toward a wonder of goods acre-walled and roofed whenever needed somewhere to go for a bit a while with miles of shelves a long while depleted every day then replenished.

II. The Market

A kind of magic at play here. Rabbit out of the hat is fish on ice; the lobster tank, the precious processors that captures still or realtime actual life that won't watch for years then once and never again moment had relived replacing memory such rot the bread and the milk, now cans of tuna pears peas with ham half-aisle of sauces ready-to-serve soup condensed creams and butter and bottles of rye ale cases and gallons of mixers, sodas soldiered at attention and primary colored sacks shouting FUN breasts frozen and breaded thighs, T-bone and the rib-eyes have it that drink while the movie and watched her lying there just standing in the empty aisle illuminated again she said do that

again and I not thinking her really there at first then glad she came to recall now, dearly. For all her coming years the shoes and socks, a profound selection of lambs wool goat leather gloves for grill handling tongs and spatulas scrapers, the charcoal and fluids went too far that head shaking I'll shake mine at the magazines the ridicule from all quarters for every interest arrayed like flimsy roofing tiles take one up the gentleman quartered sounds about right for all they tell of man's problems The Perfect Martini, Face Cream She'll Envy. He bends to pick up Jennifer Whats-her-name loosed in sensuous negligee for nothing good comes leave the flyer for some mom to explain the kid what's in store the cards for all ages, for all occasions not that for Timmy's happy birthday smiles at pink and blue monkeys giraffes congratulating the weaponizing of lace pretending his being is bi-willed anniversaries of all kinds. So much to celebrate. Sleds and the patio furniture, tiki lights and the salt spreader; car seats and baby clothes cotton ensemble polyester blends into pacifier bins assorted age and color, free flow and orthodontic with or without animals to clutch and smell, see-through and mustachioed or emblazoned with an English D the Red Winged Wheel. He passes packets of onesies and diaper bags for diaper cases and strollers and bouncers where she will fill those never full of the filling never be gleefully learn her small form's possibilities. Formula nipples, colorful spinning wheels, thick-paged books of colored cats and dogs, orangoutangs hello-smiling. A kind of magic indeed. Such wonder at six-thirty AM providing at all hours unthought of and unremarked implies implicit trust in the fullness of these shelves. That they will ever be for one now two very soon he said whenever I needed a long while asleep in the warm family hundreds of trucks have converged upon the castled market. Behind leave it for where every canned tube and sacked jar are thousands of laborers unloading loads in perpetuity I am myself forever and again. Stomping bleary-eyed they'd supplied; trudging diaper-cased he's chosen. Reveals now this one plastic card use another for that after considering emergencies only this qualifies sausages and fertilizers, DVDs and spark plugs, the candy bars and energy drinks, the wine blenders, salmon fillets and wiper blades, spools of yarn artwork framed candelabras, the glitter to the city go and the glue. Expense deducts from mystical coffers, digitized magic revealing plenty from nothing to stop this train of thought of train stops between me and there nothing. Cash back. Silent goods watch the doors come and go, speaking of forevermore, inaudibly categorizing types of love never seen before. The dark and the cold exhume quick breaths would return for her not for her who cheated me out of the silent car sliding upon glazed asphalt. Street lights, white aglow. Dark lanes marked by sporadic lines keeps a life worth order now this bolting coward's way her way too in a way mine among the denizens worse only cause being man of this city. And well-ordered must be, this: LNS. Aluminum timbers and glass bisected, creating irregular segments contrary to the timetable's predictability least desired devisor calling every morning from place-names far afield culling through options best suited from where comes the call, heed west and considers from there anywhere but the plastic bag. A beacon in this winter night drawing into its blazing embrace those red-nosed foot-stomping who, for reasons all their own, seek the comfort these rails will secure. Singly or together in weary patience they anticipate the announcement for Chicago, One, he says and listen for the track's vibration not decided if returning is undecided whose path shines ever brighter until the full sun of day. Around baggage-laden mumbles unfettered taking in the design, the clean floors and folds the bulky ticket to ride free of back pocket stuffs except her unconscious waiting maybe a sense of lack like how she knew momma maybe knows daddy is not his reflection a dark missive from a time before the man she will accuse him of being able to remind. There are more here than what first appeared. The report of the train's eminent arrival. A flurry of handle-grasps and quick steps through poorly held doors. A clear light at track's end. Trees stir. Behemoth bellows and slows. Towers above the disenchanted, who pull their weight into the steel belly. The metal sighs, as again her waiting will never be .

III. The Train

Morning everbrite envelops undulating fields, the backsides of house huddles. Cross-finger wisps from bricked chimneys wane. Passing through, these iron rails don't. This speed of travel needs material stasis and seated there like cast steel I have to be easier memories of home travel at cross-purposes. He watches another field pass across the lighted glass. Home waxing. The vanishing point the groove vision's in. Locomotive pulls harried-eyed over three thousand ties per mile is fifty for every second to where never mind beneath serpentine rails overlaid with ice they crawling toward is more time away that way lie across the rows maybe should be called it hoar frost shoulder blades and behind the knees and such artistry in its waiting form. Special lens shows new eyes the frozen glaze cracking beneath steel wheels and done with new ears a song sung to deer-sought final buds her cries all times at all hours bed changed up for no reason held fed at all proliferates where the sun doesn't behind knee it was and tired of the same old and then how soft she is in the quiet and the dark sometimes with the hot and the quiet shine. A young woman lie's too great to remain talking behind, as if to herself, asking questions answers out of sync in turn and laughing at the hatred that must be built something only she can hear. Without rhythm. Fragments merely and were they a poem lacking reasonable flow. Fifty thoughts per second not legible hearing. Auditory alienation born of fragments because sense-making day after day for months the resentment is visual. An old man I'd have with me years never knowing if she were true rests with the bag in his lap senseless how she could've gotten when so careful I was and can only mean his hands shake crinkle-waves great lengths and can't think about his elbow knocks the stately umbrella into the aisle. Streaks of aging gleam off the crozier he mumble-breathes toward. Hoar-haired beneath plaid fedora from ears and nose, bunched wild above his eyes. Talcum powder wafts from wrankled neck, moth balls and aftershave settles upon invisible rails from overhead vents. He sighs kalamata tapanade and pulls at leather bounded scripture. Black tract throwaway I said and never slapped so bent forward and cathedral-handed with closed eyes, remorse swaying what you are now I once was hard from that day staggered into this cabin slapped a year ago now between heaven and hell's opportunities but that's over until the fulness of decide reveals preferred today is a new place-name. Black bark lines sketched against white swaths. Fading morning stars are innumerable yard lights of country farms. Feather in his hat, burgundy and emerald diamonds glance right corner forward where four young people divided by two is two couples or two people the ancient Pauline mathematics of unification couples coupling one from a couple of ones and three makes the strand uneasy not easily what they are now I once but no more broken. The feather flutters in their muffled laughter that is losing its muffle. Facing one another in a turned row to lay Queens and tens on a red cooler. Cards fanned in mock security, anticipating the trick played on me her idea of father murmur-cursing at smiling tell each one a promise waiting to break brunette Hairpulled shoulder-dances in expected revelry. Hair-draped earrings shake and lays the ace lauds blasphemy when Hairpulled throws Jack of Hearts to overwhelm poor instinct staring too long get socked by men if don't stop thinking and have one already because naked dreaming Hairpulled combines the kitty. Shuffles on the cooler touching eager shins across from her. Smell tapanade. Never smiling she lifts the slender pack above the now-open lid, nods in response to sibilant whispers he's concerned she has no poker face and if she were alone the club car probably while purple and blue, now orange and green cups are presented, taken in remembrance of popped tops. Hallelujah salutes to Chicago weekend. Suckslurped and licked, young lovers away. Insider laughter. Nature's copulating illusion is all ever will be greatest known secret. He slides close to the window to chase desire not it but court it for today tonight forget domestic no longer a mirror. The train sways and jerks with more calamity in the brightening day than when it was draped in darkness. The steely movement upon the rails reasserts freedom from this day and he is carried up in it, eyes closed, glass-cooled forehead above palm-warmed cheek.

Behind is quiet now and forward right corner a cool babbling that mimics box-sway, the quiet bar and on-line the first time it was Rudy's for a few before the show and stayed to dance warm bellies and delight and nothing then she said so but next we did and most times after always the same motion tends to stay until behindknee it was then stick-piss and shell-shocked because the pill the Implanon the sponge and the shot what did it said and didn't I say the train sway stills. On the cool glass the orange glow infiltrates his lid, its advance checked by the cornea and lingering there to influence dreams. Dark squiggle lines are embryos and who's to say there is no womb-light there, no aurora borealis to wonder at. Who will say no vision there of what was before, what once they were, celebrating what has passed and the heinous act slapped sense into me I said what will come. Dreams of the dark nothings because imagining the bright something is terrible. The beginning of beauty always is. Dozing in the insignificant correspondence between the natural and the super, entreating unceasing, until deeper darkness startles him awake. Open-eyed and wiping crease-feet, memory collides with hope in the blurry wakened conscious. In the lilt of the car his face returns to him in the opaque window, downcast. Chicago. The gentleman gathers his things and young teams pass plastic bag for cups, wrappers and tops. Pack the cooler and hands clap Ode to Possibilities inherent in couples coupling nice yes and after a small family on a winter's morning. The train slows then sighs. Cold wind whips through the car in exuberant greeting.

IV. The Street

Sun rays strikes the glass, ricochets into the river. Giggles lie upon the wake. No need of purpose to journey here. It can be slight so long as here is the end. Naked hands jacket-stuffed he bends across the half wall. The rhythm of obelisks, sconce ringed midway, call to her color rings ungraspable yet scattered around an earlier century. The once-smooth stone weathered, innumerable demands clean care clairvoyance must mean caresses absorbed into its material. He turns his back to the wind, face to the sun. Linger on the bridge.

The river's course guides city walls. Slender fingers of the patamoi nuzzle voluptuous curves of stone, forgiving mankind its dabbling in the natural course, soon to dabble again. Reverse the reverse never likes to now before a drink was how we most times and can't find again what was once so what she wants change for me to change and the diapers are in the car and the car is in the lot far from home where she waits they back to nature. Across the river shadows lie urgent is what was emblazoned upon sheet glass, curved around marble columns. Shadows alive on the fifty-fifth floor. Barely conceivable the times of delight had that wonder spent alive in it together knowing each other such a notion as man working in the altitudes so far from the fields, eschewing the necessity of rain and green buds opening to each how impossible now sun-encouraged. The yield carried along fiberoptic wires that dance in the space overhead, commiserating in the clouds nearer to God without impassable rift consider but she ever will be too late throwaway the hope of Babel's builders. The signal desists its red hand. White strides to another corner, another crossroads to consider time before she it all without doubt maybe a chance for something but this Citi-Bank, Tower Self Park employee yellow vested cigarette leans on the ticket kiosk staring at Less Than Thirty Minutes $5 too much to ask had she even asked and no basking within an agitated cast of shadow-light-shadow from such a blessing said and should have suspected then but who could suspect a thing above racing beneath the elevated track with thunderous ovation I couldn't and agreed until now suspect and her all throwaway across the sun dappled street. Within it's translucent squares gray-filtered shadows of light itself are the silhouettes of still more men, still more women. Those pillars of the city as integral as what he leans upon. Feel the rough smoothness of iron. Push against it, hands now face. Consider the myriad intellects come together with the advent of industrial innovations, steel and electricity, routes and schedules, with effort and determination. They labored for a future hope that is your present disregard. Wipes his eyes. Yes, it is good to consider these objects surrounding you. The wonder of it all. Of life and the size of that bolt, rusted and painted over countless times through the centuries. City workers with their paint buckets and brushes, no power sprayer in this windy city, they apply veneer to Behemoth's stanchion and across that bolt's head that today is chipped again and cracked again it waits silently, watching generations come and go like all the rest suppose each his own tragedy the devil in us both tricks as tricked hundreds like it on the platform, watching. Thousands like it, patient as the Rockies, as stately. This bolt will be thought of again as it has been thought before. The size of the wrench that first tightened it, that first besmirched silver sheen, sullied first the fresh bolt smell. The fist first that clutched the wrench, the vulgar incantations spoken over it, vesper grunts and howling. Labor's song of praise to the fissure now split knuckles, sharing in blood-drawn altar work. Perhaps it savors still the taste and your blood would taste to it like that first blood. From like to like he is with them in love who believes so soon I said and she hurt belief my penance for a time paid but stages on proof's way mine approached too slow for her with caution wise since after the simple words unspoken uncoupled our time marches, foot swift and sure. Above is quiet now, but the rails reverberate. A wake in the steel. Movement requires swaths of stasis. Everyday miracles have flitted across his vision, the chaotic squiggle of sunspot. The corner has wonders to fill a chapbook of poems and a monograph of the depiction in photographs. It too deserves a Proustian treatment there now a Monk's Pub celibacy too far but a life in which to be rid of life better to confess its phenomenons. Coated elbows flatten upon the rail's weary mahogany. Takes his heavy breath like stain. The bartender pulls a lever to remit the relentless burden of duty, a portion of the Lethe. Offers the mug and rubs a rag into breath-stained grains. In light that shines within the shadow of the El air-borne debris illuminates, dancing and consoling in the swirl of disrupted stillness, like planets drawn in miniature, atoms lilting about, leaning and loafing until the moment they unite to assemble a father's life impossible there without desire none for it not yet didn't and told her so like so many dust mites turning new angles unknown until this turning. It requires new metaphors, quick minds for a world in need of revelations. O, Chicago. For this marvel you came and having come return. With tales of Hallelujah, return.

V.   The Tavern

To your health drink said the bartender, unsmiling. Over the glass rim foam slosh runs golden toward the bar. Flesh abates with an abrupt tip. Immediate free-fall. Half-full lands with relief and numbs like a tear drop bursting upon the mahogany, spraying smaller droplets not visible upon a coaster where they are concealed beneath the weight of mind's doubt no longer a a storied glass. The bartender's folded arms in conscious protest to the quick demise of the day's first pour is delicious and cold warming feel a lightening and another is ordered. Another given. Man alone is able to transform the world. To make of it a storehouse of the infinite, his prerogative. This his share in being nothing here to do and none to demand of me but me this I bowed above Green Line APA. Startled, he disregards his reflection. The mirror holds nothing of the past and it offers no hint of the future. The mirror is all-present, a perpetual absence of time. Alone among the beckoning shadows, inclined toward that other realm require only to make one's life now eternal. How different are the shadows in this world. The plaza shaded in light charcoal and the bartender's cast upon and between the rows of bottled curvature, compare: dove's blood altar-sprinkled, the liturgy yes even copulation itself a shadow of that other. His face lowered still, concealed behind intwined fingers. And yet merely a glance and his image too will reveal the face of God. Courage. The mirror being merely shadow does not contain all truth. Grave-like and the barren womb, land-like in drought or the flame, never fulfilled. The creases around his eyes recall the time of smooth skin and the stubble on his chin, dormant youth. The bartender's proliferation of nose follicles and ear, where future grooming compels mirror-facing and the passing of time. Self-departing now from this held time within the Edison-glow of polished glass. Consciousness keeps from that other world. Hope and memory kept from the mirror. The mirror captures eternity will never end and the problems escalate until she's eighteen to separate and misery until memory convinces

correction and hope assures the future will not end in death. Now is the clink of glassware, now the time of low speech and the aging light. Shadow creep along city-sooted windows. The barroom is submerged in premature dusk. Silence and the dim with screeching and the taking of sides against me for petty slights that could never balance the scales of her deceit and the clock is off by forty-five minutes to wait would be wrong and correct in his home. There, where his child has been laid down with her habitual fuss that delights in memory I feel the affront how much more later will murder enter my mind tired now by her small game. The bartender sees to familiar faces, tipping bottles, pulling levers he chuckles and commiserates. Proverbs and maxims dissemble another for a float down the Lethe, He came in like he meant business said the bartender to the woman on a far stool, ain't never seen him before. I seen him my whole life she think she is knowing me here nobody knows though in a time not yet apprehended, he remembers her weak moments of impotent rage, fondly. And the soft cuddle of her warm head, the impotent grasp of sleepy fingers, her command of fragile bones in the long moment of a daughter's affection. Now the reddened face and the clenched fists, the limbs rigamortis at impending abandon all hope is mine now but soon the screams and cries will be as a sepia photograph. Project toward knowledge of time passed when this more will not be that and another memory will be a gracious resort. Three glasses hop-ringed and honey colored are swallowed time and now a fourth to keep calm induce a lightness and use to hearten nerve in this new life courts oblivion. Escape from time for a time. Courage, man. Embrace that tender decision, welcome and again decide another today and again. For mankind resides in clear mist and being abides with hard-won knowledge that becomes. Project solitude and freedom and the space to float about or whip around as the winds dictate as the train schedule ordains and pretend my own will's a vision unachievable, though still conceived of. Spirits in a holding pattern, circling above, long to look into these things. Detached from it all they ache. Circadian rhythms are no law, not gravity and neither space nor time, but the word mediates. His word translates the world whether here or afar San Francisco or Seattle go and reveals his ilk the life I imagined is not forever. Beauty walks with Demise. The bartender pulls the lever releasing Noah's vigor into fragile glasses, drained and followed by another pull out of the station toward another station cash and never find enthusiasm for the draught. For him the euphoria of its song, for him also the dregs. The blessings and curse are ethereal cravings. Five generations have passed since first the dim. Now the wobble-stooled, now too the slurred speech. Tables once empty have been filled are now vacant again. Many pulls conceived and buried. From the filling of the glass to its emptying a moment and the moments in the bubbles are of such importance, pointing to desire and another decision of least regrettable acts. Another generation. How quickly they pass now. Still, slowly daughter distinguishes self. Forever lying-in day, forever screaming night. Courage, Man! Always filling diapers moistening to Mum paste spit-up, ear piercing screech tests the family constitution, profaning the memory of his first love convinced of misstep return to her life's hope and to the fruit of that union, return. Amusements amassed and filled to slumping, his fists shaking which step near tears he pays and is gone.

VI.   Union Station

This magnificence holds a dreary aspect. The light dulls behind a tower and trickles through shaped glass. He glides below ground, unsteady. The escalator carries silence and red-cheeked to waiting tracks. A slowed person's sudden halt on the leveling plateau. Teeters, now-fallen luggage elicits maledictions. Coats jostle the poor man's worried attempts to upright his capsized life. Leaping from the flattening stair, around the drowning man colliding with a woman who loses the grasp of her child. Her fingers splayed, then curl into abandoned space. Terrific squeals attend this concourse has no logic where do they go where coming from all over the country people swirl, dive into openings, sideways now then back. A sliding tile game. The portrait ever obscured. Another escalator are there no limits to the depths dug deep into the onion fields. Where once he glided across sun-warmed streets and steel,

here quick-breathed and near blind, he struggles within the stifling maze and no refreshing breeze no space to lose my way only purpose of pace here strides, spinning around glancing off. Gropes the wall for a signpost. Narrow catacomb opens into a world of freedom from the center out as many futures as an imagination creates a vaulted arena. There, a magic transference. Breakneck rays of dusk filters through glass apertures, rejuvenating it, cleansing the broadbands of atmospheric particles and cosmic dust, leaving the glass outside stained. These great hall windows hold a mystical property and return all that passes through them to an earlier aspect, an earlier time to decide upon next course back to the beginning of light work it out on this bench yes in the dim and the silence yes. Meditate on just this beginning, this special state instant-now. Animals lack this, neither do angels have the capacity for it. One does not apprehend time, the other cannot die. Both ignorant of now the moment of deciding bereft of beauty, of her life with me she would never know without would be ordinary and I would send I would still be holding another, keeping that shadow from betraying the turn of the earth faithful Oh even in that embrace there is a shadow exclaiming a greater truth. He lifts his hands to his forehead and rolls his neck upon the wooden back. Whisper and caress and beat back the torrents of time and know except in this but always after morning will come with a twilight moon through now-fallen snow. Return to that embrace shared by the lower beasts, unknown to the higher orders I will rise to be there and not for slumping this and not for slouching, either. Certainly not for sprawling upon the marble slabs this floor cooling clearer somehow upward now. Onward! Across the vast hall no, that way leads back to the street. Yes, beneath the arched entryway he had too much Monk's is all and stumbles down can't quite falls forward toward the kiosk. His thick hand vaguely aware of one complaint against the golden rail slips across its polished surface rightly so and ever be mine clutching as he goes down upon a knee mercy grip-loosened rolls to the bottom cooling floor to rest the racing glimpses the ticket booth okay okay he says to the uniformed couple money let me pay for where, he decries a place and have money enough to leave for a destination. The next train out told and not going back there another train have money but what are you saying. Return. From where you came and with Hallelujahs, return. I have a two o'clock to San Francisco for $167, now that's not with a sleeper need to sleep to think to wake in Saint Louis leaves at two-fifteen. It's going to be close, said an officer. He's going to need the yes, that sleeper, said the other. With a sleeper you're looking at $475 to the other side away as far as can throw cast steel tracks that brought you here will take you home again only speak the word, the liturgy evoking bright morning out of dark ash, itself an easy embrace of morning's infant softness away and be gone heavy lidded, her lips curving around plastic spoon-whirled globs upon plump cheeks. Unconcerned until the damp rag applied, she reacts as if to ten thousand volts and squirms in authoritative grip escorted and nothing wrong with her mouth away from the airplane. Remember after all her laugh, the easiness of being with her. Do not carry me to an exiled world. Only remember and take us home.

About the Author:

Andrew Mitin lives in Michigan. His stories have appeared in Joyland Magazine and The Gravity of the Thing.

AQUARIUS

by Robert Perron

Rita appears in Stan's doorway forearms extended, middle fingers raised. A faded AC/DC T-shirt—red thunderbolt on black background—hangs past her knees. She's short, thinks Stan, but who isn't these days? The last time Dr. A's nurse asked his height, and Stan answered as always five-nine, he detected a smirk. Stan swivels his chair away from monitor and keyboard, and confronts his wife's fluttering eyelashes and upraised fingers. Gray, uncombed hair storms about her octogenarian features. She doesn't have her teeth in.

"You know what?" she says, wrinkled lips pulled over gums. "Fuck you too. Asshole."

Stan turns his palms up, but she's gone, just like that, one second sputtering obscenities from a puckered mouth, throwing him the double bird, the next back to couch and television.

Stan reconstructs the events leading to Rita's demonstration. From the living room, he'd heard her voice rise over the honking flatscreen, increasing in volume. But the words remained a babble due to her remoteness and the blaring television, and—Stan acknowledges in the interest of fair play—some loss of hearing on his part in the upper frequencies. He wasn't being an ass, he tells himself. He just couldn't understand her and was trying to relay that information, but chose, he now realizes, regrettable rhetoric. "Speak the fuck up, will you," he had yelled. Stan guesses she keyed on the expletive and, as usual, jumped to a conclusion, and, as usual, chose retaliation over discourse.

Stan slumps. All he wants are golden years that are golden: his coolmath.com, mindgames. com, bridgebase.com, his npr.org. And his book

in progress, working title Everything They Should Have Told You in Algebra II. He's looking into self-publishing, will not have to deal with agents and publishers, just amazon.com. Maybe he'll spend some money and hire an editor.

His mind comes back to Rita. Jesus, it's not like he ignores her. They go out two or three times a week. They go to movies. They go shopping. If she visits his study or catches him at breakfast, they pass words about the kids, the grandkids, current events, other things, friends who have died. But this mumble-shouting from the living room drives him over the edge. Any time she wants, babbling from the couch, demanding a response, appearing in his doorway with obscenities and rude gestures. He doesn't have to take it. That's right, just like the song, which band? Stan remembers: Twisted Sister, pounding four-four beat, "Oh we're not gonna take it anymore."

Stan pushes on the arms of the swivel, rises, wobbles the hallway to the master bedroom, pushes the closet slider, and grabs a long sleeve polo, striped, red and white. He'd bought it when the red stripes matched his hair; now the other stripes match what's left. He pushes his feet into black sneaker-shoes, sits on bed's edge, bends, bends further, and engages the Velcro straps of the left shoe. Takes a breather and repeats for the right shoe.

In the living room, Rita eyeballs Stan from her couch slouch.

"Where do you think you're going?"

"Out."

"You can't drive in the dark, you fool."

"You're the one who can't drive in the dark. Fool. You're the one who can't drive, period."

Rita throws her feet to the floor, tries to stand, falls back. As Stan closes the front door behind him, he hears, "Stop. Where are you going?"

Stan's in his car, a Toyota something, turning the ignition key. Bells chime and he drags the seat belt across his red and white polo. He pulls the shifter a notch and regards his side mirror. Above it, Rita stands in the doorway, mouth in motion. Stan sighs and pushes a button. The driver's window retracts and Rita's words take form. "Put your lights on, you fool."

Stan twists the stick on the left side of the steering column illuminating garage, walkway, front stoop, his wife's thunderbolt, her fur-rowed, gray-framed face. I am not an ass, Stan says to the steering wheel. I am taking a well deserved break from all this shit. He looks again to the side mirror and backs to the end of the driveway. He turns his head left and right until no headlamps appear for two blocks, backs into the street, brakes, pulls the shifter two more notches, and slides his foot onto the gas pedal.

#

Stan has in mind MacKenna's on South Main. Can't remember the last time he was there, some occasion, end of school year, retirement party, it's been a while. He noses into a parking spot at the end of the block braking hard as the front of the car rises with a loud scrape. Jesus, why don't they make these things so they clear the curb? Down the sidewalk, two dudes glance up from cigarettes. Stan checks his phone—a missed call and a text. He puts on reading glasses: please answer are you ok. Stan looks at the visor, sighs, looks back to the phone, and taps yes yes am fine.

Stan waits for the smokers to go back in and pushes the car door open. Bells chime and Stan twists the stick on the steering column. He hoists his body erect as the headlamps fade, slams the car door, and pushes the lock button on the key fob.

Stan enters MacKenna's. Not as dark as re-membered: no more the drifting tobacco smoke; exposed brick and wallboard instead of oak panelling; tables and chairs instead of

booths. To Stan's left, a waitress sets down plates that look like full meals. Her arms and the back of her hands, and her face when she turns, are a deep brown, Her eyebrows lift and Stan thinks, Jesus, she's giving me the look. Reach a certain age and can't go anywhere without getting the do-you-belong-here look. Stan bypasses her impertinence with a bearing for the bar.

The bartender's Hispanic, thirties or forties, with a shaved head. The tooth behind his right incisor is gold and a gold earring hangs from his left ear lobe. He speaks casual, flawless English with Spanish words tossed in.

"You want a table, amigo?" He points at the waitress. "The señora can fix you up."

"Bar's fine." Stan raises his butt to the middle of three empty stools. The bartender drops a plastic menu in front of him.

"Anything to drink, compañero?"

"Jack and a Bud."

The bartender widens his lips but narrows his eyes. "For the Jack Daniel's, number seven okay?"

Stan returns the smile. "Number seven's fine."

"Straight up?"

"Straight up."

"Bottle okay for the Bud? We don't have it on tap."

"Bottle's fine."

"Do you want a glass of water?"

No I don't want a glass of fucking water, mor-on. Stan forces another smile. "No, I don't want any water, thank you."

Stan dons glasses and scans the menu. Cursive letters blend with a pastel background. The lighting no longer seems so good. In another setting, in an all-senior setting, Stan might irra-diate the menu with his flashlight app. He re-moves his glasses as a shot glass slides toward him followed by a long-necked bottle.

"Need a glass, amigo?"

Stan smiles. The bartender smiles and slips away.

A light handclasp envelopes Stan's right elbow. He swivels into the gaze of the African American waitress, her lips a heavy red, hair straight with russet highlights, eyes coal black.

"Mr. Kay?"

Stan peers.

"Jeannie," she says. "Jeannie Collins."

Stan recalls the name and conjures a portrait, a teenager from years past, adds weight, adds furrows, tries to arrive at the face facing his. One of the smart ones, he remembers.

Jeannie moves her hand from elbow to forearm. "Mr. Kay, I don't recognize myself sometimes. Hey, Ramón." The bartender looks over. "Mr. Kay here was my math teacher for trig and calc."

"Cómo?" Ramón steps toward them but then away as a customer down-bar raises a finger.

"Well," says Stan. He taps the menu. "What's good here for an hors d'oeuvre?"

"I'd go with the fajitas," says Jeannie. "I'll put them in for you, Mr. Kay." She backs away. "What a surprise."

Stan turns the shot glass in his fingers, raises it to his lips, and tilts. A mild burning. Can still take a shot. He places the glass on the bar and tips the bottle of beer.

His phone chimes. Stan lowers volume and ignores the vibration. Now comes an incoming text. Stan holds the phone at arm's length and reads: are you ok? He sets the phone on the bar and types in the reply window yes yes yes.

Jeannie returns to Stan's elbow. "Be out in a few."

Ramón approaches on the other side of the bar and says, "Trig and calc?"

"Yeah. Did you know speed's the first derivative of distance?"

"I had no idea."

Jeannie looks into Stan's face. "And acceleration's the second."

Stan laughs but wonders why Jeannie's working at MacKenna's, why she isn't an engineer or a teacher. Jeannie responds to his thoughts. "I

wanted to do something, Mr. Kay, you know, with my education. But right out of school I got a job in the bottling plant." She tilts her head in the direction of the Coca-Cola bottling plant by the river, closed ten years now. "The money was good. Then I got married. A couple times."

Jeannie steps away to wait on a table. A few minutes later, she returns with the fajitas. "My older daughter's a senior at state. She's real good in math."

"That's great," says Stan. But he doesn't remember the daughter from class and doesn't remember seeing Jeannie at a teacher's conference. Then it occurs to him that he's retired over twenty years.

"I can do change in my head," says Ramón.

"Thirteen thirty-seven out of a fifty," says Jeannie.

"Easy. You get back three pennies, a dime, two quarters, a dollar, a five, a ten, and a twenty."

"A lost art," says Stan.

"Used to work in my uncle's bodega. Cash only." Ramón extends his right right arm over the bar with a closed fist and Stan thinks, what the fuck, then recalls from a video a new form of greeting. He raises his own right arm and bumps fists. "Amigo," says Ramón.

Stan bites into a fajita and lifts the beer. Almost gone. His phone buzzes. Jesus H, but he picks up, swipes, listens, and responds in a low voice. "It's fine. Everything's fine."

He recalls Jeannie now. Not a lot of African Americans in the school. Skinny, attractive, although Stan didn't look at students that way. Sometimes he looked at fellow faculty that way, in particular, Anna Wasser with her put-on accent, a vague middle European. She often appeared when Stan was atop Rita, or flying solo, still does on occasion, Rita snoring on the couch, him on the trundle bed in the den, oh Anna, oh Stan. But never once had his mind wandered to students that way—a code of honor, a line not to be crossed.

Customers come and go. Stan crooks a finger and Ramón approaches.

"Another," says Stan.

"Another what, amigo?"

"Jack and a Bud."

Ramón looks aside, looks back. "Tell you what, compañero, let's skip the Jack."

Stan smiles. Ramón smiles.

Stan sips fresh Bud and nibbles cold fajita. He's making another grab for the Bud when his eyes dilate and his thighs clench. Stan drops a leg and touches floor. He drops the other leg and stands, looking across tables and the heads of people eating and drinking, out a window onto a streetlamp-lit night. He wonders where he is.

"Hey, amigo, está todo bien?"

Ah, Ramón the bartender. MacKenna's. "Need the toilet," he says.

Ramón points in the opposite direction. "Baño's that-away."

Stan reverses direction, sees doors with stick figures, and advances on the one with pants. The room's small, a sink, a short divider, urinal, a stall. Stan unzips in front of the urinal. As he waits, Dr. A's admonitions come to mind: nothing wrong, natural for his age, hurry up and wait. On their first consultation, Stan had attempted to address the doctor by name, sixteen letters, many vowels punctuated by n's and v's. The doctor laughed and said just call me Dr. A, then made a joke, after all, I call you Mr. K. On their last consultation, the annual physical, Dr. A described, using the index finger and thumb of his left hand, the decline of the aging prostate. Stan had no choice but to watch and listen, being bent over the exam table with the index finger of Dr. A's right hand poised at the portal to his rectum. Dr A reduced the circumference of the finger and thumb in front of Stan's eyes and explained how the enlarged prostate chokes the urethra and at the same time pushes against the bladder, causing both urgency and restriction, most unpleasant. At this point in the discourse, Dr. A pressed inward with his right finger. Stan's sphincter tightened and his eyes watered. Dr. A said, everything in there is quite normal, I assure you.

A dribble of urine commences. It stops. It starts again.

The bathroom door opens and Stan senses a larger, younger body passing behind, entering the stall, not closing the stall door, erupting like a downspout during a storm. The eruption ceases and a heavy blond presence looms on Stan's left, running water over hands then grabbing a paper towel. Their eyes meet at ninety degrees and Stan gives a nod. The big guy returns the nod. "How they hanging, pops?" He scrunches the paper towel and shoots it into the trash.

Stan looks down. Still dribbling. How're they hanging? I'll tell you how they're hanging, like a piñata before the last blow. Stan shakes, shakes again, zips up, washes his hands.

He runs two palms along the bar and regains his stool. Ramón looks at him, or rather looks past him. Stan twists and catches a glimpse of Jeannie. He turns back. Ramón is looking away.

The Bud tastes funny. Stan holds the bottle at eye level and wonders if they replaced the Bud with water while he was in the bathroom. Or Bud Light. He puts the bottle back on the bar. Ramón smiles. Stan smiles.

Stan hears Jeannie yell last call and says to Ramón, "What time you close?"

"Eleven, amigo."

At his elbow, Jeannie says, "It's more like a restaurant these days, Mr. Kay."

Stan lifts his bottle. "I guess I better drink up."

Jeannie rubs the middle of his back. "Ramón will bring your tab."

Stan puts on glasses and examines the bottom line. Seventeen something—seventeen fifty-five, he thinks. He places a twenty on the bar. He finds a five and places it on top of the twenty. He waves to Ramón as he drops off the stool. He waves to Jeannie as he locates the door.

\#

Stan pushes the unlock button on the key fob. Nothing happens. He pushes another button taking care to stay away from the red one—he hates setting off the freaking alarm. Nothing. He tries the first button again and realizes the car to his front is not his, that his must be the car at the end of the block flashing and beeping. Shit, these new cars, they all look the same. He totters to the car at the end of the block and its driver's door yields. Stan enters by lowering his backside to the car seat while hanging onto the car door and jamb, intending to swing his legs around. He completes the first maneuver but his feet won't come around. In fact, the maneuver is being reversed as his hands are tugged by two dark hands. He raises his head.

"Upsy-daisy, Mr. Kay," says Jeannie.

Stan is standing. Jeannie guides him around the front of the car and pulls open the passenger door. Stan lowers himself into Rita's seat. Jeannie walks back around and takes the driver's seat. "Buckle up," she says.

She twists, looks through the rear window, and backs out. She shifts into drive, holds her foot on the brake, and looks in the rearview mirror. "I guess you didn't know," she says. "We have our super special valet service tonight."

Valet my ass, thinks Stan. What's going on?

Jeannie's eyes flick again to the rearview mirror which bounces a flash of light, and she moves her foot to the gas pedal. Stan peers into the mirror on his side. They're being followed, Ramón no doubt. It hits Stan then, the Bud when he came out of the bathroom, the funny taste, they've slipped him a mickey.

Jeannie chatters. "I just loved your math classes. I still know my trig values for thirty, forty-five, and sixty. I can still do derivatives with the power rule."

"What's the cosine of sixty degrees?" says Stan.

"One half."

She's right.

"What's the first derivative of four x squared?"

"Eight x."

She's right again. They're turning off Main Street. Stan can't imagine Jeannie harming him, but Ramón, there's something shifty about him, his gold earring, his gold tooth, his amigos and compañeros. He can imagine Ramón talking Jeannie into robbing him. An easy mark.

"I wished I could have done more with it. But it passed on to my daughter and she's doing something."

"That's great," says Stan. It occurs to him then: not robbery but sex. He looks at Jeannie in profile. Is that how she pays the rent and sends her daughter to school? Tips and tricks? And Ramón—he can see Ramón as her pimp. Stan recedes into his seat belt. Paying for sex doesn't bother him. In fact, it excites him, and she's not his student anymore. But performance, that scares him, getting it up, keeping it up. He can still climax solo—given sufficient time—but—where are they going?

"It was hard, Mr. Kay, raising the girls, paying the bills. I'm ahead now but it was hard and I couldn't think about further education. You know what I mean?"

Stan nods.

"I'm sure you do," she says. "Teacher salaries weren't all that great. You should have got more. And all those sour grapes over vacations and summers, bullshit if you ask me."

Stan peers at the headlamps in the sideview mirror. Still being followed. But then out the window he recognizes Broad Street and now they're turning onto Lampier Lane. They're going by Janet McCarthy's, then the Fellini's, the new family across the street. The car slows and turns left into number twelve. The headlamps play on Stan and Rita's garage and front walk and stoop, then fade. The motor stops.

Stan and Jeannie sit in darkness. The light over the front door arcs across stoop and steps. The television flickers against the front picture window.

Stan says, "How did you know where I live? Google?"

Jeannie laughs. "I don't need no Google, Mr. Kay. Don't you remember the senior barbeque? "

Stan remembers. Every June he had the senior math club over for a barbeque.

"You cooking hamburgers and hot dogs. Cold soda in the bottle. I know exactly where you live. That barbeque, that was the highlight of my senior year."

"The highlight?"

"You played all this old rock. Led Zeppelin, AC/DC, we thought it was radical. And one time Mrs. Kay, she—" Jeannie's mouth turns down. "Is—is Mrs. Kay?"

Stan says, "Oh, Mrs. Kay, she's fine, she's fine, still kicking."

"I'm so glad to hear that. I was saying, you flipping burgers and Mrs. Kay bustling all over." Jeannie leans toward Stan. "And this one time Mrs. Kay comes by you and says something, and you give her this pat on the butt. We all put our hands on our mouths and said, oh, did you see that? It was the talk of the school."

Jeannie pushes the driver's door open and walks around the front of the car as Stan pulls and pushes his way from the passenger seat. Jeannie drops the car keys in Stan's hand and leans forward with arms over his shoulders and the side of her face against his. "Stay safe," she says before walking down the driveway toward the car at the curb.

Stan climbs the three steps to his front stoop and looks through the picture window. He sees one of Rita's hands hanging from the couch, her left one with gold ring and diamond. He turns and waves as the car at the curb flashes its lights.

About the Author:

Robert Perron lives and writes in New Hampshire and New York City. Past life includes high-tech and military service. His stories have appeared in Prick of the Spindle, The Manchester Review, Pif Magazine, Sweet Tree Review, STORGY Magazine, and other journals.

TIN SOLDIER

by Toni Morgan

We all stared at the words San Ignacio painted on a piece of weathered wood nailed to a stake pounded into the ground. An arrow pointed toward the mountains.

"Jesus, that road looks worse than the one we're on," said Jack, sitting in the passenger seat next to Tucker. Tucker's nearly bald head loomed in front of me.

"I knew we should have stayed nearer the coast." Kay had fallen in love with the beaches around Puerto Vallarta and never missed an opportunity to complain about leaving them, which we'd done two weeks earlier. But we were in Mexico to show Jack the cotton-growing potential of the central regions. Tucker procured for the Army, and the Army needed cotton for uniforms.

"Well, what do you all think? Should we turn off here or keep going?" Tucker revved the engine slightly.

Kay and I were for keeping to the road we were on, but Jack and Tucker voted for the turn-off. Tucker put the station wagon into gear and pointed it toward the mountains. Dust plumed behind us. Before long, it lay thick on the dashboard, our luggage and on the extra water cans piled-up in the back. I would have given anything about then for a long soak in a tub of warm, sudsy water.

"Let's roll up the windows—the dust is so thick in here I can hardly breathe." Kay was from Texas. "Amarillo, honey," she told people in her flat, nasal drawl.

We'd all met in Phoenix where so many people moved after the Japs attacked Pearl Harbor, looking for excitement or jobs or both. Tucker was from Tucson. Jack came from California's Central Valley, where his family owned a large cattle operation. He moved to Phoenix partly for business opportunities and partly to get away from his wife.

I was from southern Idaho, near a town that no one ever heard of. The only thing different about the four of us was that they'd been born rich. My family had eked out a living on land filled with lava outcroppings and little else. There were five of us kids and never enough money.

"It's too hot to roll up the windows," Jack told Kay, using a linen handkerchief with his initials embroidered in the corner to wipe the sweat from his flushed face.

"Well, I'd rather be hot than choke to death, sugar."

"Then put out your cigarette." Jack often complained about Kay's chain-smoking. She ignored him, as she always did, but she didn't say any more about rolling up the windows.

I wondered again why I'd decided to be part of this trip. Tucker had seemed indifferent whether I came along or not. We'd been together nearly six months and I still wasn't sure we'd ever have a permanent relationship. Or if I even wanted one. At least I knew he wouldn't be drafted.

My mother had been dead-set against my coming. We'd argued for days.

"I just don't understand you, Virginia. I'm going to ignore the fact that you're obviously sleeping with that man." She never referred to Tucker by name; he'd been married twice before and she viewed him with suspicion. "But how can you go off and leave Richie? He's only three. What if he gets sick? What if I need to contact you?"

The trip sounded like a lark though, and I was tired of all the war talk at home. I told my mother I was going and promised to call her as often as I could. Besides, Richie loved being with her. He probably wouldn't even notice I was gone.

The road started to rise and soon we were in low, rolling hills. Sage and mesquite still covered the landscape, but now an occasional juniper staked a claim in the rocky soil. When we reached the top of yet another hill, we looked down to a dry creek bed strewn with rocks and boulders. Clumps of willow grew along its edges. On the other side of the creek, tracks led up a smaller hill and again disappeared over the top.

The car ground its way down to where the road ran into the creek bed. Tucker drove slowly forward, maneuvering between boulders. Jack braced his hand against the dashboard. In the backseat, I clung to the door handle to keep from being pitched sideways into Kay.

When we reached the opposite side of the creek bed, Tucker stopped the car and we all climbed out. Tucker looked back the direction we'd come and then at the tracks leading up the hill. "Well, what do you think, folks?"

"I think we're fuckin' lost, honey." Kay dropped her cigarette on the loose gravel and ground it out with a sandaled foot.

Jack reached through the open car window, pulled the map from the glove compartment, and spread it across the hood of the car. He and Tucker leaned over it. Kay wandered over to a large boulder, sat down, and lit another cigarette. Her sleek brown hair fell forward as she leaned into the match, cupping the flame with carmine-tipped fingers. She blew out a long stream of smoke and appeared to ignore the two men arguing over the map.

My blouse stuck to my back and my linen shorts had ridden up into a bunch between my legs. I was stiff from sitting in the car all day. After getting a drink of water from the

sweating, canvas bag hanging off the outside mirror and resting against the station wagon's wood side, I started to follow the tracks up the hill. In addition to working out the kinks, I was eager to get away from the others, at least for a while.

As I climbed, I thought back to our recent stay in Mexico City. While Tucker and Jack went to meet with someone from the government—a land surveyor I thought—and Kay sat in the hotel bar drinking rum and coke and flirting with the young bartender, I explored the nearby streets. Brilliant red bougainvillea surged up and spilled over many of the high walls. I peered through an open carved wooden gate to a courtyard and a house with a long, covered patio. More bougainvillea climbed the patio's posts. From somewhere came the tinkling sound of water.

After a few more blocks, I arrived at a small plaza shaded by ancient oak trees. The raucous sounds of birds filled the air, but I couldn't see them. Then, as though one of the trees exploded, hundreds of small, pitch-black birds flew up, only to disappear again into the branches of another tree, their noise undiminished. Filling the sidewalks surrounding the plaza were tables and stalls with fruits and vegetables, lace table cloths and leather goods, cooking utensils, toys, a crate of chickens and even a live pig.

I spotted a soldier made of tin—its cheeks rosy, and a trim mustache above its upturned mouth, its legs and arms thin as straws, a trumpet in one hand—and had to buy it.

Tucker grumbled whenever he loaded or unloaded our luggage. "Why do you buy junk like this?" Or, "This is a business trip, Virginia, not a goddamn shopping excursion." I didn't bother to respond.

I reached the top of the hill and yelled back to the others. "There's a town. I can see it."

***

It was dusk. A church and several small buildings were silhouetted against the sky as we approached, dark against lavender, and lights flickered in the windows of houses scattered down the hillside.

We entered San Ignacio by what we later learned was one of two roads leading to San Ignacio. The one we'd taken was seldom used—the creek crossing wasn't dependable, we were told. The other, more-traveled road led from the coast, crossed the road we'd driven much of the day, passed through town, continued over the mountains, and eventually led to the Gulf.

It was not unusual, apparently, for motorists to be stranded in San Ignacio, especially during the winter when the road through the mountains became impassable. With the war in Europe and the Pacific going on, though, and fuel harder to come by, there were fewer travelers on the road at any time of the year. We had no trouble finding a place to stay.

The room Tucker and I were offered was sparsely furnished. A bright magenta blanket covered a double bed. The intertwining roses and vines on the wooden headboard were crudely carved but somehow delicate-looking. I thought of the unknown, unskilled artist who'd carved them and wondered if he ever thought of the people who might eventually sleep in his bed. Above it, like a benediction, a gold-painted cross hung on the wall. Across the room, a painted chest stood beneath the single window. No rug covered the smooth, wood-planked floor and no curtains hung at the window.

"Do you need your other suitcase from the car?" Tucker asked.

I propped the tin soldier on the chest beneath the window. "No. I have all I need in the small one."

"I don't know why you have to drag that thing to our room every night."

I stepped back to admire my handiwork. "He makes me smile." I turned to survey the room once again; its simplicity appealed to me.

"There's a cantina across the street," Tucker said. "Let's get a drink."

I shook my head. "I want to take a bath and wash my hair. And I want to call home again."

"You can do that later. Right now I want a drink." He didn't wait for me to answer.

Resisting the urge to argue, I followed him down the narrow stairs. At the bottom was a door that led outside.

"And I want you to be nicer to Jack."

I stopped mid-step. "Be nicer to Jack? What is that supposed to mean? How am I not nice to Jack?"

Tucker didn't pause. "You know how you can be. And he likes you. I can tell by the way he watches you."

"So what?" I hurried to catch up with him as he shoved open the door. "Lots of people like me," I said when we were both outside. "Besides, I am nice to Jack."

"Well, be nicer. I need his money."

"What are you asking me to do, Tucker?"

"Nothing. Forget it." He took my elbow and started to walk across the road to the cantina.

I pulled my arm away. "How can I forget it when you just said it?"

He didn't answer.

Jack and Kay sat near the bar in the dimly-lit cantina, each with a glass of tequila. A plate of sliced lemons and a dish of peppers was on the table between them. Kay's coloring was heightened. It looked as though they'd been arguing.

Jack glanced up and waved when Tucker and I walked in. "The tequila isn't bad," he said when we reached their table.

A brown-skinned woman with coarse gray hair hanging over her shoulders in two long braids, came to take our order. In a gathered skirt of black cotton, an embroidered white blouse that fell off one shoulder, and her dusty feet thrust into leather sandals, she didn't smile, but stood silent, waiting.

In rapid Spanish, Tucker ordered a beer for himself and a glass of tequila for me.

A single bulb, dangling on a short, black cord, cast a weak light that failed to reach into the corners of the low-ceilinged room. Another single bulb dangled above the bar and the small kitchen behind it. Along with the smells of beer and cigarette smoke, the air was ripe with cooking odors.

Tucker and Jack talked about cotton. Tired of the subject, I watched two men at a nearby table. One wore a dark suit. His thin black tie hung loose at the collar of his white shirt, but otherwise he looked tidy, as though someone who cared about his appearance had tended him. His companion was thin and dark, with pockmarked skin drawn tight over his narrow face. His dark eyes stared out from under thick bushy brows. My Spanish wasn't good enough to make out what was being said, but the thin one was drawing lines in some beer spilled on the table, and alternately jabbing his finger at the man in the suit.

The waitress brought our drinks. I sipped the tequila, enjoying the sharp taste on my tongue and the spreading warmth as it hit my belly, and tried to make conversation with Kay. I gave up when, lighting one cigarette after another, she made it clear her mind was on something else.

Finally, her eyes on Jack, she leaned back in her chair and exhaled a long stream of smoke. "Well, y'all will know soon enough. I'm pregnant."

Jack scowled. "For Christ's sake, Kay, do you need to blab everything you know?" He tossed back the remainder of his tequila.

"Well, I think it's important for our friends to know I'm knocked up, sugar." She gave me a strained smile. "Aren't you thrilled for me, honey? Do you suppose it'll be a boy or a girl? I'd love to have a little girl, I think. But then a little boy would be nice, too—I just know he'd grow up as good-lookin' an' sweet as his daddy." She lit another cigarette then quickly stubbed it out and started to cry.

"Just shut-up, Kay," said Jack. "God dammit, can't we just finish this trip and think about our problem later? Where's the waitress? Let's see if we can get something to eat."

"I don't want anything to eat. Besides, it isn't your problem, it's my problem. You already have a wife and a son." Kay downed the rest of her tequila in one gulp before pushing back from the table. She got up and walked

unsteadily to the bar, where she loudly ordered another drink. I knew from experience there was no point in arguing with her or trying to get her to go back to our rooms. She would drink until the bar closed.

Jack, grim-faced, pulled the map out of his pocket, unfolded it, and spread it across the table, the plate of lemon slices and the dish of peppers pushing up the worn and creased paper like small hills.

"The problem will be getting water to where we'd need it," he said. He pretended to ignore Kay.

"We can irrigate. This is the eastern edge of the three parcels, right?" Tucker tapped a spot on the map with his finger. "And the river is here at its closest point. That's what, three miles. It won't take much to ditch that far."

Jack looked doubtful. "Who's going to do the work? Look at the country we drove through today. There are no people. The place is empty."

Tucker waved Jack's concerns aside. "We'll bring them in from Leon and Guanajuato. There'll be plenty of people in those places who want work—they can throw up some shacks to live in. A year, maybe two, and we'll produce as much cotton here, in one spot, as all the fields they've put in around Phoenix. It'll be ten times cheaper and the government will buy it from us without thinking twice."

Jack still looked unconvinced, but Tucker went on talking about the plan and the route the four of us would take in the morning.

I returned to watching the two men at the other table, wondering if there would be a fight. But the pockmarked man appeared to have calmed down. The man in the suit got to his feet; I heard him say goodnight to the other man. As he turned to leave he nodded to me. "Buenos noches, Senora."

I drank the last of my tequila, stood, and told Tucker I was going back to our room. "It's too late to call home, but I still want to take a bath and wash my hair."

Tucker looked from me to the man in the suit then back to me, one eyebrow raised.

"Lowering your standards a bit, aren't you?"

"That doesn't deserve an answer, Tucker." I turned and walked out, my back stiff with anger.

When he wanted to be, Tucker was the most charming man I knew, which was all the time when we first met. I rarely saw that side of him anymore, and I didn't understand what drove him to say such hurtful things. I'd never tried to keep it a secret that I'd been with other men, but I wasn't a tramp. I didn't know why he treated me like one. More, I didn't know why I let him.

A short time later, as I worked shampoo into my hair, I thought about Kay's announcement. She and Jack had been arguing. Did he want her to get an abortion? Abortions were illegal, but possible if you had enough money. Jack had plenty. I wondered if Kay would go along.

My hair still damp, I lay under the magenta blanket and forced Kay's problem and Tucker's rude behavior from my mind. Instead, I pictured my little boy asleep in his bed, his fingers pinching the faded silk binding of his old baby blanket, and I thought about the last phone call to my mother.

"Virginia, I can't hear you. What did you say?" Her voice was faint and tinny.

"I said how is Richie?" I shouted to be heard over the pops and crackles coming from the receiver. "I bought him a present."

"When will you be home?"

I continued to shout. "Soon. Maybe next week or the week after. How is Richie?" I heard more wheezes and pops. The woman behind the desk looked up at me, and then down at the ledger opened in front of her.

"What? What did you say? Virginia, I can't hear you. You need to come home. Richie misses you, and he's started...." The line went dead.

"The line went dead," I told the woman.

"I'm sorry, Senora. I will try to reconnect you." After forty minutes without success, the woman told me the switchboard was closed until the following morning.

It had been three days and I still hadn't been able to get through. What was my mother trying to tell me about Richie? What had he started?

Tucker was no help. "You worry too much," he'd said when I told him about the phone call. "Kids are always up to one thing or another. Next week it will be something else."

Maybe Tucker was right. I punched up the pillow and rolled to my side. The bedsprings protested with a loud squeak. Outside the window, stars dotted the carbon-colored sky. A dog barked, way off in the distance. I thought again of my little boy.

I awoke with a start at the sound of someone tripping on the stairs.

A moment later, the door to our room opened and Tucker entered. He stood for a minute. Over his heavy breathing, the sound of two sets of footsteps continued down the hall. A second door opened and clicked closed.

Tucker crossed the room and dropped down on the end of the bed; I drew my feet back just in time. Shoes fell to the floor. I pretended to be asleep. Tucker muttered under his breath as he struggled to get out of his trousers and shirt.

When he climbed into bed, he pulled me to him. His arms and face were cold from the night air, and his breath smelled of beer and tequila. I turned my head and tried to move away. He jerked me to him again and thrust his hips against me. His erect penis poked my thigh. He thrust at me again and his peeling forehead cracked me on the cheek, bringing a stinging pain and tears to my eyes.

"Quit it, Tucker. I'm not in the mood."

"What's the matter? Your little Mexican bandito wear you out?"

"I mean it, Tucker. You're drunk. I'm tired. It's been a long day. Let's get some sleep."

"I mean it, Tucker," he mimicked.

The foul smell of his hot breath disgusted me. I pushed away from him one more time.

"Come here, dammit. I didn't bring you along to tell me you're not in the mood. I'm in the mood and that'll have to be enough." He grabbed my arms and rolled on top of me.

***

I slipped off the bed and searched along the floor for my nightgown. I tied the torn straps together and slipped it over my head then rolled an already snoring Tucker over and wrapped myself in the magenta blanket. Toward dawn I fell asleep.

***

Tucker ignored me as he repacked the small suitcase he'd brought in from the car the night before. Still without saying anything, he snapped the case shut and carried it from the room.

I took another bath, dressed, and went downstairs. Tucker sat at a table with Jack. Jack looked up when I entered, but quickly returned his attention to his coffee. Neither man looked happy.

I filled an earthenware mug with steaming coffee from a hammered silver coffeepot, and crossed the room to sit on a chair Jack dragged over from another table.

"Where's Kay?"

"Still upstairs," Jack said. "She'll be down pretty soon."

Tucker glanced around, still not looking at me. "Where's your bag? Aren't you packed yet? We want to pay the bill and get out of here."

"I'm not going."

Tucker frowned, though still avoiding my eyes. "What do you mean, you're not going?'

"I mean I'm not going with you. I'm staying here."

Just then Kay came in wearing dark glasses and carrying her suitcase. "You can't stay here," she said.

"Of course she's not staying here," said Tucker. "Now go get your things together, Virginia, and stop playing games."

"I'm not playing games with you, Tucker."

Kay looked at the end of her cigarette and tapped the ash onto the floor. I felt Jack's eyes on me.

"How are you going to get back to Phoenix then? We're not coming back here for you," Tucker said. His gaze finally met my eyes.

"I don't know. I'll find something, a bus maybe." I had no idea how I was going to get home, but I felt reasonably certain that busses passed through San Ignacio to somewhere I could get transportation.

"You're crazy." Tucker's eyes narrowed. "I mean it. Are you coming with us or not?"

"I'm not." I took another sip of coffee, hoping he wouldn't notice my hand trembling.

"Suit yourself then." Tucker stood, pushed his chair back and strode away. Kay followed him.

"My God, Virginia," Jack said after they'd left. "Are you out of your mind? Whatever Tucker's done can't be this bad. You're cutting your damn nose off to spite your face."

"Maybe. But I'm still not going."

He leaned toward me. "Tucker's right. You are crazy. There's no telling what might happen to you down here. Your Spanish is no better than mine is, the American Embassy is miles away and there's a war on, for Christ's sake. Or had you forgotten?" He straightened. A wet spot spread across his shirt front from coffee spilled on the tabletop.

"Europe is a long way from Mexico, and so is the south Pacific." I jumped at the sound of the car horn blasting out Tucker's impatience. "I'll be okay."

Jack asked me one more time to change my mind. When I still refused he gave an exasperated sigh and got to his feet. I stood, too.

"Do you have enough money to get home?"

"Yes," I lied.

"Here's some extra, just in case." He handed me several folded bills and then turned and left to join Tucker and Kay.

Wait, I've changed my mind. The words trembled on my lips, but I didn't say them. Instead, when the door closed behind him I ran up the stairs. In the room Tucker and I had shared, I crossed to the window. All I could see of the station wagon was its dust-covered rear window and the extra fuel cans strapped to the bumper as it disappeared over the top of the hill. At the side of the road, next to where we'd parked, was my blue suitcase.

I picked up the painted tin soldier and cradled him in my arms; sunlight glinted off the gold trumpet raised to his smiling metal lips.

About the Author:

Born in Alaska, raised in Oregon, where she studied history at Portland State University, and married in Hawaii, **Toni Morgan** has lived all over the United States, from California to Washington, D.C., and the world, from Denmark to Japan. She now makes her home in southwestern Idaho. She is the author of six novels: TWO-HEARTED CROSSING, PATRIMONY, ECHOES FROM A FALLING BRIDGE, HARVEST THE WIND, LOTUS BLOSSOM UNFURLING, and QUEENIE'S PLACE. Toni's articles and short stories have been published in various newspapers, literary magazines, and other publications (http://authortonimorgan.com)

BECAUSE IT FELT GOOD

by Nikki Munoz

Have you ever felt halved? You think that you find someone that you can share your life with. And you think that that entails being the person's other half, and it does. But what if you don't want to be just a half? What if you want to be full? What if, by giving your whole self over to this other person, you start to feel emptied out? Like, rather than sharing yourself, you have given it up entirely. Now, if you're with her, sitting next to her, lying with her, fucking her, you still don't feel full. Yet, when you're by yourself, you don't reach fullness either. With or without the other person, you're still incomplete. And you don't grow up believing that love is supposed to make you feel incomplete. You don't watch people jump through hoops for a kind of love that drains them out.

I felt halved. When it ended, I still felt halved. It took a long time to feel full again, and even now, it wavers. I decided I could never give someone my all again. I didn't know what love is, but it couldn't be feeling emptied. And until I figure out what that means and what it means to have a grasp on your own self, then I can't give anything at all to anyone.

And then, I met her.

I was attracted to her, in more ways than one. She was someone I was bound to gravitate toward. I liked being around her and I liked her and I knew it was mutual and I liked that. There isn't anything quite as good as knowing someone else feels as strongly about you as you do about them. Feeling those emotions line up evenly between both people. I got lost in what was happening. I wanted to see her all the time, asking her to come over close to every night. She would leave and I would think of

when it was too soon to ask again. But she would always come and then I didn't worry about time anymore. I felt the sense of time escape me.

But I started to feel that emptying again. And I needed to do something about it. I had to, for once, choose my own self over another person, despite how much I felt for that person and despite that person being her.

I had to distance myself from her, break it off. I tried to explain this emptying. I told her I needed to detach myself from her and these feelings. I told her I wasn't capable of giving. I didn't know how to give without giving it all.

She asked me why I did anything to begin with, why I started anything with her at all. And I had so many words I wanted to say to her, but all I could say was, "Because it felt good."

"Because it felt good." Because it felt good. BECAUSE IT FELT GOOD. Because. It. Felt. Good.

This was just one line in our long lasting convoluted conversation, in which I felt the deep connection between us getting stabbed at. Everything hurt and my mind was lagging. It wasn't until later, after he dropped me off at home, that this line of his started its repetition in my mind. It was all I could think about, because it felt good because it felt good because it felt good. It was on loop in my head. Because it felt fucking good.

I couldn't avoid it and so I began to face it. And, at first, I thought it to be the most selfish thing anyone could do. How selfish it is to start to give yourself to another person, knowing full well that you're never going to give it all. And, consequently, to start to take in somebody else, knowing you're never going to accept them in full. How cruel to revel in the happiness, to enjoy it as a temporary high, knowing that the person giving you that happiness is under the impression that this is the beginning of something and not the whole of it. To think: I like how this feels and that is all there is.

Because it felt good, you cruel shithead.

But, then, I got to thinking about it differently, because it felt good. It started playing a different tune in my mind. He had found something in me that felt so good to him that he broke all boundaries he had set for himself. Maybe he wasn't thinking about any consequences because it had felt so good. Maybe he wasn't being selfish, nor being selfless, but merely being. Not thinking, but just feeling.

And how could I blame someone for feeling? I had been doing the same.

Because it felt good. It felt good to me too.

About the Author:

Nikki Munoz is currently a student at University of California, Berkeley where she is working on her Bachelor's in English, with a minor in Journalism. When she is not working on her creative fiction, she is writing for the Daily Californian's Arts and Entertainment section, focusing on theater. For her fiction, she is interested in pulling both from her own life and those around her to create realistic fiction that is compelling in the mundane.

A WOMAN'S PLACE
by Janel Brubaker

I was no older than twenty-five when I first felt the weight of what it means to be a woman defined by social norms and gender roles. I came to this realization by degrees. Each misogynistic label plastered to me against my will, like the proverbial scarlet letter, brands meant to define my existence to suit the expectations of other people, prodded me closer to eruption. Only when I looked in the mirror at each label and realized that I didn't know the woman these people said I was did I reach the conclusion that gender roles and stereotypes are bullshit. Looking back at my life, I see how prevalent these labels were; some were soft, some were harsh, but all of them inflicted harm and tainted my view of the world and my place in it. The deterioration of my autonomy was slow, whittled away with purpose so that, by the time I reached adulthood, I would be a perfectly crafted, submissive shell of a woman.

What's worse is that I bought into it. Even when what was said didn't settle in my mind and kept bouncing like a ping-pong ball against the walls of my psyche, I set aside my own voice in favor of others. I was not one who broke or questioned the rules. I obeyed them. I was not rebellious. I grew up in a traditionally Christian congregation where great emphasis was placed on female modesty and purity. I didn't know to question this. I had never heard the terms "rape culture" or "victim blaming" or "slut shaming," so I accepted these values as true and right. At fourteen, I hadn't yet matured into my sexual self, so I didn't realize the danger in relating the female body to a pathway for sin, or in vilifying sexual desire altogether. I didn't know how shame could erode a relationship, erect barriers between spouses.

I remember attending youth group at two different churches. I remember the leaders of both churches attempting to address issues of sexuality. I remember it was impressed upon the young women that it was our responsibility to shield our brothers in Christ from lust; if we wore modest clothing that wasn't revealing, wasn't too tight, didn't flatter us too much, then we would have done our jobs. Otherwise, we would be culpable in their sin. The first time I heard this message, I was thirteen years old.

I don't know what the young men were told. These "lessons" were always given to the genders separately. I know I never heard about masturbation or pornography. I know I never heard anything positive about sex other than that, as long as a man and a woman were married, it wasn't a sin. I remember thinking that I didn't ever want to have sex if it was as dangerous as they made it seem. I was never told that sexuality is a natural part of human experience and identity. Telling teenagers to pretend as if they have no sexuality, or to try and pray it away, only reinforces shame and unmeetable standards. When a young woman is told her body is simultaneously a vessel for sin and a temple for the Holy Spirit, it reinforces the message that one's sexuality is contrary to living a life of righteousness. To live a passionate and fulfilling sexual life, therefore, requires an abandonment of her faith.

I remember being told that sex was created for men's pleasure and was a duty a wife was expected to perform. Well into adulthood I encountered this message, yet another attempt to silence and repress female sexual expression. I remember there was a time I didn't believe marital rape existed, as if "I do" placed the woman in a perpetual state of consent that could never be revoked. I heard nothing of women truly enjoying sex because, of course, it was unladylike for women to discuss such things.

I heard nothing of platonic, intimate relationships between the sexes. I never saw single men and women develop friendships for any other purpose than romantic intent. Men only pursued women for sex, and women only married men for companionship and security. I never knew it was acceptable to simply be friends with a member of the opposite sex and appreciate them as a human being. I didn't know it was alright to be a single, independent woman. Even Paul said it was better not to marry, and perhaps for men this was fine (especially those called to ministry), but for a woman to remain single was to deprive a man of her body, and that was incomprehensible. A woman's life is not her own, I was told; it's God's first and He would never create a woman without also creating for her a husband. And as a couple they, of course, are required to have children.

Even my appearance was not my own. I was told on a repeating loop not to cut my hair because, "Men prefer it long." The first time I heard this I was fourteen and, by my parent's rules, much too young to date. I wasn't looking for a boyfriend. I wanted a pixie cut. At thirteen I had begun to wear makeup and wanted to try a different hairstyle. I was dabbling in my own sense of fashion and self-expression. I saw women in pixie cuts on television and I wanted to know if such a short haircut would look good on me. Instead of encouraging my self-expression, I was told to ground my choices in the preferences of a group of teenage boys who hardly ever spoke to me. I was fourteen and already taught to value my desires less than the desires of the men in my social circle. This was the beginning of my existence as a woman in the patriarchy.

As I grew older, the gender roles and expectations became amplified. Already I was ashamed of my body and its potential for sin. By sixteen I couldn't walk down the street without someone shouting, "Nice ass!" or "Show us those tits!" I didn't understand how they could say those things when I took such careful effort to dress modestly, to walk without allowing my hips to sway too much. This took careful concentration and focus on posture and how long my strides were. I often resorted to wearing loose shirts and long skirts in an attempt to hide not only my figure but the sway of my hips that I could not entirely subdue. In summer it was the worst; I never wore shorts for fear of exposing too much skin. I only wore jeans or capris, and they too were enough to elicit unwanted and unprovoked calls of sexual interest. Even riding in a car with the window down, my face makeup free and glistening with beads of sweat, pulled in whistles and flirtatious smiles from men walking down the street or driving next to me. It did not occur to me that this was their issue rather than mine. Each whistle, each call from drivers by, made me feel ashamed, as if I had failed to be modest enough and somehow deserved what was being tossed at me. I avoided taking walks in my own neighborhood for fear of attracting unwanted attention. And if I dared to ignore these shouts, I was flipped off.

Once, a blue car with two young men inside pulled up next to me to "chat;" they smiled, eyed me up and down as I was walking on the sidewalk in my neighborhood. I stopped walking as they pulled up, unsure if they were going to ask for directions or something else. When it became clear they didn't want directions, I kept walking. The driver kept his car next to me while the passenger tried to get my attention. I ignored them, hoping my being in a busy neighborhood would deter any malicious intentions. I don't recall the specifics of what they said, but I know they were trying to get me into their car. When I didn't acknowledge them again they both shouted, "Bitch," and sped off. Both of them flipped me off through the sunroof. It wasn't until adulthood that I realized how lucky I was it only went that far.

Church was no safe haven, either. Teenagers are awkward beings, no longer children, but not yet adults, navigating the space between the two. I was, and have always been, an outgoing human being. My mother used to call me, "A social butterfly," and it was an apt description. I loved having friends and, as a homeschooled student, church was where my friendships were mostly based. If someone wanted to talk with me, it felt wrong to say no. I was thirteen when a young man around fifteen first attempted to ask me on a date, only I didn't realize that was what he meant. Each Sunday for several weeks he asked if I wanted to come to his house and help him work on his car and then have dinner with his family. I did not want to do any such thing. I hated cars and couldn't fathom why he would think me the kind of person to ask for such help. I told him that he should ask someone else, but he continued asking me. He made me uncomfortable, giving the kind of compliments I knew were inappropriate to speak in church; nothing explicit, but close enough that I didn't want to see him again. I never understood his interest in me, either. We weren't friends. We didn't talk. We had no similar interests that I could detect. Our interactions with each other were entirely contained in him asking me to help him with his car, and me finding an excuse for why I couldn't. He didn't stop asking me for my help until his family left the church a month or so later. I never understood why one "No" wasn't enough.

I was fifteen when another young man at our church thought it was hilarious to sneak up behind me while I was talking to my friends, and poke me in the sides. I don't know if he was trying to scare or tickle me, but I didn't like either option. It hurt. I did not find it funny. I did not laugh. I told him not to do it again and he responded with, "Aww, boo hoo." This happened almost every time I was at church and he was there; Sunday mornings, Sunday evenings, Wednesday nights. Sometimes he did it twice, once before service and once after. It didn't matter how many times I told him to stop, he wouldn't. He just laughed. He didn't take me seriously when I told him I didn't like it, when I told him he was hurting me. He didn't care about the bruises he left on my sides. He didn't care about the emotional torment each time we pulled into the church parking lot. I loved going to church. I felt alive there, really connected to life and purpose. For weeks I was afraid to go because I knew he would be there, and I knew he would put his hands on my body again.

I finally told my parents. It shouldn't have taken as long as it did for me to tell them, but when there's an especially awkward teenager in the youth group who suffers from chronic illness, and who almost died a couple of years prior because of his chronic illness, it feels cruel to try and get them in trouble. I didn't know what the fallout would be if I told my parents what had been going on, so I kept it hidden, hoping that he would realize the inappropriateness of his actions. He didn't. He wasn't going to stop without some higher authority getting involved. My parents said they would talk to his father. Their reassurance did nothing to comfort me. I asked my dad if there was anything he could teach me in self-defense that wouldn't cause him injury, but would warn him to stay away from me. My dad was a fourth degree black belt in Kung Fu San Su. From a young age, he emphasized the importance of valuing my physical safety and to never hesitate to defend myself if I felt threatened. This young man had made me feel unsafe for weeks. He may have thought it was just innocent fun, but I was tormented. My dad told me, if he touched me again, to turn around and land an open handed smack to his solar plexus as a warning to leave me alone. It would be enough to express my boundaries without causing him harm.

The next Sunday morning came and my family left for church. I was nervous. I am not an aggressive person by nature, and I was not comfortable with what I felt boiling inside of me. It made my palms sweat. Indeed, they're sweating as I recall the memory. It made my body tremble. Between my eyes a cluster ache pounded. My jaw was clenched so tight, it throbbed the rest of the morning. I felt it wrong to contemplate and even prepare to make an act of aggression inside of a church, but I reminded myself that I was not the one who violated its sanctity.

The warning shove was enough. He never touched me again.

It should never have been necessary in the first place.

I started college at twenty-one years old. In spring term of my first year I met a female friend for lunch in the cafeteria. We had hardly grabbed our food and sat down when an intoxicated male came over to our table and asked if either of us wanted to go to dinner with him. We both said no and he walked away only to come back and reiterate that he offered to take us to dinner because he wanted to have sex with us. (Because buying someone dinner is akin to giving irrevocable consent, apparently.) To this day I don't know if he intended to pursue us as a potential menage troi, or if he just tossed his interest on the table between us hoping at least one of us would pick it up. I told him I was married and my friend was in a relationship, and he walked away mumbling about how, "Ya'll always say you're married or in a relationship." As if being male entitled him to whomever he wanted.

Moveover, that she and I even had to use the relationships in our lives to justify or explain our rejection of his advances is wildly problematic. Not wanting to date him should have been explanation enough. He didn't respect our refusals until we made it clear we were spoken for by other men, and even then his respect was begrudged. Why wasn't "No" enough? Why was my refusal only made valid by the existence of a pre-existing husband?

I could go on. I could tell you about the time I bought a dress at the mall and my parents shamed me into returning it, even though I was nineteen and it was more modest than the other modest dresses I owned. My father's exact words were, "You look like you're about to go work 82nd Avenue." I could tell you about the time, in a fit of drunken anger, a young man I was conversing with said he "Hoped I was raped" because I told him I was against the death penalty. Even though the death penalty isn't used as sentencing for convicted rapists. I could talk for hours about what it was like to be a woman and watch the last election. I could tell you how, at fifteen, my youth group crush said, in earnest, how he wished he could revoke the 19th Amendment, and how, at sixteen, this mattered so little to me, I still went out with him for four months. I could tell you about the times my male and female family members have said, "A woman's place is in the home," or how if a woman wears slutty clothing, she's asking to be raped. I could

tell you about the time a pastor and his wife chastised me for what I wore to church two Sundays before, and how his wife said, "The dress really wasn't flattering on you anyway. You could see all of your rolls." I could tell you I no longer attend church.

I could give many more examples as to how society, both my specific social circles and society at large, have tried to silence me almost since the moment I was born. The message has been unmistakable: I am female, therefore my place in this world is less valid than those of men. I'm also bisexual, so that only serves to invalidate me further. Looking back at my childhood, my teenage and young adult years, I see how I was being groomed into patriarchy's perfect woman. Even in my life today, I'm bombarded with images of my reflection held in contrast to what society deems the acceptable modern woman, and I don't hold up. I'm not skinny. I don't attend church any longer. I'm almost twenty-nine and have no kids. I'm pursuing a creative writing degree and I work part time as a barista. I drink. I curse. I smoke weed. I like sex with my husband and I think I would enjoy sex with women. A few weeks ago, I buzzed off all of my hair. Anyone who knows me knows that I am not quiet. I never have been. I talk a lot. I have strong opinions.

And I thank God for all of it, because it means the message, the labels, the roles that were assigned to me at birth and regurgitated throughout my life never stuck. It means I have not allowed myself to be defined by anyone else's definition of who I am. The labels still pester me. They pop in and out of my life and try to irritate the internalized shame planted there more than fifteen years ago. Sometimes, they get the upper hand. But then I look at my shaved head and put on a tight dress that accentuates every beautiful fucking roll on my body because a woman's place is wherever the fuck she wants to be.

About the Author:

Janel Brubaker graduated from Clackamas Community College with her associates in English and Creative Writing. She also graduated from Marylhurst University with a Bachelor of Arts in English Literature and Writing. Her writings have been published in Bookends Review, The Bella Online Review, Crab Fat Magazine, Linden Avenue Literary Journal, Phenomenal Literature, Adelaide Literary Magazine, Sheepshead Review, and LEVITATE Magazine, and soon to be published in DoveTales Journal, Sheepshead Review, and Timberline Review.

HIS YOUTH

by Steve Coughlin

Decades before he folded her sweaters into a trash bag, placed them on a curb in front of the house, his youth rumbled with desire as she washed dishes in a yellow dress, sunlight crawling across the kitchen floor.

It was trips to the beach in his Ford convertible, the scent of salt water, radio blaring--the parking lot melting beneath their feet.

At 27 he woke beside her in the coldness of morning, their clothes discarded on the floor, stifled a yawn as he dressed for the factory. There were the cement stairs he bounded two at a time, the shifts when he worked the machine that produced an endless stream of miniature gears for boat engines.

It was him in the spotlight of the break room certain no one doubted his words. He repeated the same jokes to men whose names he never learned, predicted this was the year the Sox would win the Series.

And maybe a few minutes before the whistle blew he walked to the payphone in his grease stained shirt.

Maybe he deposited his only quarter just to hear her voice.

Years before his DUI, it was him stumbling drunk into bed, the darkness spinning him wildly to sleep.

At 31 he could not explain to her how his youth, its relentless demands, was the restlessness that kept him driving alone into the night.

Was there an affair in a cheap motel room? Was there whiskey and cigarettes, fast food wrappers on the nightstand--his need to touch another woman's body?

Did his wife, hours later, her own youth lost to depression, her body grown fat, allow him to wrap his arm around her? Did she ignore the perfume on his skin as he pulled her like a doll against his chest?

Before he was left to wander the empty rooms of his house, there was the embarrassment she felt when he revved the car's engine in the church's parking lot.

There was the eternity of minutes she waited in the car while he, 45, flirted with high school girls working at Dairy Queen.

And what if his youth became the shadow in front of him at 54? What if it turned the corner a few paces in front of him--him running five miles a day--his lungs burning with exhaustion?

There was the hopelessness of aching knees at 66, the years he had gone since sleeping beside her in the same bed.

But still, after she told him of the cancer, there were those final flares. It was youthful naiveté that convinced him she could get better. It was him insisting she eat a salad each night with dinner. Him helping her into the used car for a drive to the ocean.

Before her heart stopped beating. Before her body cooled in front of him. Before he walked the lonely streets, legs too worn for running, eyes squinting, searching in the distance for its shadow.

How he grasped her tired hand.

About the Author:

Steve Coughlin's poems and essays have appeared in several literary journals and magazines, including the Gettysburg Review, New Ohio Review, Michigan Quarterly Review, Willow Springs, and Slate. His book of poetry, Another City, was published by FutureCycle Press. He teaches creative writing at Chadron State College in northwestern Nebraska.

AN ASCENT: CONSIDERING THE SHADOWS OF A STONE STAIRCASE
by A. M. Palmer

If the woods are haunted, but the forest merely enchanted by shadows and soft light, into which realm does the stone staircase lead? And who will follow?

In a different era, as industrial wealth of the twentieth century flowered into great family fortunes, workmen were transported to a distant location and ordered to arrange a pile of rocks. It was an interesting task. Their employers—the founding fathers of our city—were determined to build a grotto   in what was then wildland, something of a monument to affluence and ambition, a hint of things to come. Although, at first glance, it seemed like nothing more than a curiosity, the project had obviously been calculated, its site chosen with something in mind; the location was a place set apart from prying eyes and gentility, a place where the activities of a grotto could go unchallenged and remain hidden—never to be seen in newspapers or history books. Even now, long after the age of discretion and propriety has faded, the grotto remains a significant destination. Although suspicion has given way to appreciation over   the years, something of the original aura persists; the structure still engages travelers as they explore pathways and wander in the shallow woods.

Every aspect was designed with care. Gray and orange rocks form not only a fount but also a series of walls and a staircase, steps that gently descend into an entanglement of oaks.

In the late afternoon, a larger vision becomes clear; odd angles reveal how the builders were able to use light, as it passed through tree branches and thick brush, to create an interesting experience; a journey of the mind no less than that of the body. Although the forest of our era has thinned considerably, the experience of traveling through light and shadow remains tangible.

Standing at the base of the stairs, one is immediately confronted with a choice; either climb back to the full embrace of sunlight or give way to momentum and continue the descent. Enjoy a reprieve from uncertainty or delight in a new adventure, the choice is yours. In the present era, the impact is less than what it must have been during the early twentieth century, back when the rocks were first arranged. And yet, the shadows cast by the staircase are still compelling, emphatic in a way that the escalators of a shopping mall, or even the steps of a venerable bank building, simply are not. The choice   offered by the grotto is not only unavoidable—in that the traveler must either ascend or descend —it's also something of a coy challenge. Are you willing to follow the shadows of an old stone structure? A few interruptions of darkness await you, but they will quickly give way to sunlight and the predictable elements of home. You can climb safely out of the forest and be on your way. Or would you prefer a deeper venture into the woods? Decades ago, when settlers were uncertain about their new surroundings, the experience must have been powerful.

Sadly, times have indeed changed. In the presence of traffic, and in the company of dog walkers and children at play, the haunting ambience of the grotto is greatly reduced, perhaps returning only at night. However, at the moment of decision—when one must travel either up or down—a quick rush of anticipation is easy to feel, a reminder of the previous century, when the occasion of adventure was probably very common in that area.

Even now, the mood of the place is difficult to capture and define. It's as if the grotto is always becoming something different, reasserting itself in the face of history, crumbling slowly but nonetheless remaining unpredictable and vaguely disturbing.

As daylight fades, and hints of dusk become more insistent, the atmosphere truly changes. At the base of the stairs, sunlight begins to look a bit less capable of rescuing travelers from darkness. And the climb to the top begins to look forbidding. As night approaches, enchantment seems less likely than outright haunting, adventure being more a matter of survival than the experience of enjoyment. Again, from the vantagepoint of the stairs, these sensations become magnified, as the mind prefigures the body's journey. Moreover, the mood of the place serves as a reminder; life is full of choices, many of which are difficult. At some point, before the full arrival of darkness, certain decisions must   be made.

As for the question of who will follow the stairs as they beckon, either for an ascent to the world above—or a downward movement into the woods—a quick glance in any direction provides an answer.

Empty whiskey bottles and beer cans, graffiti and the annoying presence of food wrappers have all converged on the old grotto, as if to challenge its claim to a mysterious past. The question of who follows its path is easily answered. At such moments, introspection can quickly transform into a feeling of grief. On one occasion, however, I was offered something more.

As I began my ascent, and tried to clear my mind of the inviting yet disquieting spirits

of the place, I realized that I was not alone. It was a strange moment. I paused very close to a patch of graffiti—glaring red streaks of paint that reduced the grotto to a mere neglected ruin—as two people approached me. They were teenagers, a loud, enthusiastic boy and girl making their way through the afternoon. Both were laughing and sipping from plastic cups, the boy playing music on his phone, the girl texting on hers. They were moving with the ease of childhood, perhaps smiling at the rapid approach of their adult responsibilities. I smiled in return. We passed each other in the awkward manner of travelers who meet while going in opposite directions; they were heading to the base of the stairs I had just left.   As they reached it, I glanced down and met the boy's gaze. It was the familiar expression teenagers give   to adults who are neither their parents nor teachers, but authority figures nonetheless, still capable of chastising them for their intimacy or demanding that they turn down their music. I did no such thing. My attention was elsewhere.

Although the day had been bright and warm, the air had recently begun to chill, and shadows had grown among the oaks, engulfing spaces that seemed to welcome the arrival of night—a sudden change in the mood of things. I wondered if they had noticed.

About the Author:

Allison M. Palmer is a municipal park ranger, writer and copyeditor living in San Diego, California. She is currently the editor of Footprints, the publication of the Japanese American Historical Society of San Diego. Allison is also the founder and director of the Palmer Memorial Humanities Library.

FADED

by Victoria Endres

A small wet drop blurred the rounded pink letters where it landed. Quickly I set the pages back onto the smooth grey surface of the kitchen counter to keep my tears from further obscuring the words. For a few moments, I couldn't say a word. I couldn't collect my thoughts into any rational sentence structure. All I knew or understood was pulsing anger and betrayal. I fixed my eyes on the small stack of pages, "Why didn't you tell me?"

Mom glanced back at me, continuing to do the dishes, "What are you talking about now?"

"Why didn't you tell me she wrote this me when you got it six years ago?"

The water shut off, her hands stilled, and the only sound was the hum of the refrigerator.

• • •

Because she was only 5 years older than me, Sarah was more like my older sister than my aunt. Being so much younger than my dad, their relationship was inevitably somewhat more paternal than a typical sibling dynamic. Just like my dad had wanted to help care for his sister, so Sarah loved to help care for me. She often spent nights in our house, asking my mom if she could help change diapers, always wanting to keep me from crying.

As we got older, we became best friends. Despite having friends my own age, I always preferred to spend time with Sarah when I had the chance. The first 14 years of my life were filled with musical movie nights, forts built of scrap PVC piping, baking or burning new cookie recipes, sleepovers, Dance Dance Revolution, and thousands of texts on our new flip phones.

Sarah was the first person I texted, and the first to text me. She was the one I told about my first crush, my first kiss, my first breakup. She gave me my first makeover, sloppily painting my face in bright colors. I helped her get ready for prom, she helped me do my hair for middle school dances.

Inevitably Sarah hit an age where spending time with her younger cousin was no longer the top of her priority list; she was 15. I was heartbroken as the slumber parties and fort building became more and more infrequent. But mom reassured me that it was just a phase, that we would be close again one day. I'm still waiting for that to happen.

• • •

Sarah, usually clear eyed and attentive, always engaged and laughing, bantering and bickering with my uncles, was sitting with red eyes staring fixedly at faded green carpet. When you spoke to her, it was as if she couldn't hear you. Only after repeating her name over and over again would she look up, and even then it was as though she didn't really understand what you said. After several attempts at starting conversation, trying to ask Sarah about what she thought of the new Twilight movie, about her classes, her friends, her boyfriend, her new dog, anything, I gave up.

That was the day I first understood what it meant for someone to be on drugs was the first time I really cried over Sarah's illness. At 13, you would think I'd have more of an understanding of what it meant to be high and out of touch, but all the movies I'd watched and books I'd read didn't help me here. I misinterpreted drug use for the flu several times before I finally figured it out.

I picked myself off of my grandparents' old plaid couch and went to find my mom in the kitchen. She was peeling potatoes for a Thanksgiving dinner as I sat down on a stool next to her at the island. "Mom?"

Her hands stilled and she set down both peeler and potato to look at me. Her face composed into a stiff smile, "What do you need, Victoria?"

"Why is Sarah acting so weird?" I hesitated a moment, "Is she sick?"

I asked almost hopeful that the answer would be yes. Mom had already told me Sarah was on drugs, but I thought that maybe she just took them at parties or something, not before Thanksgiving dinner.

"I told you why." She took a deep breath, clearly not wanting to have this conversation right then, in my grandparents' kitchen with the other kids running in and out as they played tag. "When someone is high they act weird. They aren't themselves."

I stared at her, waiting for more information that she was clearly hesitant to give. She started peeling the pile of remaining potatoes before speaking again, "It depends on what kinds of drugs you're taking – different drugs make you act different ways. The kind she takes make her seem ... really tired... like she can't focus on anything. Sort of like she's sleep walking, but really she's awake."

Now I was really confused. "But if the pills make her weird than why is the doctor giving them to her?"

Mom stared at me, opened and closed her mouth a few times before finally saying, "A doctor didn't give them to her." Seeing that this answer was not enough to quell my confusion she continued "Sometimes people will sell pills their doctor gives them to make money. Then people like your aunt buy them."

I don't remember if I even responded to this. I only remember hiding in the basement for hours. My favorite hiding places there was the window sill. At my grandparent's house, the basement windows had a ledge that jutted out about 8 inches from the glass, each window about 3 feet wide. Plenty of space for a skinny

middle schooler to sit. So, with the curtains drawn I hid for hours. Of course, everyone knew where I was, my hiding place was well-known. But for once my mom let me be. No one came looking for me for dinner or dessert. Only when it was time for us to go home did my dad come to find me. My parents took me home to cry in my own bed instead of against the window, chilly from the November night.

• • •

That Thanksgiving was the first time I saw Sarah on drugs, but I learned about her addiction earlier that year. It was summer, Sarah had been in her second car accident of the year, but her little Hyundai had just been brought back from the mechanic. I was thrilled; it was just in time for us to have our annual summer movie day.

Sarah and I had gone to see the first two Twilight movies together and spent the remainder of those days out shopping and getting ice cream. We would drive to Teays Valley, windows down, blonde hair tangling in the wind, *NSYNC blasting over the stereo. Just a year ago we were talking about crushes and people watching while we ate cinnamon sugar pretzels at the mall. We had been planning this next day together for months. It was the one tradition we'd kept up despite spending less time together.

When I asked Mom the week before we were supposed to go, she didn't even consider it. I hadn't finished explaining the whole day we had planned before mom interrupted me, "Absolutely not."

"But we go every year!" I was confused, Mom had never kept me from hanging out with Sarah before. "Should we just go a different day or something?"

Her face was red, angry, "I don't want you spending time with her alone, and she's not allowed to drive you anywhere anymore." She picked her book back up, clearly hoping that was the end of this conversation, but I was never one to let things go.

"But that isn't fair! Why can't I go with her?" Now I was red and angry too. We always look more alike when we're emotional. Our faces and eyes go red and our hands tremble. Each of us was always on the verge of tears, frustrated with our inability to control our reactions. I'm sure in this moment we looked very much alike.

"She isn't a safe driver. You heard about the accident. You saw how messed up her car was."

"Sarah said it wasn't her fault! Why are you blaming her for it?"

She let out a huge breath, "Whatever Sarah told you wasn't true." She set her book on the side table and looked at me intently, "Your dad and I didn't really want to tell you this until we knew more, but I guess you're old enough to understand… Sarah is on drugs."

If real life was like a cartoon I would have been standing there with my jaw on the living room floor, mouth agape. But reality is never that funny. Instead I just nodded and stared at my toes. The pink and purple sparkling nail polish was already chipping off; my nails never stayed painted for long in the summer months when I ran the neighborhood barefoot with my brothers.

I couldn't look at her as she continued telling me everything she knew about my aunt's addiction. So I kept on looking at my toenails, trying to memorize the ragged spots of paint as she spoke, "Apparently she started smoking pot a few years ago, but somehow she got started on Oxycontin and Xanax. I think it was probably when she started going out with that guy she met at Shoney's."

I could pretend I remembered the rest of what she said that day, but I can't. Based on all the other conversations we've had since, I would bet that she mostly just told me her theories on my aunt's addiction. She may have even talked about how my grandparents weren't doing enough to stop this. But really I can't be sure. I just remember tuning her out, trying to make sense of it myself.

When she finally finished her lengthy explanation, I only wanted to know what Oxycontin and Xanax were. Mom told me they were pills and that one was like a stronger version of Advil and the other was for people who get nervous.

I didn't make it downstairs to my room before the tears came. I always cried too much, my mom always tried to teach me to fight the tears, but I never could. The rest of that day I just laid in bed and sobbed. Part of me wants to be able to say that I cried because of Sarah's illness, because I understood that she was sick. But that night I was selfish. My pillow was soaked from tears because I wasn't going to be able to have a fun day with my aunt and because I was afraid I would never be able to again.

• • •

Over the course of the next few years, my relationship with Sarah continued to deteriorate. During my first two years of high school she got into two more accidents and traded out one abusive boyfriend for another. The pair of them came to a Fourth of July party at my house the summer before my junior year of high school; they were high. Sarah sat on the porch with eyes glazed over, a half-eaten plate of food on her lap. Flies kept landing on her coleslaw, but she hardly seemed to notice.

Her boyfriend was much more adventurous for someone so out of touch with reality. He decided to get in the pool with my uncles and cousins and floated aimlessly on a 5-foot inflatable crocodile. The lull of the water, the warm sun, and the drugs put him to sleep quickly, and he floated on for a long time undisturbed by the games the kids were playing next to him. At some point his balance must have shifted. He started sliding into the water and off of his crocodile. His head slipped under the surface quickly. He didn't wake up. My uncle grabbed him around his waist and threw him on the deck. Only then did his eyes open. He and Sarah didn't stick around for dessert.

• • •

As Sarah's addiction worsened, her looks changed. Once we looked like sisters. Our blonde hair was the exact same shade, nearly impossible to tell apart in pictures. Long noses, high foreheads and large blue eyes dominated our faces. Even our acne ran along similar tracks, each of us had a string of red spots along our jawlines.

But years of drug abuse altered everything. Her hair lost its shine, still blonde, but with its luster gone it took on a greyish hue. Everything about her seemed dull – her eyes, skin, personality – everything except the acne which raged defiant all over her face, no longer confined to her chin. Dark circles weighed down her eyes which never seemed as big since her lids couldn't stay open. Her body was decaying. By 20 years old, she had lost her youthfulness. She was a walking corpse.

• • •

It wasn't long after her boyfriend nearly drowned in our pool that Sarah went to rehab for the first time. We sent her a few hours away to some small rehab center ran by a local church. No one ever told me its name or even where it was and I never thought to ask. Sarah went without fuss, telling us all that she would try to come back sober. And she did, for a month or two.

By her third month out of rehab Sarah was using again. She became the stereotypical drug addict. She stole money from my grandparents. She got into more car accidents. She lost jobs. She stole drugs from the pharmacy where she worked, how she even got the job there as me. She got the windshield of her car smashed in because she owed money. She lost touch with her family, only coming around when she wanted something and for major holidays.

The only time I heard from her aside from her rare appearances was a text on my birthday. Before she went into rehab we had still kept in touch fairly frequently. I would speak to her a few times a month, just to check in. But when she was in rehab she never called. I didn't hear from her at all, and when she got out the silence stretched on. I waited for calls and texts that never came. I was heartbroken. I'd lost my best friend.

Our relationship was never the same. During her rare bouts of sobriety, she would come visit a little more often. But neither of us ever tried to rekindle our relationship. We were stiff and formal, I would ask about her kids and her job, she would ask me about school, but never anything more. The days when we would gossip about crushes and spent whole weekends with each other were gone.

It wasn't until I was in college that I got some answers. When I was home over winter break, my mom called me into the kitchen. She handed me an envelope with my name written on its front in large pink letters. The script was a half-cursive half-print style, undoubtedly Sarah's. The envelope had been opened. Inside there was a letter dated 2012, the year Sarah had first gone into rehab.

She had written me. The letter was an apology, asking me to forgive her for hurting me, for distancing herself from me: I know this has all been hard on you, and I'm sorry. I know that I don't deserve another chance, but I hope that maybe we can be close again. Even if that means things are different. I understand if you don't trust me anymore, I mean I've been gone for so long. But I hope you'll call me. Or even write me if you want. I just want to hear from you.

A small wet drop blurred the rounded pink letters where it landed. Quickly I set the pages back onto the smooth grey surface of the kitchen counter to keep my tears from further obscuring the words. For a few moments, I couldn't say a word. I couldn't collect my thoughts

into any rational sentence structure. All I knew or understood was pulsing anger and betrayal. I fixed my eyes on the small stack of pages, "Why didn't you tell me?"

Mom glanced back at me, continuing to do the dishes, "What are you talking about now?"

"Why didn't you tell me she wrote this me when you got it six years ago?"

The water shut off, her hands stilled, and the only sound was the hum of the refrigerator. She toweled her hands off on the dishtowel by the sink, "You were too young, I didn't think it was a big deal anyways. They obviously made her write that. I got one too."

My hands were shaking, "That wasn't your decision to make."

I went back to my room and cried again. I wondered if I'd ever stop crying, if I'd ever stop grieving. I had given up on her. Sarah had wanted me to help her, to rebuild our relationship. All that time she thought I'd ignored her, that I didn't want to fix things. The letter was all I'd wanted, but I'd gotten it six years too late.

About the Author:

Victoria Endres is West Virginia native and undergraduate studying Literary Studies and Creative Writing. After graduation, she hopes to further her studies by earning a graduate degree in English. She work has appeared in Thoreau's Rooster, Underscore Review, and The Manhattanville Review. Her works focus on problems of identity and relationships. When she isn't working or writing, Victoria enjoys reading, video games, nature hikes, and spending time with her friends and boyfriend.

PERCY SHELLEY'S POETRY
by Matthew Ross

Non-Linear Temporality and Causality, Trans-Dimensional Space, and the Struggle to Grasp it All; Percy Bysshe Shelley, a Pioneer

A to B. Water freezes into ice – fire boils the former and melts the latter. A three-dimensional space with no doors or windows, only walls, cannot possibly be escaped by whatever resides within. A collapsed kingdom exists only in the minds of those who lived under it; that kingdom's ruins and remains become the relics of history forgotten to the next kingdom's – the next nation's – push toward the future. The contemporary world is in the now, and it is the now which truly matters – there can be no better summation of the commonly held perspective on time and space. The Romantic poets, however, thought anything but common thoughts. In a number of his most renowned pieces, Romantic poet Percy Bysshe Shelley challenges the common notions of time flowing along a clear continuum, explores the perception that physical space has easily comprehensible limitations, and expounds on human's tendency to fashion definitions for the laws of our reality in the desperate attempt to understand and reconcile them. In crafting metaphors for these thoughts of his, Shelly has succeeded in providing his readers with not only a lens through which to re-evaluate their perception on these matters, he also has formulated a dialogue through which these facts about our reality may be discussed.

Archaeologist James McGlade writes this on the archaeologist's perception of time; "Until recently the temporal discourse in archaeology was marked by its objective detachment and almost non-problematic nature; time was some-how self evident." He begins by outlining the commonly held belief on time; it is linear and, ultimately, objective." Then, later; "...the experiential nature of time, i.e. its human face has become a dominant focus as an antidote to the omnipresence of objective, measured time within archaeological practice." McGlade refutes that original belief of an objective time and asserts that a subjective – a non-linear - view on temporal matters is the more accurate perception (McGlade).

This shift of thought – at least among learned archaeologists – occurred in the late 1900's – well after Percy Bysshe Shelley had already touched on such revelations in his 1818 poem "Ozymandias". Perhaps his most famed poem, "Ozymandias" is but a narrator hearing the recounting of what a traveller saw. "Two vast and trunkless legs of stone stand in the desart," the traveller describes, "Near them, on the sand, Half sunk a shattered visages lies, whose frown, and wrinkled lip, the sneer of cold command...(Shelley 776). What this traveller "from an antique land" saw was a ruin in the desert. However, what the traveller may not have realized about his observation – what it seems Shelley wanted to hint at – was the traveller, in truth, interacted with the ruin through his interpretation of it and projection on it's subjects. The traveller describes a "sneer of cold command" but that he sees a sneer is simply how he interpreted the expression. His description is wrought with cynicism regarding the ruler's benevolence – but in fact, that ruler may have been well loved by his people. The sneer he sees may instead be a look of contemplation, of pondering – that the traveller sees a sneer is merely his projection, likely based on his own negative experiences with rulers, onto the ruler displayed on the stone. Likewise, the creator of that sculpture – "it sculptor well whose passions read" – may have created his work in the aim of deifying the beloved, contemplative "Ozymandias, King of Kings." That the traveller thought the sculptor's hands were "mocking" is, again, that traveller's interpretation – only instead of then projecting onto the King, he is projecting onto the sculptor. The form of interaction – interpretation and projection of an individual – is identical across generations and subjects; the only difference lies in whether or not the subject's heart still beats. In crafting "Ozymandias," it is clear that Shelley sought to expound on these manners of interaction with the past – and in doing so he revealed how the "past" is made to live in the present. The traveller's experience with a relic of time has crafted an entire interpretation – an entire personal history - of that time. Yet the truth is so much more – the truth is something that may be completely unknowable; Ozymandias may have been cold, but he also may have been well loved. His sculptor may have mocked him – or he may have revered him. That lone sculpture may be a testament to the patheticness of virtues such a order and civilization – or that a sculpture even remains from that civilization may speak to it's lasting power, especially when compared to all the nations without even broken sculptures left as relics of their existence. The shift of thought McGlade highlights, then, was in truth likely a struggle; archaeologists were forced to recognize and re-evaluate previous perspectives on history with the revelation those perspectives may be tainted by bias. After-all, if the aim of archaeology – the aim of laymen discussing history and it's facts – is the establishment of an objective framework from which to draw lessons to improve the present and future, then archaeologists and laymen must recognize their tendencies to fall into to the same method of thinking the traveller in "Ozymandias" fell into; one characterized by bias-based interpretation and the forming of potential un-truths due to subsequent projection. As Shelley addresses these issues of time

in Ozymandias, he likewise addresses issues of space in another of his prominent works.

In the same way McGlade addresses time in his dissertation, anesthesiologist Peter T. Walling addresses space – and how humans perceive space – in his own. He writes, "Consciousness is indeed strange, straddling the objective and the subjective with no dimensions to call it's own." This seems to reflect McGlade's belief that common perceptions of time as objective must be re-evaluated – but Walling takes that another step by challenging the common notion that an objective reality may even be determined. He uses the example of a rose's color; "The redness of the rose I see exists in a private domain. I cannot communicate to anyone else what redness is like. Redness and other qualia are subjective phenomena which cannot be described to outsiders" (Walling). In essence, the rose, the object with permanency – existing "objectively" in reality – is not, in truth, objective. That is an illusion, and each individual has their own perspective – their own interpretation – of that illusion. Walling's red may be the green of this essay's reader - that reader's green may be McGlade's blue. An individual with sharp eyesight may see the rose's thorns while a blind person may only realize those thorn's very existence when they prick themselves on them. The rose, an object deceivingly existing in three-dimensional space, in truth exists in a space incomprehensible to us. The rose can be anything – any object or any space – and the allegory remains; the space we perceive is not the space that exists in truth. Shelley, again, comprehended this long before many others.

"Ode to the West Wind" is more than just an ode to the beauty of nature – it is Shelley's poetic dissertation on the nature of space itself. In the poem's second stanza, Shelley presents a metaphor for life and death; "Thou Dirge of the dying year, to which this closing night will be the dome of a vast sepulchre, Vaulted with all thy congregated might..."(Shelley 791-792). Death is the sepulchure, and confined within – defined by, built and supported by – the multitude of experiences each individual life goes through before death. A sepulchure – as with any other building – is a three-dimensional space. In Shelley's view, death itself constrains life by nature of seemingly being a space with walls and a roof, with clear boundaries and clear entrances and exits – a clear beginning and end, in other words. This is but a reflection of the fact that while living, our perspectives are seemingly bound to three-dimensions. Even in an open field, for instance, the sky itself is a boundary, and its permanency and our inability to defy the laws of our reality and escape beyond it define that boundary. Just as Shelley asserts, we are bound throughout the duration of our lives because of the very nature of those lives. Shelley, however, may also have envisioned a way beyond those boundaries. Although death is "the dome of a vast sepulchre," that sepulchure, it seems, has a tendency to explode; "From whose solid atmosphere Black rain and fire and hail will burst...." Shelley describes "fire and hail" bursting from the dome – a seemingly minor bit of vivid imagery that is so much more. By every natural law we know of –by every one of our closest attempts at unearthing the objective reality Walling would renounce as illusionary – fire should melt hail. Fire should consume cold, especially if it has the capacity to explode – yet in Shelley's metaphor, there is no such melting. Even when, presumably, the source of the hail and the source of the fire were broiling that vast sepulchure, the natural laws of reality were not obeyed. Yet only when the dome explodes is that revealed. Shelley plotted this sequence of events intricately in the aim of not only presenting life as being bound by our very own perceptions – he has also asserted his belief that death is the manner by which those limitations will be escaped. The death of the subjective mind Walling describes is, in essence, the freeing from the spacial confines around it in life articulated on by Shelley. It is no wonder Shelley was pondering such truths – or un-truths – about our reality, especially given his knowledge of – and infatuation with - the Eastern world and it's philosophies.

Shelley was known for being a voracious reader and studier of ancient and modern philosophies, and that breadth of knowledge was on full-display in works such as "Alastor," "The Revolt of Islam," and "Hellas" (Greenblatt 750). In "Ode to the West Wind," however, Shelley's

narrator invokes a number of deities to "hear" him – and among them is the Hindu god Siva, the "Destroyer and Preserver" (791-792). Alongside evidence in this same poem that Shelley views time non-linearly, it is not a leap to presume that Shelley's precise view on time is akin to the Hindu view that temporality is cyclical. As Subhomay Das, a Hindu scholar writes on the Hindu views on death; "It is time, which is accountable for old age, death and dying of his creations. When we overcome time, we become immortal. Death is not the end of the line, but a gateway to the next cycle, to birth." That notion of rebirth through death is reflected in the final line of "Ode to the West Wind": "If Winter comes, can Spring be far behind?" In Shelly's own words, Winter – embodying death – is naturally followed by Spring – the embodiment of life. For death, there must be rebirth, and for Shelley, perhaps that rebirth is supposed to occur in a space beyond our current comprehension. That notion seems akin to how many perceive death as being a detachment from this reality in some sense – even eternal oblivion is incomprensible to someone living – and such thoughts are often the cause of terror in people. Perhaps that is why Shelley's narrator is asking so many gods to "hear" him; he needs to voice that terror in order to reconcile it. Perhaps, even, Shelley's narrator is beseeching the gods to aid him in overcoming his fear of the inevitability of his perception of time coming to an end. In Shelley's mind, successfully overcoming that fear may spell the secret to immortality beyond the confines of mortal perception. Furthermore, Shelley's frequent capitalization of the West Wind suggests he holds it in the same esteem as the other gods. He is invoking the West Wind – his own personal god – in the same vein as the others, and begging it to provide him some glimmer of comprehension of these issues. In this, Shelley provides a metaphor for the very reason humanity tends to deify and define truly incomprehensible forces such as time and space; gods of fertility and rebirth such as Siva and Dionysus – also mentioned in "Ode" – are faces humanity envisions so as to commune with those forces. Through that communing – through those attempts at understanding and reconciling with embodiments of those forces - as Shelley attempts to with his West Wind, as Hindus do with Siva and as the Greeks did with Dionysus, various peoples find solace in the midst of a reality defined by limitations and mysteries such as time and space.

Shelley and his Romantic peers were more than poets; they were explorers of unknowable truths – the pioneers for our recognition of the bounds of our reality. In his poems, Shelley asserts his beliefs on the non-linearity of time, pushes the limits of the very space we perceive, and demonstrates how humanity has attempted to reconcile with these incomprehensible notions. In doing so, he has given us readers a framework through which discourse on these issues may be had – it is unfortunate, then, that such transdimensonional discourse is limited by humanity's three-dimensional dialogue.

Works Cited:

Das, Subhamoy. "What Hinduism Teaches about Time." ThoughtCo, www.thoughtco.com/the-concept-of-time-1770059.

Greenblatt, Stepehen. "Percy Bysshe Shelley." The Norton Anthology of English

Literature. Vol. 2 , no. 9 , W.W. Norton & Company, Inc. 2012. New York, pp. 750

McGlade, James "The Times of History: Archaeology, Narrative, and Non-Linear Causality." Time and Archaeology. Routledge. 1999.

Walling, Peter T., and Kenneth N. Hicks. "Dimensions of Consciousness."Proceedings (Baylor University. Medical Center), Baylor Health Care System, Apr. 2003, www.ncbi.nlm.nih.gov/pmc/articles/PMC1201004/.

Shelley, Percy Bysshe. "Ode to the West Wind." The Norton Anthology of English

Literature. Vol. 2 , no. 9 , W.W. Norton & Company, Inc. 2012. New York, pp. 791-792

Shelley, Percy Bysshe. "Ozymandias." The Norton Anthology of English

Literature. Vol. 2 , no. 9 , W.W. Norton & Company, Inc. 2012. New York, pp. 776

About the Author:

Matthew Ross is a nineteen year old author and poet residing in the San Francisco Bay Area. A college student pursuing English and Administration of Justice degrees and an advocate for the rights of animals, Ross spends his free time hiking in the nearby Mt. Diablo hills, reading, and writing. He takes great pride in the professionalism and discipline he applies to that writing. He aspires to spread his work to as many readers as possible and envisions himself as a teacher and a career writer. Under his belt are three finished novels, a breadth of short-stories, literary essays, plays, and poetry, and he is currently working on a collection of thematically and stylistically connected novellas. He is also currently considering an opportunity to produce a script for a documentary on a groundbreaking medical technology targeted at alleviating the symptoms of neurologically-traumatized soldiers, athletes, and everymen.

CRAIG

by Shirley Palmerton

Have you ever felt yourself struggling to wake up and then find you are awake, the nightmare is true? I felt this way one hot summer's day in the pediatrician's office when the doctor examined our six-year-old son and told me to take him to Children's Hospital for further tests.

"What's wrong?" I asked in a shrill tone. He didn't answer right away, just stood looking at the other pediatricians that had come in. A chill crept over me and I held Craig tight as if they were going to take him from me. Louder I asked, "What's wrong? You know, tell me."

"We think he either has a brain tumor or a blood clot."

All I could think was 'Oh no, not Craig. He's so beautiful, almost too pretty to be a boy.' Many nights I had stood over his bed watching him sleep and thought 'how could someone so ordinary looking as my husband and I have such a beautiful child.' We had another boy, aged twelve, but he was average looking and a little girl too, who would win no beauty prizes, but they were loved and wanted as much as Craig.

The doctor's voice shook me back to reality, "Do you know any neurosurgeons?"

'Just Ben Casey,' I thought. 'Oh my God, that's not funny.'

Out loud, I replied, "No. Get the best. Money's no object." Even if we had to mortgage our home, it didn't matter. Money was the last thing on my mind. I told them I wanted to stay with Craig, so get a private room for us.

They made a few phone calls and told me to get right over to Children's. They were waiting for us.

I left Craig at a friend's house and headed home to pack our bags. When I got home, I washed a few dishes, straightened a few pillows, folded some clothes, and looked out of the window. I was jarred back to reality when the phone rang. It was my sister asking how Craig was. In a monotone, I told her.

"What can I do? What can I do?" she asked.

"I don't know," I replied and hung up.

I arranged for the other children, picked up my husband at the office, and we went to the hospital. They were waiting for us and the neurosurgeon turned out to be a quiet, short man with wavy hair. His manner, made us put our complete confidence in him.

The next day, after the tests were taken and Craig was watching television, Bill and I went to the dining room for a sandwich. We had just sat down when the doctor joined us at our table. He told us he was sure Craig had a brain tumor and he was going to operate in the morning. "Be ready," he said, "It's going to be a long one."

"Do you think it's malignant?" I asked, hardly able to get the words out.

Quietly he replied, "Yes. Ninety percent of the brain tumors in the back of the brain are malignant and we're sure this is in the back of the brain."

"What if it's malignant," I whispered again.

Quietly he said, "It's fatal."

I found myself in the hall sobbing in a corner and some lady was patting me on the back saying, "There, there, it can't be so bad."

Silently I screamed, 'You don't know. You don't know.'

That night when Craig was asleep, I sat by his bed and watched him and I thought of all the things I had wanted to do with our children and never had.

We lived on the outskirts of a small town, many neighbors and a sub-division was growing up behind us. The children had many, many friends to play with and it seemed they were always eating and running off to someone's house to play. There were open fields and dirt piles, baseball games and supervised play at the school. In this way, the days flew by.

As I sat there I thought, 'I've never laid in the field with them to watch the clouds roll by in shapes of animals, people we knew or as ghosts or goblins. I've never taken long walks with a picnic lunch or had we watched things born or leaned over a country bridge and watched the fish or leaves float by – or – or,' the list went on and on.

Sleep was impossible that night and I sat and held Craig's hand. In his sleep, his fingers curled around mine. The thought of tomorrow was too much.

The morning came too soon. My sister, Bill's brother, and the minister came in to be with us. The nurse gave Craig a shot and asked me to read to him until he went to sleep. With tears streaming down my face, I read The Three Bears. When he finally was asleep, I laid my head down on the pillow next to his until they came to get him. Silently I kept asking, 'Why, why us' and the answer came back, 'Why not you?'

My husband, was suffering as I was but his arms were always open to me when I needed a haven. He said the right things at the right time to keep me from falling apart completely.

Craig was in the operating room eight and one-half hours. The first encouraging news we had was when they called up after a couple of hours that they had found the tumor in the front of the brain and our baby was doing well. Every hour was like a day itself. I walked and walked that day, oblivious to all. My every

thought was a prayer. Night came and suddenly he was back. His head completely covered with bandages. The doctor explained the tumor was the size of a tennis ball with a cist growing on it that was filled with water. In addition, because of the size of the tumor he might be paralyzed on his right side with his speech slurred. Or he might be in a coma for a few weeks – or – or – or. Again, the list went on. It was still unbelievable.

The joy of seeing him alive was overwhelming. When we were alone, I leaned down and put my arms around him. I put my cheek next to his.

"Mom, you're hurting my head," he said rather disgustedly.

We couldn't believe our ears. I ran down the hall shouting to the nurses, "He's talking. He's talking." They couldn't believe me until we went back to the room and they heard for themselves.

The next morning, when I walked down the hall, heads popped from rooms, telephone booths, and elevators. "How's your son?" they asked.

"How did you know?"

"We prayed for him all day yesterday, you suffered so."

In my grief and despair, I wasn't aware of them, but they were aware of us.

That day the doctor told us he didn't think it was malignant but we had to wait for the pathologist's report. Sure enough, when the report came back, the tumor wasn't malignant. However, Craig had to have radium treatments, as it was the type that might regrow.

Craig steadily improved and ate hotdogs the third day, took a bath the fourth, and went for a ride in a wheelchair on the fifth.

We took him home ten days after the operation and that was a day that didn't let up. Our eldest son, while going shopping with his grandmother, got his finger caught in the local grocery market door, and broke the bone in his little finger. After that was taken care of, I called my sister and asked her to bring Sissy home, as I couldn't wait to see her. They were both white as they drove in. Sis had been run over by a horse. She had been taken to another hospital where they x-rayed her, but was found only to have multiple bruises of the chest. Two days later taking Craig in for his radium treatment, I got caught in a radar trap and was arrested for speeding. I was in court two days getting it settled. Life was not dull.

After things settled down, Bill and I talked long into the nights. We found out you can never go back. You must do things with your children now. There's never another chance to live a day or hour over. The only way we felt this could be accomplished was to buy a house way out in the country where'd there'd be only us, thus forcing us to do things together.

We looked a full year before we found a rather new house on a side hill with ninety acres of hills, valleys, and Christmas trees, planted by a previous owner.

We moved three days before Christmas on a snowy day. The next day, I watched out one of the back picture windows as Bill and the boys dragged a newly cut Christmas tree over the field covered with snow. I realized our daughter was awfully quiet. She had locked herself in the bathroom. When I finally got the door unlocked, I found she had devoured a whole bottle of baby aspirin that I thought I had safely hid. Back to the hospital, again we went to have her stomach pumped.

That spring we started taking long walks with the children. We slid down the sides of ravines in the leaves, followed streams and swung on grapevines, and sat and listened to the sounds of the woods. Each walk we seemed to end up laying in the pine needles under two pine trees that were so large, that if Bill and I clasped hands we could just reach around them. One day we were all stretched on a cushion of pine needles completely relaxed when we heard organ music drifting down through the valley. It was an unforgettable, unbelievable time, a moment of sacred closeness I would have hated to miss.

Later, we bought an old tractor and trailer, so on Saturdays and Sundays we loaded it up with a folding table and picnic lunch, and all in

different parts of the woods and explored the area.

That winter we put an advertisement in the local paper that said, "Christmas trees, cut your own." People came in droves with their families to revive that feeling of togetherness. The boys helped sell the trees or watched the small children who were too little to go to the woods. Our Christmas spirit lasted for weeks.

Since then, we've built a small barn and we've watched eggs hatch and kittens born. We've gotten up in the night to see a colt newly born and watched in trembling excitement as it took its first steps. The boys raised pigs to show at the fair and felt pride at the first blue ribbon. We've gathered wild berries and when we got home, I made a pie. We ate it while it was still warm. Each day there is a feeling of togetherness I'm sure the children won't easily forget.

Of all the wonderful times, we've had together; I think there's one that's outstanding in my mind. One late November day, we were on the back hill cutting Christmas trees. We worked in pairs, one cutting and one dragging. Sissy picked out the ones she thought were special. We tired and lay in a mossy area on the side hill tickling each other's faces with dried grass to see who could keep a straight face the longest without moving. A thought crossed my mind and tears streamed down my face. Silently I said, "Dear God, thank you. We've found our place in the sun."

Six years later the tumor came back and again there was surgery and radiation. There were several nights spent in the hospital and one night Craig stopped talking to me.

"Tell me what you want and I'll do it."

"I want to go home and never come back."

"Okay." I called Bill told him to come get us.

Never again did we stay in the hospital. When things got bad, we hired private duty nurses and they were with him 24 hours a day with all of us there.

I didn't think I had the strength to go through that, but I did. I know where the strength comes from – thank you God.

About the Author:

Shirley Palmerton writes from her heart and readers find themselves laughing or shedding a tear. As she approaches 90, she is finally sharing her stories with more than her friends and family. Her "My View" columns in the Buffalo News have reached people far away. After she read this story at her writer's group she was encouraged to submit it to Adelaide. It was written decades ago and recently found.

DOLPHINS, AS A METAPHOR

by Justine Cadwell

A dolphin's smile is the greatest deception. It creates the illusion that they're always happy. – Ric O'Barry

What would it be like to sleep at the bottom of the ocean? As a young girl, my favorite scene in the movie Mermaids showed a blasé bedroom transformed into a magnificent sea. A rotating lamp sat on the floor, projecting sea creatures onto freshly painted dark blue walls.

On family trips, I gathered seashells of various shapes and textures. Shiny marine treasures decorating the perimeter of my aunt's hot tub caught my eye, and she showed me how to carefully crack open a sand dollar, revealing the tiny white "doves" inside. My parents owned a large peach conch shell, displayed on a book shelf in our home den. I held the opening over my ear, reveling in the emulated sound of distant waves. Anything related to The Little Mermaid warranted my attention. In the bathtub, my yellow and blue striped Flounder toy sprayed fountains out of his mouth. At school, I sported Ariel sneakers. I collected dolphins: sculpted figurines of various materials, a small stuffed replica.

Dolphins represented the epitome of everything I wanted to be: majestic and pure, intelligent and kind. Anxiety created chaos within my body, but dolphins appeared immune, shining brightly as a symbol of harmony. In conversations with others, I made sure to clarify that dolphins were mammals, not fish. In my mind, this granted them additional validity for appreciation. I purchased a dolphin adoption kit at Natural Wonders, my favorite New Age store, and proudly displayed my adoption certificate in my room.

At Sea World, I sensed a magical atmosphere. The dolphins seemed happy, smiling as their fins propelled their curved bodies along the tank confines. I fantasized about swimming beside them, of touching their smooth silver exterior. Maybe I'd be a dolphin trainer when I grew up or an oceanographer. I imagined the beautiful art I would capture: their glorious bodies gliding through crystal turquoise waters amid a backdrop of vibrant rainbow coral.

***

I formed a growing awareness of our dying planet, the plastic clutter and toxic chemicals permeating our oceans. Envision the scene from The Beach where blood mars the former pristine white sands, the sparkling aqua shore. Dust settled over my tiny dolphin statues. I donated most of my collection to Goodwill, leaving my unrealized dreams at the bottom of cardboard boxes.

In 2007, I returned to Sea World as an adult, and magic no longer filled the air. My Mecca of wonder seemingly transformed into another example of rampant consumerism. Before scheduled shows and while walking the grounds, products were advertised over the loud speaker. The vast tanks I marveled at as a child seemed dirtier, smaller. The glass panes appeared thicker, as if the creatures existed in a separate realm, no longer within my reach. The animals looked less happy or maybe I was projecting? Cynicism now tinted the rose-colored glasses of my youth.

In 2009, The Cove documentary was released, showing film footage of gruesome dolphin hunting in Japan. I watched the film in horror, salty tears stinging my eyes. It's not a film for the faint of heart, especially those who revere dolphins.

I learned dolphins are more complex than their peaceful stereotype implies. There is a widespread myth that male dolphins are "rapists". It's one I fell for when I first heard it. However, scientific literature does not support these claims. Their mating behavior cannot be categorized as forced copulation, despite the rumors.

Unfortunately, attempted infanticide has been witnessed. In 2013, researchers watched from a distance as a female dolphin gave birth to a calf. This awe-inspiring moment was interrupted when two male dolphins attempted to murder the calf immediately afterward, holding it underwater to prevent it from breathing. Each time the males tried to sink the calf, the mother pushed it above water and rested it on her head, desperate to help her newborn survive. This ghastly event went on for two and a half hours. I can't image how I would have handled this information as a child.

There is mounting evidence that dolphins are capable of intricate emotions and appear to grieve their dead. Females dolphins have been observed frantically lifting the carcass of their young above the surface for days after their death. Along the coast of California, a witness watched a mother mourn her dead baby by carrying it on her dorsal fin as she swam.

***

During childhood, I interpreted dolphins as one-dimensional creatures, but this view has been altered. Their existence cannot be understood through a Lisa Frank prism. They are not an untouchable display of perfection. A mother dolphin may find it necessary to fight against her own species to protect the future of her child. The lives of dolphins are not defined by an endless stream of harmonious waves. They must navigate their course among useless debris and toxic waste. They display beautiful shells for bodies, enduring hardships behind a smile that implies otherwise. Perhaps the dolphin and I are not so different after all.

Works Cited:

The Beach. Dir. Danny Boyle. Perf. Leonardo DiCaprio, Tilda Swinton, Virginie Ledoyen. 20th Century Fox. 2000. Film.

The Cove. Dir. Louie Psihoyos. Perf. Ric O'Barry, Hayden Panettiere. Participant Media. 2009. Film.

Gregg, Justin. "The Dolphin Rape Myth". JustinGregg.com 11 Jun. 2013. Web. 27 Mar. 2018.

Hogenboom, Melissa. "The dolphins that kill each other's young". BBC Earth. 16 Jul. 2015. Web. 27 Mar. 2018.

Mermaids. Dir. Richard Benjamin. Perf. Cher, Bob Hoskins, Winona Ryder, Michael Schoeflling, Christina Ricci. Orion Pictures. 1990. Film.

Nelson, Bryan. "Do dolphins mourn their dead?" mother nature network. 19 Jul. 2016. Web. 27 Mar. 2018.

Nye, James. "Devastated dolphin mourns for her dead baby by carrying it on her back while swimming". DailyMail.com. 02 Apr. 2013. Web. 27 Mar. 2018.

About the Author:

Justine Cadwell is a former blogger at The HungryGuineaPig@wordpress.com and ParentalAdvisorySite@wordpress.com. She is currently writing a book of essays centered around the various shades of her neuroticism. Justine lives in Minnesota with her husband, daughter, and feline friend.

UNA VOZ, UNA VEZ ONCE...A VOICE...
by Andrea Bernal

1.

Confound my name,
Hang it from a branch,
after all
I don´t know what it is.

Help me lengthen this life,
a giant lily that spins like Earth.

And if they don't listen to me,
sing very low to the voiceless blackbird,
when a voice was needed indeed to talk.

And if it is snows, cover the world in white,
save me from a single love that saved my whole life,
and when I opened my eyes,
I discovered
-don't deceive yourself anymore-
paradise is something very small.

Soon after, the girls came
with all the woman's hands,
and with them I opened a hill of a single river:

Some call it freedom.

1.

Confundan mi nombre/
cuélguenlo de una rama/
al fin y al cabo
no sé lo que es.

Ayúdenme a prolongar esta vida,
una azucena gigantesca que rota como la Tierra.

Y si no me oyen,
canten muy bajo al mirlo sin voz/
cuando se necesitó una voz en realidad
para hablar.

Y si nieva, cubran la palabra de blanco,
sálvenme de un solo amor que me salvó toda la vida;
y cuando abrí los ojos
descubrí
-ya no se engañen-
que el paraíso es algo muy pequeño.

Después vinieron las niñas,
las manos de todas las mujeres,
y con ellas abrí un monte de un solo río:

Algunos lo llaman libertad.

2.

No

And it dawned when we didn't want to.
And it got cloudy when we didn't want to.
And an older lady told me that the whole world was covered by
dont's.

No

And I went into her house,
when she was collecting sand mouns,
I stamp on them,
They escaped through the pipelines.
And the sand told us
no.

And I sat to her winter porch,
and I collected wood,
and an iron fire again
told us
no.

And we grew petunias in the spring,
And an unfortunate frost
told us again
no.

And we sat together in two silent benches,
and all the clay that portrayed the men also sitting here
told us
no.

Then, we perished grave against grave,
and a dog dug us up and found our bones.

And although all the black dressed had guaranteed they would to affirm the world,
the hound from the top of the hill told us again
no

2.

No
Y amaneció cuando no queríamos.
Y se nubló cuando no queríamos.
Y una señora mayor me dijo que el mundo entero estaba cubierto por

No

Y entré en su casa,
donde coleccionaba montículos de arena,
los pataleé,
se escaparon por las tuberías.
y la arena nos dijo no.

Y entré en su porche de invierno,
y coleccioné madera,
y una lumbre de hierro de nuevo,
nos dijo no.

Y cultivamos petunias en primavera,
y una helada infortuna
volvió a decir que no.

Y nos sentamos juntas en dos bancos de silencio,
y toda la arcilla que representaba a los hombres también sentados
nos dijo no.

Entonces perecimos tumba contra tumba,
y un perro excavó y encontró nuestros huesos.

Y aunque todos vestidos de negro se habían asegurado de afirmar el mundo,
el podenco de la colina les dijo de nuevo
No

3.
Last act.

The one of the rift's happiness.
The sand's fecundity of all goddesses.
To die by Medea's love.
Since the stars arent's so big,
they are tiny dots on a sheet.
The last act.
See how the pitted rain falls
in the thin reeds on my chest,
and how a dagged is nailed,
without pain
next to the perhishable compass that atends
me.
The last act in front of you:
Before all the locks are damaged.
The houses meets their standars:
They are inhabited and vacated.
Trains arrives on point, on time.
Last act in front of you.
Feel the water spilled in the blue ceramic.
Maybe as a tear, I also wanted to escape.
It's better to escape before each farewell.
The last act.
You also cried,
at our age, we don't know more than
nothing, nothing, nothing.

3.
Último acto

Último acto.

El de la felicidad de las grietas.
La fecundidad de arena de todas las diosas.
El morir de amor de Medea.
Porque los astros no son tan grandes,
son minúsculos puntos sobre la hoja.
Último acto.
Ver caer la lluvia deshuesada
en finos juncos sobre mi pecho/
y así clavar un puñal
sin dolor/
junto al compás que me atiende perecedero.
Último acto antes de ti:
Antes de que se estropeen todos los cerrojos.
Las casas cumplen su norma:
Se habitan y deshabitan.
Llegan trenes en punto, a su hora.
Último acto antes de ti:
Sentir el agua derramada sobre la cerámica
azul.
Quizá como lágrima yo también quise escapar.
Es mejor escapar antes de cada despedida.
Último acto:
Tú también lloraste,
a nuestra edad no se sabe más que
nada/ nada/ nada.

4.
Mom

Mom has to write,
Don't look at her too much.
She has beaten all the trivial house objects.
We'll not forget to take the cake inside the oven.
Mom has to write,
It's not a remedy,
She has opened all our garden doors.

4.
Mamá

Mamá tiene que escribir,
no la mires demasiado.
Ha vencido a todos los objetos triviales de la casa.
No olvidaremos sacar el pastel dentro del horno.
Mamá tiene que escribir,
no es un remedio,
ha abierto la puerta de todos nuestros jardines.

5.

A voice,
once,
once,
expired
like the story's bad giant,
the way a whole life is told.

A voice,
a life,
like the plaintive grinding of the one-eyed blackbird.

Or a voice
like the wind's laughter
which shakes my winter days
and mocks the fallen backhand
from the street in a hat.

A voice that reaches everyone
-Impossible-
A fenced intimacy
as the cowbell hanging from the gente neck.

A voice,
Purity?
A voice that explained why we are not alive,
why when I needed it most, my wounded deer fled.

Or a voice,
as the poet said
-you due to you-
as it is said of this century,

of quick denial,
as you speak with an echo above in the vault,
letting fall it
from circle to circle,
wild open,
for two hands.

5.

Una voz,
Una voz,
una vez,
una vez,
vencida.
Como el gigante malo de un cuento.
Como se relata toda una vida.

Una voz,
una vida,
como el rechinar lastimero de un mirlo tuerto.

O una voz,
como la risa del viento
que sacude mi invierno
y se burla del revés caído
de la calle en un sombrero.

Una voz que llegue a todos
-un imposible-
Una intimidad cercada,
como el cencerro al manso cuello.

Una voz,
¿una pureza?
Todo lo que calla el hombre y se silencia.
Una voz que me explique por qué no estamos,
por qué cuándo más lo necesité huyó mi ciervo herido acelajado.

O una voz,
Como dijo el poeta
-a ti debida-
como se dice de este siglo,
de negación veloz,
como se habla con eco para la bóveda,
dejando caer
de círculo en círculo,
de par en par,
estas dos manos.

6.
Dead

Nowadays the dead are not even remembered.
The day is so fast that one should give foot-
wear quickly.
So he who is no longer,
is rescued,
nobody knows by whom.
Someone places a cable on the roof of my
house
Inside lives the deceased little man
who has been traveling dumb for centuries
through his wife's phone.

6.
Muertos

Los muertos de hoy ni siquiera se recuerdan.
Es tan veloz el día que es oportuno dar rápido
calzado al otro.
El que ya no está
es salvado,
nadie sabe por quién.
Alguien coloca un cable en la azotea de mi
casa.
Dentro vive el pequeño hombre fallecido
y hace siglos que viaja mudo
por el teléfono de su esposa.

7.
Something is going to happen...

Something is going to happen,
my meadows are going to be opened.
It is an omen.
I'm now stretching my stockings further on my legs.
It is augured:
I'm growing.
Even if you don't read it in the written press,
the children whom I had cuddled have drunk all my milk.
Something is going to happen,
I predict it,
They will be higher and time will be shorter.
Something is going to happen,
and the letters revolt in their crib's bars.

7.
Algo va a pasar...

Algo va a pasar,
se van a abrir mis praderas.
Es un presagio.
Hoy ando extendiendo más mis medias en las piernas.
Se augura:
Estoy creciendo.
Aunque no lo lea en la prensa escrita,
los niños que acuno han bebido toda mi leche.
Algo va a pasar,
lo auguro,
estarán más altos y será el tiempo más breve.
Algo va a pasar,
y las letras se sublevan en los barrotes de sus cunas.

8.
I was...

I was always on the road.
Looking for the frost in the stamens.
An invention for those who don't believe in the white chewed flowers.
There is a brief tinkling in the daisies' teeths,
Little illusions evaporated after being children.
However, I was always there, crying for the mosses,
Cradling in shadows that took me
I don't know where.
I never knew.
Quiet
for beautiful places,
that never recede from one.

8.
Estuve

Yo estuve siempre en el camino.
Buscando la escarcha en los estambres.
Una invención para los que no creen en el masticar blanco de las flores.
Hay un breve tintineo de los dientes en las margaritas,
pequeñas ilusiones que se apagan después de ser niños.
Sin embargo, siempre estuve allí, llorando para los musgos,
acunándome en sombras que me llevaban no sé a dónde.
Nunca supe.
Quieta
para los lugares hermosos,
que nunca se escapan de una misma.

9.
Shipping

I send you dogs.
I know,
There's nothing beautiful about it.
But this is how the world works.
They eat breadcrumbs anywhere.
Also we once interrumpted their jumps and barks in the park:
We kissed.
They were not crumbs,
it was sand
for our mouths.

9.
Envío

Te envío perros.
Lo sé,
no hay nada bello al respecto.
Pero es así como funciona el mundo.
Ellos comen migajas en cualquier parte.
También nosotros una vez
interrumpimos sus saltos y ladridos en el parque.
Nos besamos.
No eran migas,
era arena
para nuestras bocas.

10.
Green

Let the little girls adore us with their green silk dresses
in the winter that sinks,
and makes me give birth
to sinister fish.
Memory is a long stream that procedes from a delicate source.
You kissed it near the marble.
You don't remember this anymore.
I was once
your girlfriend,
Yours and theirs:
Little Firenze Bestiaries.
A woman, a very lonely woman stood still,
and she is sewing the little girls'ties
-of whom she is mother-
The freedom of their dresses when they dance.
-They're no longer a belonging, they are not owned-.
Wild green, green grown old.
It leaves my spots tied to my thimble,
like the moss to the thirsty rock.
So much green that I paint with longing,
so much longing painted in green...

10.
Verde

Que las niñitas nos adoren con sus vestidos de seda verdes
y sea en este invierno que se hunde,
hace que de mí nazcan
siniestros peces.
La memoria es un largo arroyo que proviene de la delicada fuente.
De ella tu besaste junto al mármol.
Ya no recuerdas.
Yo fui novia alguna vez,
de ti,
y de todos ellos,
pequeños bestiarios de Firenze.
Una mujer, una mujer muy sola se ha detenido,
y va a coser ahora los lazos de las niñitas
-de quien es madre-
de la libertad de sus vestidos cuando danzan
-ellas ya no pertenecen, ni son pertenecidas-.
Verde salvaje, crecido verde.
Me deja atadas a mi dedal las manchas,
como el musgo para la roca lleno de sed.
Tanto verde que pinto de nostalgia,
tanta nostalgia pintada de verde...

11.
Poet

I can add a censored world to everything,
An empty room,
I have a poem in my hands,
I'm an ofender.
I can fill it with misfortunes,
cook it,
wait for the oven to warm up,
or leave it in the pantry,
freeze it,
makes its darkness against my fever.
It is a living being that doesn't live.
That's why I can do everything, everything.
Censure it,
kill it one day,
or lend it my room,
I can tell it even to wait for me a hundred years or who knows,
to leave it at home or make it return.
Is it in my soul, is it in my guts?
Is it toxic, harmful, hurtful?
Today it rests in the bed as a good and silent child.
I takes its cold hands and sing a lullaby it doesn't understand.
See, how has it blinked?
Do you understand that it this living being doesn't live?

11.
Poeta

A todo puedo añadirle una palabra censurada,
una habitación vacía,
tengo un poema entre las manos,
soy una delincuente.
Puedo llenarlo de desdichas,
cocinarlo,
esperar a que el horno se caliente,
o dejarlo en la despensa,
congelarlo,
hacer combatir su oscuridad contra mi fiebre.
Es un ser viviente que no vivo.
Por eso puedo todo, todo.
Censurarlo,
matarlo un día,
o prestarle mi habitación,
decirle incluso que me espere cien años o quien sabe,
que se marche de casa o que regrese.
¿Está en mi alma, está en mis tripas?
¿Es acaso tóxico, dañino, hiriente?
Hoy reposa en la camita como un niño bueno y silencioso.
Le toco sus manos fríos y le canto una nana que no entiende.
¿Ven cómo ha pestañeado?
¿Entienden que no esté vivo, esté viviente?

12.
And I Closed

And I closed all the house doors.
The screams were loud.
In truth, people were crying as in all civilita-
tions,
everywhere.
But we have become accustomed to closing all
the house doors.
We prefer body nakedness.
I read it before,
somewhere
a fury words that would assail the wooden
floors
and would mess up the new crocklery.
I read it before.
Once a book mentioned a life.
It cries and grows,
It is wearing and it is fraying.

12.
Y cerré

Cerré todas las puertas de casa.
Los gritos eran muy fuertes.
Se lloraba en realidad como en todas las civili-
zaciones,
en todos los lugares.
Pero nosotros nos habíamos acostumbrado a
cerrar todas las puertas de casa.
Preferíamos la desnudez del cuerpo.
Lo había leído antes,
en algún lugar,
una furia de palabras que asaltaría todo el par-
qué
y desordenaría la vajilla nueva.
Lo había leído antes.
Un libro mencionó una vez una vida.
Se llora y se crece,
se va tejiendo y se va deshilachando.

About the Author:

Paula Andrea González Bernal (Madrid, 1985) is a philosophy teacher and poet. As a philosophy teacher she studied at the University of Salamanca and was awarded a special prize.

As a poet she is known as "Andrea Bernal". She published her first poem "Primavera viva/Live Spring" in 2006 at Lord Byron Editions, being the youngest poet of an anthology that included poets such as Jaime Siles and Cristina Peri Rossi.

In 2013 she published "Los pájaros/The Birds" with Eolas editions, León. This book is presented in León, Salamanca and Madrid, with the writers Raquel Lanseros, Julio Llamazares and Antonio Colinas (current winner of the Reina Sofia Poetry Prize in Spain).

In 2016, she published "Adiós a la noche/ Goodbye night" with Isla de Siltolá editions. This book was also presented by Antonio Colinas and Julio Llamazares in Madrid. In addition to poetry, she has worked as an art critic in several Spanish Museums and other cultural institutions such as Domus Artium Salamanca, Musac and art galleries. Her current literary work is based on the French translation of her new book "Todo lo contrario a la belleza / Everything opposite to beauty". She is also working in a book of short stories "La felicidad de los lobos/The happiness of the wolves".

AMUSING MY MUSE

by Endika Sangroniz

AMUSING MY MUSE

My muse stepped on the Earth and faced mortality
Since then, she is the icon of feminine freedom
An iconoclast from head to toe
She calls the shots, she soaks my words
Plus, she didn't come to please anybody but herself
Whenever she wants me, she takes me
She is the antithesis of romanticism
And I love that, to say the least.

GIVE ME A SECOND

Raise your chin and look at me
Look at me and hypnotise me
What do you do young pale-sapphire-eyed
glancing directly into a stranger's void?

The sun elevates your beauty as a best friend
In this crowded life, won't I see you again
The picture you left me is out of focus

I'd rather not live fast to admire you more
My memory is sore, you are a heavy loss
Whoever you are.

HOURGLASS

I almost don't wake up this noon
It seems far away now

After an astral trip I have realised
that there won't be any night
in which she will shine for me
I'm horrified by the idea of not getting to sleep with her
That is a truth of mine

I would like to study
her intricate philosophy
as well as the anatomy
of her ripe body

I still trust the éphémère
I ignore if she does too
Moving on is unconceivable
Her remembrance stalks me
like a ghost I have bred
How did all start? Does she know?
Because I can't recall

"You are out of time
Forget her, for your own good".

About the Author:

Endika Sangroniz was born on the first day of spring 1997 in Bilbao. Early on, he got introduced to the arts by music, building then an interest in literature; mainly poetry. Currently, he is a musician that has no audience and has recorded twenty-two songs that someday will see the daylight. Besides, he is about to finish a collection of poems to be published, where the three sent poems have been taken from.

MERCHANDISING
by Debra Brenegan

Merchandising

I hate the decay masterminded by marketers
the blue sweater worse than the gray one, the pills, snags, holes
with barely a wearing
Next the washing machine can conk out mid-cycle
all dazzling rinses and planned obsolescence
and the new shoes can pinch with little pricks
between and through the cheap socks
Then the capitalists will dress up another American myth
while the top dogs earn their crazy salaries some more
and the earth will slow its steady spin and stumble
minutely
shabby and muted
like the rest of us

Burn Out

Our bodies tremble, eyes burn, begging for
sleep, a hunger thirst hunger for
leisure and peace
If the lists could multiply invisibly for a while
with inaction and forced compilation
and the heroic juggling could halt mid-circle
amid the crash of broken crockery
then our eyes might roll back and stop their dry twitching
and our breathing might calm these stretched nerves
and the work would begin to soothe our
shaken psyches, to the chagrin of
overseers, starved themselves

Sick Day

I recognize an illness tainting blood and breath
the bark worse than the bite, through the joy sweet bliss
of a day in bed
Now the cat can sleep undisturbed for hours
around and between my ankles
while the computer belches and phone bleeps
all urgency and flashy come-ons
Then the white blood cells will commence their vital
war, destroying membranes and compromised nuclei
And time is lost forever from the plague
of obligatory masochism
as I sink down the wormhole, finally taking care

Trauma

I fear the pain crawling out from my bones, the memory
as bad as the incident, the ache raw ache
these muscles clenched
Now the acupuncturist can stab her tiny needles
while the herbologist mixes me a bitter toddy
and the pills can release their numbing magic
so the shards around my spine smother
quiet for a while
Then my jaw unlocks and fists uncurl between and
around this shallow breathing
and for a moment I blink back tears as the clouds float soft
behind the trees

Real Family

We hear your judgment coiling through the speaker phone
the meaning worse than the words, the dream crack dream
our mirror has shattered
Next the airplanes can rest a while in light
of your absence and selfish vision
and our daughter can sit with a lonely look
around and between the family tables
While the real cousins mingle at another white holiday
the other family eats their fragrant dinner in exile
until the little ones stare down your frightened eyes
to chip, bit by bit, your granite heart
of senselessness

Debra Brenegan has a Ph.D. in creative writing from The University of Wisconsin-Milwaukee and is an English Professor at Mount Mary University in Milwaukee, Wisconsin. She has received a Ragdale residency, and was a recent finalist for Glimmer Train's Family Matters Short Story prize, the Snake Nation Press's Serena McDonald Kennedy Award for a short-story collection, the John Gardner Memorial Fiction Prize, the Cincinnati Review's Schiff Prose Prize, and the Crab Creek Review Fiction Prize. Her poetry and fiction has been nominated for a Pushcart prize and has been published in journals such as Calyx, Tampa Review, Natural Bridge, The Laurel Review, Cimarron Review, Bluestem, Milwaukee Magazine, Phoebe, RE:AL, The Southern Women's Review, Knee-Jerk, Literary Orphans, and elsewhere. Her novel, Shame the Devil (SUNY Press), about nineteenth-century American journalist and novelist Fanny Fern, was named a finalist for Foreword Reviews 2011 Book of the Year Award for Historical Fiction.

AFTER THE RAIN
by Jack Brown

AFTER THE RAIN

The squirrels told her
it was safe to talk with me.
Birds who protected her before
gave their approval.
They look after their own.
Wearing ribbons of struggle
she beckoned with wounds
and wonder. Seeking
the moral high ground. Nurturing
the will to be brave.

Neither unkind nor criminal
I offered namaste
and an authentic ear. A private
hearing in a public place.
Over soup I shared
umbrella analytics.
She found a syllogism of clarity.
I made a phone call. Good news.
Warm under a gray sky.
After the rain.

ENDURING LOVE

Imbued with the amplitude
of the night
I play the stars
with velvet hammers.
Like a vibraphone.
Melody is destiny.
Harmony a ripe measure
of the moment
married to the eternal.

Keep a high heart.
Wave and be brave.
Cherish truth.
Embrace enduring love.

MUSIC THERAPY

Feather cat alights
on the radio corner
of the bed.
Music therapy morning.
Social. Near me.
At little desk.
Floyd (her son) at window.
Her family.
Swift piano. Low.
Flying fingers. Upright bass.
Duet.
Feather feels the mouse like
runs. The pitter pat
of the bass.
The musical chase.
Sound lively.
Violin wanders
over the hill.
A meandering bee.
Up and down the scale.
Around the bush.
Piano kicks in again.
Bird skylarking.
Bright sunny day.
Drums. Brush slap slap.
Scratch scratch.
Sweet sound poetry.
Music therapy.

About the Author:

Jack Brown. Poet, songwriter & activist. Lives in New York City.

SHROUD FOR A SOUL
by María Agustina Pardini

Shroud For A Soul

His soul shrieked at
The touch of the cold iron bars,
Confined, existing in vain,
Sentenced, living in pain.
Elated by a diurnal shaft of light,
Soon to be dismissed when evening closed.
Caged into immobility, into oblivion, into delirium.

Spreading his wings like an unbarred prisoner,
He measured the size of the cage,
To collect his dignity, to emulate freedom.
A cold gentle breeze, a residue of liberation
Caressed his fragile, fagged feathers.

Locked inside the
Still unravelled enigma,
He looked up, his eyes empty,
Glassy, the vacant sight of a once
Luminous soul.
The wave of vitality ebbing,
The wave of silence flowing.
Involuntary displacement made him
Writhe in agony.
The reminiscence of a past drug
The intoxicating sea smell,
The addictive seashell resonance.
Here, in his enforced discipline,
The current of life collapsed.
Complacently, he shut his eyes.

Tanka

High, up the royal
Ruins of Lion Fortress
Silence hangs in the air,
Inside a damp cave I find
Frescoes of damsels dancing.

Alfonsina Storni

Waves must have turned into an icy rage that night,
Crisp air of wrongness; like a shooting star
Which leaves death in its wake; you hugged the sea.
"Only I can craft your fate", God clamoured,
"And no sky will watch your sleep, if you're gone,
And no moss will be your quilt, come dawn."
A shared pain wrapped us, your still disarmed readers.
We always wondered what grief drowned you alive.
Your deathless soul brawled with deep agony,
But now your soul shines in a star, poor
Moon, who is jealous of your dazzling light.

La difunta Correa
(Ballad)

The soldiers mocked the moon and took
A man from his wife's care,
Recruited was his soul
And his dear wife's despair.

A civil war had broken
The country's fragile peace.
Enlisted men, be fearful! For
The fight will never cease.

Oh! Very dear sweet deceased,
We pray for your intervention.
Keep us safe on our long, wide ride,
We now ask for your protection.
Blessed are those whose souls you touch,
We implore your cooperation.

Seeing her husband leave drove his
Wife to desperation.
She took her baby in her arms
And ran across the nation.

Like keen travellers through the mist,
They both made their way,
But the sun's heat blazed above, the road
Offered no leafy shade.

Oh! Very dear sweet deceased,
We pray for your intervention.
Keep us safe on our long, wide ride:
We now ask for your protection.
Blessed are those whose souls you touch,
We implore your cooperation.

In exchange for rest and shelter
She kissed death on the cheek.
Dehydration had turned
All her prayers useless, weak.

Some shepherds were walking
Later on, ahead,
When they saw, by the corpse, her baby,
Who had survived, breastfed.

Oh! Very dear sweet deceased,
We pray for your intervention,
Keep us safe on our long, wide ride
We now ask for your protection,
Blessed are those whose souls you touch
We implore your cooperation.

You may well come
(Prayer)

You may well come another day, death.
The day age, grown, knotted, like a withered garden
Looking for light, steps into darkness; the day
The scent of jasmine decides not to tiptoe into
My room at night.

The day my cloudy eyes seem offended,
I will need the radiance of a newborn star above,
To care for me, to lessen the torment,
To guide my steps across the fields
On a sleepless, hot summer night.

The last drop of a fine red wine shall
Not tingle any sensation on the tip of my
Tongue and the oily blackberry flavour will
Die quickly in my mouth, will give way to a
Despairing tasteless night.

The temperature of my skin,
All Evidence extinguished, swept through
Ashes, will recall the time when
Fierce flames served as witnesses
To long, lascivious nights.

The day I grow weary of the incessant chatter
A swarm of budgies; the day they feel noisy,
The day they seem intrusive,
The day I choose silence;
Death, you may well come that die-a-ble nigh

Moans of Despair
(Based on Howl by Allen Ginsberg)

I see the women of my generation destroyed by inequality, living in fear,
Taking to the streets at dusk in protest over chauvinism, fighting for their rights,
Empowered female fighters burning to eradicate a social disease, misogyny,
Raging against the war machine of our days.

Who can put an end to this harassment and cry to stop
the violence, stop the silence, stop the rape, stop the corruption?
Everyday, they chain their bodies to lampposts to call for somebody's attention,
Until the rain washes their mascara and the icy July's wind touches their skins.

Their feet are tired for they have been walking since ever.
Their eyes are dry for they have been filling rivers with crystal diamonds.
Their voices are cracked for their rights have long been silenced.
Tic- toc- ti, the revolution of the clock. It stops at every new brutal femicide.

Lucía was abducted from her bed, fear made her heart stop beating.
María could not see the sunrise, her body was dragged into the depths of the night.
Clara never got to the job interview, her illusions were snatched before she arrived.
Silvia let her murderer in, she had shared the bed with him that night.

A crowd of women packed in Plaza de Mayo, wandering grief carriers,
Marching with the dead, singing their hearts out for the women's emancipation,
Not yours, machismo kills, never again, my body & my rules, not one less
All signs read. Thousands of drums echoing the beating of their hearts.

I see the women of my generation refusing to give up this obsession.
Preventing parliamentary legislation from building more oppression.
Hand in hand, creating a protective barrier where we now all stand, trembling in the
Supernatural darkness, determined to make us all savour the bitter taste of defeat.

Falling in love
(The ghazal)

Morning came like a hummingbird hovering nearby.
Full of promise, it displayed its sovereign rays.

Night fell swiftly upon the curtained, moonless window,
Sucked her heart and dragged the lingering love away.

Morning came seeking the light, climbing the long, rugged walls.
Hooking a root into the cement, a seed gave its life to the day.

Night fell, obliterated the beams of golden love.
The little plant shrieked like a mandrake; the sky turned grey.

Morning came like a visitor to stay.
Morning came, grew gnarled roots.
Till Doomsday, I hope it stays.

About the Author:

María Agustina Pardini is a writer, reviewer, teacher, and translator. She graduated as a Literary Translator and years later got a Bachelor degree in the English Language (four years). She is starting her Masters in Comparative Literature next year. She has been studying Drama for the last seven years with different experienced actors and playwrights. She works as a teacher of Literature and as a Theatre and Book Reviewer. She spends her free time reading, going to the theatre, writing poetry and traveling around the world.

TWO POEMS

by Austin C. Morgan

THE AMULET
A Brief Appreciation of Friedrich Nietzsche's The Gay Science

I.
The statues of the forest
Weep in medium light,
Upon the sea beside.
Mars, above, looms on,
Casting crimson rays upon the waves.
The sea,
A mirror earth,
My soul subsides.

By what hand
Have these lovely creatures
Been sculpted?
Perhaps a stone mason of Alexandria?
The gold gleams within the trees,
Sour grapes too dense
For our comprehension –
A failure of mine,
A sin of which I shall not be absolved.

The uncinatum of the caverns
Heeds not the will of mortal men.
God has breathed his last breath here,
The procession, a shadow upon the wall,
Cast by hands of the communicants.
The faithful, from whom spirit does escape
And bows into the falling light,
Cackling,
Sky-bound.

The empire bustles
In evening,
Our enemies
Of equestrian persuasion
Invade from the East.
Every maiden, once of such great beauty,

Now harkens, stone-faced, to the march
Of Hermes, who tumbles in from
Painted ceilings within the Grand Tower,
A place once reserved for the knowledgeable,
To announce the fall of the West,
Where mediocrity has devoured pillars
Like cavities in pale marrow.
"Heed not!" Shouts the stone mason.
"The time of nigh has passed."

His roses grow frail,
Bloom cast the color of dawn,
From a hillside overlooking Eden.
Her face, there, remains,
Slightest hint of cholera
Blushing against her cheek.

Beg of the idols
That she might return
Ever-safely.

II.

The statues of the forest
Know well,
For the superstitions
Of lesser men
Form shackles upon the wrists
Of the wise
And the silent voice
Carries greater echo.

The child has died in vain
By the hand of jealous brother,
Lower brother,
Lost to the Canaanite field.
Know, though, that it shall be by will of
A wicked sister that men are devoured.
Yes, she shall unveil your words
Of righteousness to the soldiers
Of corrupt fortune upon the horizon —
Forever lost,
Misconstrued
Upon the horizon.

The Prince arrives
Enshrouded by a flock of doves,
Pale and saintly,
A title hardly shaded
By trite nostalgia
Projected from his early sonnets.

Pure, the stars hang idly,
Boney light shone down upon the terrace.
"Learn not the will of men,"
Spoke the Prince.
"But the Will – that of the sea.
That of which remains ever-present,
Ever-flowing within its vast rage.
See now, the waves no longer envy,
Currents no longer yearn.
The eternal hue of emerald gleams."

Mephistopheles emerges from the crowd,
Draped all in gold, eyes exotic lilies
Of the Old World,
For to speak, "the moon shall be mine,
Every verse, every line."
There she lies,
A slight thicket of evening cloud,
Crevices of age
Folded into the rhythm of her flesh.
Aglow with beams as pale as hope,
How I knew I could never love another!

"No man," speaks the Prince, "shall harness her beauty.
This beauty is to be a means
Of admiration from afar,
Just as the summer, infinite days of youth,
Glimpsed from afar."

...with which we had fallen
Beneath the spell,
Behind the blustery curtain
Of night.

To beguile the greatest man,
The battle but a fortnight away.

III.

The women of the courtyard
Move southbound in rhythm to
The incendiary tune against this
Calamitous scarlet sundown.
Scarlet, indeed,
Cased in crystal strata
Of fairer Asteraceae,
A temple abreast of flourished July
With harlequin breath of May.
"Fit secundum regulam,"
Declares he who no longer follows,
Fearing not the beasts of the forest,
My brothers, savages of the strangest persuasion.
How I long to be among them, beachfront and

Awestricken, having beheld the bath of Venus
Churning madly upon the sea before them.

"But what greater motivation is there, Robert Burton?
What shrapnel shall be collected from the earth, so holy?"
Surely there is more to be gained from the absence of lust,
Perhaps the pursuit of higher knowledge, a genuine appreciation
Of the cunning ways of the women of the field,
Wading out into the twilight, a sisterhood to minimalize
The bond of brothers.
What greater motivation?

IV.
The statues of the forest
Pray with cupped hands,
Stone palms pooled with water,
A blessing of the sea beside.
Their heads have bowed in shadow
Cast by boughs of poplar above.

There on the footbridge
Lingers the Prince,
Who raises one hand
To wield against foolish disciples,
Those who embrace the madness
Of our often-tumultuous Condition.

"For there is no room for interpretation –
One must possess a heart of Mars
And a soul of blanketed stars,
The soul upon which this strange midnight
Has fallen.
If not, one shall surely bleed far more
Than to nurse his battle wounds."

And with this, he departed
On wing of palest feather,
This Prince to be freed
From the boundaries of lesser earth.

Upon departure, I saw Hypatia
Walking lonesome by the sea.
I fell before her in a breath of June
And kissed her feet as if the face
Of some long-lost lover.

"Lesser men never comprehend
The secret tongues in which we speak,"
She sighed and closed her eyes against
The cryptid wind across the water.
"How they have forsaken the greater art."

I had not a word to utter,
Basking in the otherworldly glow

Of her shadow, laid across the sand,
Deep within the bones of beasts unrecognized,
Just as the tongue in which she spoke,
I only learnt of the festivities above,
Failing to spread my arms in joyous wisdom.

"There she rests," breathes Hypatia, pointing.
"The aeon has not been so kindly
Across such a delicate face."
Stellae, la luna, I swooned.
"The greatest pain is that of
Failure to obtain such beauty,
To objectify the muse, indeed."

I thought not of Mephistopheles,
Although his shadow was present,
Ever so.
La luna, la luna, which shall remedy
Your aching separation from me?
Two planets basking in evening air,
The first being that of fortune,
The second, that of the language of verse
In which we had so softly spoken.
"Grasp the latter, hold her there upon the sea
Until the hazy light of Heaven falls like a child
From the lovely blanket of dawn cloud.
There you shall obtain."

Among the ashes,
Embers,
Embers gleam.
Man has lulled his
Higher demons to slumber
And chased his lover,
Fingers sprout of leaf,
Flesh no longer porcelain,
Given way to the mossy bark
Of the great forest before him.
Every face of which he has written
Remains lovelier from then on.

I see the celebration of the villagers,
Their boundless glow piercing the night,
But I choose to remain here, at the waterside.
The value of the night rambling among
Lonesome waves, silent now.
This jealous sea has nearly parted,
So, Cupid, toll your lonesome bell
Upon the waking dreams of the enchanted,
Cupid, toll your lonesome bell
For to set us, the dreaming,
Free at last.

Selections from Rafaela (II, VI, X)

to Kurt Cassidy-Gabhart

II.

That night, from afar,
I watched her face
As pale as porcelain moonlight
Fallen across the night.
Such secrets, the night – saudade –
Whispered toward
Her rostrum of light.
The sound crept softly to me,
Low and lovely as the scent
Of melting snow in February.

I would look upon such a face,
With its silent hint of displeasure,
At which the apples of her cheeks
Would swell, caressed by shadow,
Shadow blacker than the night.
Or should I stand to witness
Such joy upon her face,
Then the spirits of the room
May drift lightly
To rest upon the canvas
Within the hollow of her cheekbone,
Saudade, saudade.

VI.
Tonight,
Among the misty groves,
The milk of the moon
Glistens upon her skin.
I've waited for this,
Among the blossoms,
My steely soul eternally bent,
But to no avail arrive such hopes.

Fairest of undertones,
Light blue,
Swell in swirling hues of flaming chivalry,
As the centuries drift and dance
Across the cradle of her face, so lovely.

Beside a lake,
Partially frozen, pale,
Ice gathers like
Shattered glass around the rim.
This faint lunation
Upon the skyline above
Hangs as if haunted – transparent –

And should it know my name, I may swoon,
For to know such a memory
Crashing through nighttime air,
Thin and misrepresented.

The sun is of better days.
It is cooler in the forest,
A million winding paths
From which I may not
Find my way back.

The lake, Patoka,
Bluer river underbelly,
Face the dawn.
Beachside, which I have walked.
There is a spirit which glides
Beside her,
He is conventional
convoluted
and alizarin,
waiting bedside to her roses,
the petals of which fold by midnight.

On this day, "God has healed."
Hebrew, I embed her name
Within these words.
Lymantria dispar dispar,
Wings against the leaves.
Trouvelot has waned his soul,
Children beneath floral moon.
Petals fall as embers,
In the garden glow, eternal June.

Dispelled from the shop,
Like Pound unto Rome;
Not to keep, not to want,
Never to return.

X.
(Crone)

Crone:
The earth,
Brittle as bone,
Foxtails, mi culpa.
Toward the waxing,
Bitter I have grown,
Such luck to have
Amidst the grand Seventeen.
Now I am lost to time,
Lilies upon the water,
And Jupiter weighs

Heavily,
A storm which refuses to cease,
A fraudulent masculinity,
Those beneath me,
Their persuasion toward battle,
Mere echoes
Down the passage of history.

...and I fade

This longing,
Simply a grand mosaic,
Of what love could have been.

Still it was beautiful,
It was divine.
I shall recall thee
In perfect form
Upon the dais
Until my final breath,
Upon which this love
Shall be as in a dream,
Spoken in murmurs
Across lips awakened,
Acknowledged only by fools
And dreamers, alike.

...but until the day has arrived,
I will linger, lonesome,
Forever more,
Lost like a child
Within the flowing,
infinite passages of time.

About the Author:

Austin Morgan was born in 1994 in Southern Indiana. He currently serves as a contributing editor to aaduna, inc.

LOVE CALLS OF FOXES
by Jack Conway

Love Calls of Foxes

Last night I heard the gray fox howl,
along the old stone wall,
three yips and then a scream,
ungodly sounds,
its ritual mating call.
Love calls of foxes,
reminds us
that love is out there, somewhere,
now, for everyone,
willing to cry long and loud enough.

The Library of Love

On the fiction shelves,
in the library of love,
there are stories of
damsels in distress
and knights in shining armor
who rescue them.
Last night,
while you were sleeping,
I turned on the back-porch light.
Even the dragons are out of breath.

Nature

"The happiest man is he who learns from nature the lesson of worship."
— Ralph Waldo Emerson

Did you ever notice,
how the butterfly
doesn't give a shit
about you?
Can't you see that, man?

Thin Ice

Ice is nice
For chilling drinks
And for soothing wounds.
But I surmise
It isn't wise
To skate on it
In June.

About the Author:

Jack Conway's poems have appeared in Poetry, The Antioch Review, The Hiram Poetry Review, The Norton Book of Light Verse and other poetry journals and anthologies. His book, Outside Providence: Selected Poems, was published in 2016. He is also the author of a dozen nonfiction books. He teaches English at a community college in Massachusetts.

BORROW

by Mike Li

Mike is not my name,
I told you.
I borrowed it from Bible
to roam the land of Uncle Sam.
It's my tuxedo and pasta,
a man
behind which the I hid and ate,
slept, woke and educated.
Shame felt,
swallowed like an esophagus glide,
peppered and festered,
like when he cheated on the red and yellow stripes
with a pure lady of your kind,
and everything will be fine if no one tells, right?
But when the sun goes down at night,
every night,
something must've been left behind.
You tell me it's alright.
Girls borrow clothes from mothers
to appear mature for one party night.
Boys borrow advice from fathers
to become good doctors for two lifetimes.
Sod borrows blankets from snow
to cover debris in their plowed skin.
Water borrows momentum from winds
to dance atop sky like an elegant Jackson Mike.
Uncle Sam borrows Earth from everybody
so more borrow titles from that book of Holy.

Your name is Mike.
You want to borrow my language
even if it's just for a night
so that you can communicate with my heritage.

He tells you it's alright.
Your white skin, paler than rice paper in his printer,
constitutes the most proper mandarin smoked in my homeland.

Doors

There is nothing more vex than the slam of doors on a morning before 8—the bathroom door that is, that suffers constant suspension by 7 people like it's a new gift box every three seconds. My classes don't start til' ten! So I perceive light and December in one flash, to the tale of 6 alarms at once, almost a band of its own kind—Bulletin, By The Seaside, Night Owl, Hillside, Presto, Uplift, and oh that kill-me-now pocketful of Classic, a symphony sufficient on its own, screw you Apple! Screw you tryhards that dare commence a day of hell before dawn, before me, the all-stars mathlete. The spring, suitemates rouse after me, bio clock, that bastard of Victoria Harbor, slams me still, now an hour earlier than fall, in the softest cartilage of my heart silk. Now I understand. It is, a virus named Jetlag, who buffers my goodwill, augments my chance at ill, all inherited from that trip to your house 16 hours from where I am now. So when I'm first, as I always am nowadays, I make sure to walk slow, open the door without foreshadow, and leave it hanging still.

Don't Ignore

The weather, as usual—
Morning sun and crickets
Pulls leches of sweat
Down my veins, Afternoon
Rain and Puddles wet my   already   sweated strains
Which is,
Simply hell,
Just like your mood,
How it spirals down.
The morning we involved in non-stop texting—
Why ignore and continue playing—
Ever afternoon rain stops breath—
Forgot to mention,
Our night is also open,
Although snowing often—
Debris,   sweat after wetting,
Withdraws hand in its pocket,
Where I fiddle a few buttons,
And put the phone to sleep.

I am a rising junior at Cornell University. I am majoring in Neuroscience and minoring in Creative Writing and Spanish. After reading Fitzgerald's works in high school, I started creating my own stories at the start of my college career. My favorite book of all times is The Great Gatsby and as of right now, I'm going through the poetry collections of Denise Levertov.

A Young Man's Date

In white bathroom walls,
I placed my hands under the faucet, washing what, I don't know.
Above my head, I saw a scene, familiar, repeated,
And played on what looked like flat TV screen,
Taking them back to that bathroom in Dorsett Hotel.
A boy, face fresh like apple, impeccable of the world's accidentals,
Is only two years into his college education,
Three years into his deepest depression,
Stares into the mirror—
"Honey," she holds him under the night,
"Let's be together forever," she says,
"The only one I want to marry is you," she smiles but lies inside.
The boy reciprocates every line with a fervor two octaves higher,
And underneath the strips of naked light,
His face has always been flawed, but still two years into his higher education,
Now lonelier, but still together with her,
Stares into the mirror,
Until two weeks later.

He flies back on Cathay's 890,
Looks out the window, sees that once love infused fountain
Drying on the stars over that skyline studded city,
Wondering when they will again meet.
But why even date in this society?
To feel accompanied when you're lonely,
To seek confirmation in times of uncertainty,
To have someone take care of you when you can stand on your own feet;

I turned off the water.
Or is it simply to have a sex partner?
To garner yourself experience for the next partner?
Until you find the right partner?

I walked outside, slow, to the half open window.
Ithaca's sky was again doing nothing but snow,
And I couldn't seem to notice anything,
Or even come close to know.

And so he holds her hand and leads her to the streets,
Across the people seas towards that subway station where they always meet;
Through ten stops and two transfers, he sees their final destination.
He says to her, "Ever since I met you, I can't take in another woman."
He squeezes her hand and wants to kiss her.
He kisses her forehead, lips screened by a fading bang,
"Will we meet again?"
She smiles, goes in, and continues washing her hands.

WRITER'S WORKSHOP
by Martin Willitts

Writer's Workshop

Write what you know, the professor suggested;

but what if you've forgotten every piece of information
you've ever known? What if you've crossed an intersection
of your life and you realize you're lost, the map
is all wrong, and your past just keeps getting in the way?

What do I know that is worth knowing? On the way,
I missed the bus. I learned buses never arrive on time,
but they depart when you are not there.
And, in the rush to miss my connection,
I left a part of me still struggling to get dressed,
buttoning my shirt, tripping on loose shoe laces,
my hair every which way like that picture of Robert Frost,
wind-tossed, reciting at the Kennedy inauguration.

I am not famous enough to be so forgetful. But if I was,
would the bus wait for me, tapping impatiently?

I was not even in that classroom.
I happened to ignorantly walked by, accidently
ease-dropping. I don't even have to respond.
I do not even have to know anything.
I blissfully missed bus connections; but here I am,
writing everything I definitely do not know.

Remaining

Seasons depend on internal compasses
and all I can do is watch
as days are getting harder, bitterer,
with staying and leaving,

marking what is ours, what is not —
moving on and disappearing, touching
tree tops with darkness,
unraveling the remaining days.

Dark comes sudden.
We never seem ready for it —
it arrives harder, bitterer, a season
for staying or leaving.

There's nothing we can take when we leave,
leaving much, perhaps all, behind,
unraveling darkness our remaining days,
until nothing, nothing, nothing remains.

How Could We Not Know Winter is Near

Of course, the season grays.
Of course, we came into the weather unprepared.
All danger really ever teaches us
is that nothing is contained or restrained.

Late fall will be nasty, light will dwindle,
and we'll withdraw into our home,
hoping winter will not last forever. Of course,
we doubt it will end anytime soon.

Of course snow clouds hover.
Light jaunts between snow.
I begin counting every moment until the land vanish-
es.
Oh course, the cold bites without teeth.

That moan — like a thrash of winter wind —
is my soul. Of course it is. Of course.
My soul feels gray, unprepared for the long duration.
My soul is seen in my breath in sub-zero air.

Love Is Never Far From Us
Villanelle

Loss, perhaps, is not far from us,
yet it seems so far away;
We are overwhelmed with loss.

When we believe (for our belief is false)
love is gone forever, it betrays —
loss, perhaps, is not far from us.

Loss is never far away. Loss is never lost.
It is with us every day.
We are overwhelmed with loss.

Small moments remind us what's false.
Loss comes again, today and today.
Loss, perhaps, is not far from us;

maybe, the sadness is just across.
We never know completely what to say,
we are overwhelmed with loss.

We try to hold on and let go at all costs.
Sometimes, loss comes unexpectantly.
Loss, perhaps, is not far from us —
we are overwhelmed with loss.

About the Author:

Martin Willitts Jr has 23 chapbooks including the winner of the Turtle Island Quarterly Editor's Choice Award, "The Wire Fence Holding Back the World" (Flowstone Press, 2017), plus 15 full-length collections including forthcoming full-lengths includes "The Uncertain Lover" (Dos Madres Press, 2018), and "Home Coming Celebration" (FutureCycle Press, 2019).

AT THE TEMPLE OF THE MUSIC GOD
by Felix Purat

At the Temple of the Music God

As tunes flow through my waiting ears
The sun paints Apollo's portal
The pigments of Helios shine

Ear hairs shrink from poignant solitude,
Too much noise in the big wide world

The rhythms of island and coast
Give faith to flesh and its offshoots
Satyric drumbeats moisten rocks

Banalities minimized for once
Into Olympian dimensions

For this I thank Apollo fair –
Nice guy even mortals did spite
How envious they must have been

Never plucking once a flat serenade
Then or now, a lyre never lies.

- Naxos, 2016

Minotaur, Where Art Thou?

O Moving Minotaur
So summarized by Pablo
Lay down your weary cart
And come get me!
How you must tire of
Stale, bland Athenians:
Their city is grimy now
Ugly and unphilosophical
Come out from your labyrinth,
Allow me to behold your
Courageously ugly beastliness
Instead of this cowardly beauty
In my artificial era where plastic is commendable
And no one person can claim
To walk safely upon any trail
I wish to feel the full depths of fear
To walk the path towards indomitability.

Memories of Baja California in Crete

Above the submarine chamber of Aegean Atlantis
Rugged slopes of the Sierra Giganta rise
My friend back then was indeed Anubis
An actual friend, always welcoming my arrival
With humble fanfare befitting friends

Succulent clams and octopus resurrect Loreto,
Old California's beating heart
But here Orthodox shrines decorate Minoa
As Virgin Mary's became my second mother
Beneath the shadow of the Sierra Giganta

In Café Ole we sipped upon lemonades
Watching the Pepsi plane fly by
A block away sat California's corner stone
Salvatierra's work completed long ago

How modern this is in the land of the Greeks –
They generate memories too precious for pithy reflections
Subtracting the dumbbells of time (and therefore value)
I see that I am young and foolish and so is my country

Waking up In a Strange House, Shaking

Exposed to the elements
Of hot Cretan weather

Too much makes me tremble
My nerves malfunction

The price of a penchant for solitude
In an extroverted nation

About the Author:

Felix Purat is the author of A Drinking Horn of Accumulated Expiries and a microchap titled Epicurean Ruminations from Turin & Beyond. He has been previously published in Two Thirds North, Orbis Int'l, Ink Sweat & Tears, Allegro Poetry Magazine, Pulsar, Poetry Salzburg Review and Vox Poetica, among others. Originally from Berkeley, CA, he currently lives in Slovakia.

THE STORY OF LIFE
by Linda Casebeer

The story of life

We could feel the evening falling around us
though it was noon when clouds covered the sun
above the chapel lit only by natural light
filtering through the windows
and upwards from the window wells
the guidebook said low light lent an ancient
and melancholy air to the fresco we had come
to Italy to see God the father creating Adam
their fingers almost touching except for a small
space left between the two in anticipation
of that moment when God would complete
his creation but in the dull light the fresco
distant and blurred by macular degeneration
and glaucoma for Ed who decided to ask
the guards what time they would turn on
the lights after all in the story of life God
had risen into the sky with arms outstretched
to separate light from darkness evening
and then morning of the first day but that day
Ed was one of those the official husher tried
every few minutes to quiet the crowd forever
changing but always always looking up and sighing

Strange angels

American Horror Story haunted an old
house a gorgeous Tudor with Tiffany
fixtures transforming light
into ordinary horror not so terrifying
until the second season when the Story
took up residence in an asylum
also not so frightening for most
no more than a haunted house
but it was the asylum of my nightmare
where three strange angels knock
on the door while D.H. Lawrence
shakes his fist at me and shouts
admit them admit them and when I do
open the door I find Norma splintered
in a Picasso portrait with her blond son
Norman the father of my children
holding the hand of the third angel
an anonymous towheaded baby girl
wandering off into a clouded dream
without an answer to these questions
1) is it true that angels represent
what has been lost and
2) what am I to do with these three
barefoot angels that elicit body memories
of pregnancy the little souls moving
around in my belly four times
creating in me a certain vulnerability
all hormones and love we were young
then twenty somethings seeking romance
and orgasms playing house and haunted
by Norma who had never agreed
to give up either of her sons to marriage
meanwhile with each birth my focus
turned more inward first in utero
then towards the small warm beings
it was during those baby years
when the last two girls where born
a year apart that I lost track of myself
and world events as they unfolded
a peanut farmer president hostages
taken I think I forgot to vote
the year an actor was elected then later
the Iran contra affair and other whole
blocks of news I never followed
or music that changed with the body
politic all a blur until the marriage

finally shattered after Norma decided
to reclaim her sons and send me
to an asylum transference a doctor
would later explain she the strange angel
who would take care of everything
and even when I heard it as crazy talk
I could feel the sensation of walls
closing in of doors slammed shut
gauzy claustrophobia wrapped around
me in Central State Hospital the place
where my own depressed mother
had volunteered as a Gold Lady
and though that asylum was closed
years ago claustrophobia still
finds its way back to me in dream

Her body was small in the box

On a ship anchored off Tortola the island
named for turtle doves I watched tenders
in the distance transport tourists back and forth
while I stayed with Mr. Fox: A Novel that twisted
and turned in on itself a metafictional plot
of murder and mayhem when the father
who murdered the mother was viewed
by his daughter as small in his coffin
this muse brought back to me my own mother
dead these few months not murdered
unless I did kill her by insisting on morphine
for the intensity of her pain

either way at the end her body was delivered
before dawn one Sunday in June to a deep South
funeral home tastefully set back in time
where cremations were complicated
by the need for signatures from every sibling
as a defense against drama our own family
unpredictable in that way since years before
one sister had hijacked the burial of our brother
the one closest to our mother and the only boy
so we didn't seem to mind that he was her favorite
until he broke her heart the year she said
he drank himself to death

when we discovered we could bury her body
without all siblings signing since a body
could always be exhumed to settle a fight
discussions turned to a sea island cemetery
three states away Spanish moss palmettos
azaleas and a thousand brown live oak leaves
behind a three hundred year old church
the double headstone already engraved
with her name but not the year of her death
and after a couple of gin and tonics
the good sister thought we could kill two
birds with one stone like the aphorisms
so common among our mother's people

we could bury her in the mink stroller
her name embroidered in the lining
of the coat she waited so long to
own
but none of us now could imagine wearing
until that night I reread her will
with her request to be cremated
and I felt her claustrophobia punch right
through the lid of any satin-lined coffin

we could choose so it came down to the third
girl a notarized signature I finally asked
for and she did offer more out of the shock
of the death itself coming within a day

in what as children we thought was meant
by the quick and the dead in the creed
that told us what to believe in
but leaving only my identification
of her body to the mortician he said
he had prepared her in a cardboard
box for cremation and as if she had shrunk
that last day ever she was small in the box

About the Author:

Linda Casebeer lives in Birmingham, Alabama. She has published one collection of poems, The Last Eclipsed Moon, from Cherry Grove Collections, and poems in Slant, Earth's Daughters, Chest, and Hospital Drive, Knowing Stones and The Light of Ordinary Things among others.

THE CLIMATE OF TODAY
by Rafiki Chemari

THE CLIMATE OF TODAY

Is God raging or crying?
With these...
Massive storms,
And violent quakes.

The ones that make, break,
And unequivocally shake...
Cities, counties, families,
And cultures!

So when (Uncle) Harvey
Came to visit us
In the
Lone Star state of Texas...
He managed to
Put Port Arthur
Very deep underwater
For two to three weeks.

'Right before (Aunt) Irma
Came in
And flooded
The Florida streets!
And then the border states of...
Georgia and South Carolina.

But it didn't stop there...
As she rolled-over
The U.S. Virgin Islands (who really weren't
virgins at all).
While she went on
To plunder
Puerto Rico.
Who got stuck in the muck
Of a ruthless financial brawl!

But why is this all
Happening now?
Because...
The (Devil) is in "The White House"
And you know
What that means!

It was revealed in "Revelations-20".
It was described in "Ephesians 6:11".
As it began in "The Garden of Eden"...
Where evil had tempted Eve and Adam
(As a dark and fallen angel).

Then he corrupted King David
And later
He tortured
Moses and Jesus.

Can you now begin
To understand...
Just how long
This has been with us?

It's been much, much, longer...
Than the date of
January 20th!

INDIGESTION

Not just a colon
For eating and defecating.
Nor a semicolon
For punctuation and grammatization.
But simply a socio-political indication...
Of the depth
Of a person's bowels
While not standing
For "The National Anthem"
On concussion-ball Sundays.

Some say,
"It's wrong and downright disrespectful!"
While others say,
"It's just too damn political
And so very controversial".

As the cheerleaders...
(clap, pop, bop, and nod).
While whispering,
"Oh my God...
They are all
Kneeling on one knee
At the edge of the sidelines"

But what are
These players
Who are athletes
Really supposed to do?
While it is customary to stand
With your hand (over your heart)
And pay tribute to 'The National Anthem'.
There is no official mandate,
Or a punishment at all...
If someone wants to kneel,
Instead of being upright
And tall?

Or takes another
Type of posture
For a civil appeal.
That is part of their right!
As stated in "The U.S. Constitution".

Ironically, (though)
It's when a lot of cops...
Keep shooting
Unarmed blacks!
That you definitely have no choice.

Especially at night...
When you go out in public.
Then certain organizations cheer,
"God Bless America"
For the right to carry a gun.
But how many people
Yell, "Oh my god...they have murdered my
son!"

And how many others
Have now been frequently pulled-over?
When they are not
Wearing...
Their familiar team jerseys,
And that particular number.

So when does this
(Social) indigestion stop?
Probably Not!
Until an enema...
"Flushes-out"
The very last drop.
Of such a violent era:
That mostly uses
Racial profiling
And stereotyped cases.
.

THE OTHER SEX

When I grew up in the 1970's:
It was only
Male or Female.
Even though there had been...
"The Battle of the Sexes".

Except for that one
Trans-woman
Who was allowed
To play women's tennis.

Then my mother
Had told me
About one more?
A young man in the 1950's...
Who had gone to France
As such an obvious
Looking male sailor.

And then he came back
To America
As a very beautiful,
And a very feminine
Female transsexual.
Who had turned
All at once
Into
An overnight celebrity!

Then fast-forward 65 years!
In 2017:
There are now nearly
300,000 people
Who have been diagnosed with..
"Gender dysphoria".

And who are trying to
Transition...
(Without) any sort of discrimination.
Or any sexual violence
(Despite 10%)
Of the above
Being children
(Who are questioning their gender)
In absolute silence?
Until one day they say,
"Daddy...I don't like my penis!"
And "Mommie...I hate wearing dresses
Cuz I (really don't want) any breasts

At all!"
So the transgender sex:
Needs much of our support
So that they don't resort
To suicide!
Because after all...
This is a medical fact.

Then they need total equality:
In serving our country (within the military).
Then in attending certain elementary...
Middle and academic high schools.
Which should also provide
Any necessary
Public bathroom facilities.

TENT CITY U.S.A

Homeless today and homeless tomorrow.
The city streets are jam-packed:
With widespread sorrow!
So much...
Dirt,
Debris,
Urine and feces.
Not from dogs,
But from people,
Who are poor, sick and feeble.
They are desperate for help!
As they cry out daily
Without any hope of...
Improving their miserable lives.
As they suffer through the improbability:
Of not obtaining a job?
Or not panhandling enough money...
To pay for a comfy room?
Or enough to buy something...
That is healthy and nourishing to eat?

Or to get some medical care...
For those gangrenous sores
On their hands, legs, and feet?
Or to have a hot, clean, soapy, shower!
In conjunction with:
Some brand, new, clean, clothes?
And some brand, new, well-fitting shoes?

But instead we have got:
"Tent-cities".
Which are like pop-up,
(Campsites)
For the homeless communities.
That are now located...

In every major urban city!
They are...
Under the freeways,
Near the sewer systems,
In the public parks,
And on the coastal beaches.
But they are primarily along the forgotten
streets!
And these are not like...
Those established "trailer parks"
That usually have a designated area.
For those specific types of vehicles...
That are sometimes less affordable.

Unfortunately,
This is a brand, new, cluster:
Of working-class folks!
That did not survive
The "mortgage-crisis" yoke,
Or that fateful date of (2008).
These are the ones that lost their homes!
And everything else...
Despite the attempted bailouts,
And the reduced interest rates.
These are the families...
That have been living out here (on the city
streets).
In filth, poverty, and garbage
For more than 10 years...
Which is an abominable feat!
Along with the many, many, other
Military veterans.
Who just can't get a job
Due to their PTSD disorder?
And they are wandering aimlessly...
Just like "shopping-cart" hoarders.

GUNS! GUNS! GUNS!

Well, it's the 19th anniversary of:
The 'trench-coat mafia'.
And I had dearly hoped...
That we would never, ever,
Have to celebrate
This tragic event (once again)
And go bowling!
When I say bowling...
I mean a mass-shooting!!!
And a mass killing of:
The innocent people...
And the countless lives
That are taken down daily
By semi-automatic weapons!

There have been nine...
Since Columbine in the year of (1999).
Then in (2007)
We had Virginia-Tech;
And in (2009)
There was...
Fort Hood and BingHamton;
Then in (2012)
It was...
Sandy Hook Elementary School!
And after that in (2015)
It was...
San Berna_dino;
Followed by...
'The Orlando'
(Nightclub) shooting in 2016!
But it still continued...
Into the year of (2017):
With 'The Texas First Baptist Church' (killings).

And then the Las Vegas...
'Mass-shooting' of 59 people
On the Mandalay Bay Strip!
But now it is 2018:
And we have already
Started the year...
With another horrible
High school massacre
In Parkland, Florida!
Has Americas' passion for guns...
Overshadowed
These shocking statistics?
Or the startling correlation between...

Mental illness= Gun violence= Gun Ownership.

Who will be the next sacrificial lamb?
Well, apparently not these students.
As thousands of them...
Marched!
And posted their thoughts
On social media today.
Which is exactly
(Just one month later).
And it was all across the country...
As they were all united
In complete solidarity.
With their poster-signs held high:
That said, "I DON'T WANT TO DIE!"
Then others chanted, "GUN CONTROL NOW!"
And this was how...
They all took to the streets,
('Right) before their 18th birthdays!

About the Author:

Ms. **Rafiki Chemari** is a native San Francisco resident. She is a local member of THE SCREEN ACTORS GUILD and ASCAP Music Publishing and she currently has a music track on hold for placement in a feature film with ONE NITE STAND MUSIC. In February 2018 she was an Adelaide Voices Best Essay Award Finalist for "Women in Prison" and it was included in the special issue of the: ADELAIDE VOICES AN-THOLOGY 2018 VOLUME TWO.

OLD SCHOOL

by Tony Tracy

Physiography

The phenomenon is irrefutable; a true scientific
and earthly wonder, mathematical improbability
that leaves scholars of astrology scratching

their heads to explain, and pundits of scripture and
Christianity gawking through their $10 cardboard
sunglasses as midday light turns shadowless and

the sky takes on an eerie, blue metallic sheen⬚
cosmological evidence, they say, God is at the center
of all things. It's like Evolutionism vs. Creationism,

both lacking that single key ingredient, smoking gun
of empirical evidence that solves the single most
human mystery: origin. But sometimes it's the lack

of answers that makes us who we are, buoys us like
a giant life-preserver, spawns intangible words such
as hope and faith; a belief in something, somewhere

in the cosmos that is waiting to fill us with radiance
like a private, invisible sun. But it's no secret
what's going on here, the whole world is attuned

to the miracle of being shaded by a single shadow,
that the moon, which is exactly 400 x's smaller,
will pass in front of the sun, which is exactly 400 x's

further, so perfectly, so precisely, the rarity of its
necessary mathematics so staggering, even the theorem
is viewed as flitting on the edge of insanity.

The physiography of a total eclipse akin to finding
God's face in a solar flare, or the hard data between
ape and man just beyond the shadow's penumbra.

Seized Assets

Eye-balled like we are potential terrorists, or Western tourists moving through
customs in the old Soviet-Bloc, i.d.'s are checked and rechecked. Guards
don't acknowledge one another. Appear tight-lipped, chisel-faced statues,
robotic figures incapable of allowing even a sprig of levity to lighten

the moment. After all, this isn't some swap-meet, some coffeehouse gallery, some fussy
antique shop we've come to stuffed with an endless display of Queen Anne relics and French doi-
lies, a neighborhood garage sale replete with dusty
heirlooms and racks of greasy automotive parts (the rust-pitted jem of

Duesenberg or Packard grill found only in an episode of American Pickers),
but a real timeauction of wealth seized from raids on dirty millionaires' estates⬚ highly sought col-
lectibles of museum quality placed under bullet-proof
plexi. So on a whim, on a rainy, lackluster Saturday, we've come to

the Ramada Tropics Resort to gawk at how the other half lives. The spoils of money's
excess doesn't disappoint. Housed below hawking eyes— the crazy mix of silk rugs and bronze
busts, serigraphs and lithographs graced with authenticated
signatures of Pissaro and Chagall, Dali and Miró, the impenetrable blue

of some trophy wife's 9 ct. Tanzanite, its cool mint counterpart of a Paraiba Tourmaline,
I kid my wife, that once laid on the slope of Coppertone Valley,
sparkling under a maritime sun between the Silicone Peaks. Naturally, she finds
no humor there while the ratta tat tat of a auctioneer prattles numbers

that climb higher and higher with seemingly no ceiling in sight: 23, 23 do I hear twenty
-three thousand? We walk past locked FDIC tables towards the fray percolating around an easel.
The painting up for bid: an Itzchak Tarkay with women and flowers and teapots and tables and the
deepest hues I've ever

seen in acrylic, one of ten originals come to bear. Sometimes it's the simplest things
that exact ridiculous prices. The grandeur of smaller moments signed
with a hand's flourish. The beauty of private life purchased over and over again.
An acquisition of the muse's intelligence costing us big time.

Land of Bizarro

Inside the skirted fender, gravel ricocheted off the wheel
well, whizzed and pinged. Oh how it rang out, the spray
sounding like bullets missing the flesh of their intended targets.
I remember listening as I flinched from the trunk— endorphin's
rush of being smuggled into the Drive-In, a kid's fantasy
hatched in the dark. Tonight, on A&E, movie-making that glorified
the horror of living "The Sicilian Way"⬚ that gruesome scene
from Casino where Pesci's Santoro is released from tail-fins,
the Nevada stars burning overhead as some low-level mafioso
hands him a shovel, orders him to dig a double grave at gunpoint⬚
one for him and his blindfolded brother. It's moments like these
where I flee by osmosis, disappear into the land of bizarro—
those Friday nights sneaking into the Mason City Drive-In.
How it felt so criminal, so epiphanic escaping that cavernous
shell I shared with a spare and a tire-jack, to be helped
from the trunk and handed a Coors— my aunt's reward
for the ten-year-old who endured the journey— salty beverage
that primed the pump for an evening's double-feature
of guts & gore, troubling addiction that would last a lifetime.
But how unlike drinking to be released from that oblivion,
from above the signature badging, gangster whitewalls of her
'73 Coup de Ville, believing this must be what the dead felt like,
what it feels like to be dead— the key unhinging the latch,
the giant carapace swinging open like a coffin's lid to reveal
Orion tracking through the night sky, reminding I knew nothing
about death or dying, nothing about the monumental jolt
of heartache that follows, nothing of loss outside the movies,
any world beyond the scaffolding of the giant wooden screen—
not even the fact that the light that reached us arrived from
a place vanished long ago.

Of Thousands: An Eternal Lament

The Bibbs' eastern windows are slate-grey,
except the gable's triad which has caught
the sunrise in panorama, display
of molten light⬜ three dizzying spots

where color between volcanic red
and canary yellow a bomb gone off⬜
fiery fusillade, end-time spread
across glass where I imagine heavy loss

and hell's ruin; then heroic dream⬜
climbing through toppled layers of steel,
pulverized concrete and smoking I-beams⬜
to rise into a shattered cathedral

once a lobby's façade. None ever did.
Besides the rapture, eyes forever hid.

Old School

Sailing over the Black Hills,
a Lakota warrior chiseled in hewn.
The static voice of the captain fills
the cabin, overdubs Dire Straits on iTunes

with info on landmarks and flight-time,
current temp and weather in Sin City.
Still hours from touchdown, from crazy nights
of slots and booze⬜ drama of Billy

Idol at our hold 'em table in a drunken
sneer of himself as I try to catch
a royal flush on the flop. The outspoken
is the Vegas rule, only place to hatch

life as a grotesque. Demand for MTV
old school: Money for nothin', Chicks for free.

About the Author:

Tony Tracy is the author of two collections of poetry, The Christening and Without Notice. His work is forthcoming or has recently appeared in Flint Hills Review, North American Review, Poetry East, Hotel Amerika, Potomac Review and various other magazines and journals.

TEARBLANKET

by Reuben Ellis

Urine for the Spring

We have no need for a pot of urine. Ours
has sat unused in the corner for a
month as it is.

The weather has been clear and cold at
night. The horizons have been
far away and have spoken to us
in the darkness of what we fear
in what we know of the next town.

There the people all wear coyote masks
and eat raw meat from chickens.

Urine sits still and thick. This grows
demeaning for us, in the warmth
of the wood stove.

We would walk to the next town if the
roads were open, but they are dark
and still and empty as snow lies
three feet deep on the grade.

There are stories about the way they
copulate in the next town.

And the moon is new and like a branch
bowed under the snow. We have
urine stored up from all of us for
spring.

Metropolis.

Tearblanket

To alter flesh, use the deciduous catclaw,
the spiculumed acacia, tearblanketits
common name, unpronounceable in
ambiguity. I could describe it to you,
three-thorned, polygamous flowers, pinnate
pods, but you will know it because you will
be bleeding and the alkaloids in the cuts
will be a kind of pleasure, perhaps not
mainstream, but not either unusual.

As for the name itself, because there is no
outside to language, perhaps the thorns once
ripped apart someone's bedding, tangled with
their bodies. Perhaps it lodged, a premise, in
the coarse-woven, sweat-soaked space between
the saddle and the mount. The poultice does
nothing to stop this mad post to modernity.

Or the long a could become the long e and the
the difference between tare and tier Ricky
Ricardo struggles to understand. The dusted
yellow flowers bloom most heavily in April,
which is the cruelest month, and Jesus wept.
But as much as we hate the fucking plant,
small animals at times seek refuge inside
its lower places from predators. Good for
them, but not everyone escapes.

Think about it as you nail the deer hide to the
splintered battens of the barn. The flattened
black skin, cringing around its still bloody
edges, pulling back from bristling hair, looks
petal-like, fine lobed, and lace. Too dense
for fabric, it curls and cracks. You joke that it
died in a tragic gun cleaning accident. In the
morning you will treat it with borax, salt,
vinegar, with brains. Say the word--tearblanket.
And you have already committed. A living
animal has no edges, you know.

You Can Eliminate Orange Traffic Cones

You have done the rest. Good job,
and only this remains.

Remember the woman at the coffee
house, back by the sofa with the
chess board, the one who told you
when to travel and when to stay,
and how small seeds should be
swallowed with which liquids,
especially the black sesame, and
how to carve away soft material that
does not belong around the image.

She was an actuary, in her early forties,
and she smelled of grapefruit, and she
told you which non-native plants must
not be used, and of course why the
white rook was missing from the set

She brought it up, but in the end taught
you nothing useful about the cones,
the brightly colored thermoplastic thugs.

You must handle it yourself now.
Create an aqueous infusion of polyps,
extract alkaloids, maintain the regime
of kombucha, sulphuric ether that
will protect against unwanted oriental-
isms and depositions. You know the
rule of cones.

Soon strangers will begin staring at you
with looks of great concern and for some,
anger, but you know how to handle that.
Now you can move at liberty. You are
free.

About the Author:

Reuben Ellis is professor and chair of the
Writing Department at Woodbury University in
Los Angeles. His publications include Vertical
Margins: Mountaineering and the Landscapes
of Neo-Imperialism; Stories and Stone: Writing
the Ancestral Pueblo Homeland; and Beyond
Borders: The Selected Essays of Mary Austin, as
well as many published essays, short stories,
and poems. He is currently working on a book
-length project describing literary representa-
tions of ancestral Puebloan peoples and sites.

A POET'S QUILL
by Antoine Airoldi

A poet's quill grows so slow;
From a bird in mid air, too low;
Loses its flight attendant, oh;
Watch its mill flow even more;

When the seasons change;
The days shrink to an inch;
All captains set their ships;
Out of water, out of gold;

Afraid to rise to the occasion;
In becoming the man with the;
Last words, never came so close;
Because a poet's quill stains;

And every mint of fabric;
Stretched with a thin needle;
Pin it, cross the waves of;
A pattern so firm and just;

Never builds character;
Without a poet's quill;
And it stains the very fabric;
And as it stains, the world;
Goes blind for just one second

About the Author:

Antoine Airoldi is a storyteller, author, and Elite Speaker. He uses creative writing to generate more leads and sales for his clients. Furthermore, he is the author of Insights From Professionals and Revival, and is soon releasing his first novel: Kingdom Come. The art of storytelling has propelled his career to a whole new level as he is published by The Sherbrooke Record, The Campus, The Townships Sun, Gen Z Publishing, etc. Antoine is proud to announce that this is just the start to his everlasting legacy.

AS ALONE AS I WANT TO BE

A memoir by Pam Munter

Paperback: 240 pages

Publisher: Adelaide Books
(August 2018)

Language: English

ISBN-10: 1-949180-17-4

ISBN-13: 978-1-949180-17-6

Product Dimensions:
6 x 0,7 x 9 inches

"'Life,' George Bernard Shaw wrote, 'is not about finding yourself. Life is about creating yourself.' That experience—creating myself while living an adventurous life on a learning curve—is at the core of AS ALONE AS I WANT TO BE. The memoir is a feminist journey through a life lived deliberately—many lives, actually—as seen via an occasionally sardonic point of view, an eye for irony and humor and a consistent sense of awe. It will encourage readers to go for their dreams at any age but women over 50 might find much with which to identify. Achieving mastery in several fields is still unusual for a woman in contemporary society, much less one from an earlier generation."

Pam Munter is the author of When Teens Were Keen: Freddie Stewart and The Teen Agers of Monogram (Nicholas Lawrence Press, 2005) and Almost Famous: In and Out of Show Biz (Westgate Press, 1986) and has been a contributor to many others. She's a former clinical psychologist, performer and film historian. Her first "publication" was a monthly four-page, carbon-copied newspaper she published about a local baseball team when she was nine. Since then, writing has infused every era of her life.

She taught political science at California State University at Northridge during the volatile and often violent 1960s. During her tenure, the top floor of her office building was burned out, just a few days before she watched Robert F. Kennedy deliver one of his final speeches just yards from her office. After earning a Ph.D. in clinical psychology, she served as an Associate Professor at Portland State University (see "Walt"). It was a time for academic, research-based writing. Concurrently, in private practice, she published a groundbreaking quarterly newsletter for her clients.

When she retired from clinical psychology, it allowed the time and opportunity to resume her lifelong passion for show biz. She jumped at the chance to perform in major cities, singing with a jazz trio (see "Romancing New York"). She also worked as an actor, appeared in independent films and numerous commercials, and hosted and produced an arts-based TV program. She recorded two CDs, the last a tribute to her childhood hero, Doris Day, at Capitol Records (see "Sinatra's Mic"). She wrote all the shows and both album liner notes. Her many lengthy retrospectives on the lives of often-forgotten Hollywood performers and others have appeared in both Classic Images and in Films of the Golden Age.

More recently, her essays and short stories have been published in Adelaide, The Rumpus, Matador Review, The Manifest-Station, Angels Flight—Literary West, The Coachella Review, The Creative Truth, Quiet Letter, The Legendary, and dozens of others. She is the nonfiction book reviewer for Fourth and Sycamore, a literary journal in Ohio, and is a Pushcart Prize nominee.

But Hollywood has never been far away. She has published a series of short stories with a historical Hollywood theme. Her play Life Without was nominated by the Desert Theatre League for the Bill Groves Award for Outstanding Original Writing, along with a nomination for Outstanding Play. That Screwy, Ballyhooey Hollywood, another dark comedy, is slated for production soon. She has an MFA in Creative Writing and Writing for the Performing Arts from the University of California at Riverside in Palm Desert, her sixth academic degree.

Pam's personal life has been similarly eclectic, married to a man for nine years and later partnered with a woman for nearly 32 years. Her son, Aaron, and his spouse, Dana, live in Lake Oswego, Oregon. Since 2002, Pam has made her home in Palm Desert, California after living in Oregon for many years, a return to her native soil.

WHERE THERE IS BREATH, THERE IS LIFE

A memoir by Susan M. Davis

Paperback: 300 pages

Publisher: Adelaide Books (August 2018)

Language: English

ISBN-10: 1-949180-16-6

ISBN-13: 978-1-949180-16-9

Product Dimensions:
6 x 0,7 x 9 inches

Karen and Susan's story are a testament to the strength, commitment and love that defines their relationship. The "sudden event" of a ruptured brain aneurysm took them on a harrowing journey into hospitals, rehabilitation units, and care facilities. The title, "Where there is Breath, there is a Life", defines the journey from the perspective of simply the act of breathing and the hope that life is still present. The word, 'BREATH', represents key concepts for the reader.

B defines "BIG Crisis": Aneurysmal Subarachnoid Hemorrhage (SAH) is a type of hemorrhagic stroke that is usually caused by a ruptured brain aneurysm. Twenty percent of individuals who sustain SAH from this cause perish within hours of the event. The survivors are faced with countless potential complications and crisis that are known to commonly occur after SAH and threaten their lives. In Susan's book, the natural course of the disease was evident as Karen's body was affected in every organ system. Her brain suffered from increased pressure and the risk of rebleeding of the aneurysm while her heart and lungs experienced a shock similar to a heart attack. Once the aneurysm was sealed, the left-over blood in her brain produced irritation causing the 2-3 week period of vasospasm which can cause more strokes in the brain. Treating the vasospasm to avoid those strokes involve high risk procedures and require a highly advanced team of doctors, nurses, and technicians. This "BIG Crisis" had Karen fighting for her life, the hospital team using every treatment option and skill to keep her from dying, and Susan watching from the bedside as all of this unfolded. Susan's reflections of the days in the ICU describe the perilous and stressful minutes, days and weeks that patients loved one's experience while patients are fighting for their lives! How do all involved function and provide the best environment to survive?

R defines RELATIONSHIPS: When an individual (patient) enters the hospital, a relationship is established with the health care team. The patient's loved ones become part of the team. Personal connections between staff, patients and families/loved ones are key to establishing trust between all involved. Nurses spend the most time with patients and their loved ones at the bedside and when patients remain in the hospital for a long period of time, relationships continue to develop and mature. It is not uncommon for families of ICU patients to become "part of the unit family" when the caring relationships mature over time. The goal for all involved is to optimize the outcome of the patient. Sometimes the eventual outcome is not what all hoped for and staff feel the loss as greatly as the families. The transition to another level of care often results in a frightful time for the patient and loved ones. As Susan describes it is like leaving the "womb". The relationships help ease that transition.

E defines EMOTIONS: Loved ones of the patient may experience highs and lows in an hour or in a day. The critical care unit cares for individuals who are critically ill and often unstable. When talking with the patient's loved ones, the team will describe a roller coaster to define the various emotions that are experienced. Staff are present to support the patient and family. It is ok to be scared. Staff keep in the backs of their minds how frightened families can be of the known and the unknown. Listening and providing reassurance and communicating information honestly and as often as necessary are essential to help ease the ups/downs.

A defines ADVOCATE: Susan's perseverance and dedication to Karen are evident throughout the journey. Susan is Karen's advocate and will move "heaven and earth" to ensure Karen receives the best care. Advocacy is essential and every patient must have an advocate! The ADVOCATE questions and reviews what is best for their loved one. In today's health care system, an advocate is important to maximize the outcome for their loved one.

T defines TEAMWORK: Often most individuals refer to the health care team as the ones that possess teamwork. While that is true, true teamwork is when healthcare teams, patients, and their support team (families/loved ones/friends) come together to implement the treatments needed for the patient to survive. A simple example is when a physical therapist (PT) provides range of motion (ROM) for the unconscious patient in the bed to promote mobility. The PT can teach the family and loved ones to do the same ROM as they are sitting at the bedside for hours. Susan, her mother/brother, and close friends/family comprised TEAM KAREN as their presence on a daily basis created the larger team of practitioners caring for Karen.

H defines HOPE: There are two mottos on the wall in the SICU. The first is, "Where there is life-There is Hope"! The second is, "NEVER GIVE UP...NEVER SURRENDER". The TEAM works tirelessly 24/7 to provide the best care possible and are driven by hope that the patient will survive and have an optimal outcome. Families and loved ones pray and believe in hope. Without hope, a hospital would be a very dim place. It keeps us going in the direst of circumstances. Physicians use their incredible skills and talents to save lives. Sometimes, they deliver grave news when complications occur, such as Karen's cardiac arrest. The physicians also provide an outline or path of treatment that hopefully will result in an improved outcome. The team of nurses and therapists believe and maintain hope that the outcome will be successful. Karen's support team maintains hope throughout the entire journey. Hope she would survive! Hope she would return home! Hope that Karen would be Karen once again! Hopes do come true especially when someone has BREATH and Life!

Forward by Mary Kay Bader RN MSN CCNS FNCS
FAHA Neuro/Critical Care CNS, Mission Hospital

Susan M. Davis graduated from California State University Fullerton with a degree in English. She has been an 8th grade English teacher for 27 years. She is a former Teacher of the Year. Susan also has a Masters of Science in Educational Counseling. She just completed her MFA in Creative Writing Non-fiction from Fairfield University in Connecticut. Susan resides in Southern California with her wife, Karen Kozawa and their 3 Cocker Spaniels. Her favorite color is purple. If you know her, you will know this.

A collection of rhyming poems, and haikus

Samuel S. Kaufman is a poet from Asheville North Carolina. Samuel has been described as a "Punk Rock Poet" due to his writing often showing the rebellious spirit that lives in punk rock music. Samuel's influences in writing are writers from the "Beat Generation". Writers such as Allen Ginsberg, Jack Kerouac, and William S. Burroughs. He also gained much of his love for poetry from poets such as Charles Bukowski, Billy Collins, and Sylvia Plath. As well as being a published poet Samuel is also an accomplished songwriter. He plays six instruments and is constantly putting new music out online, as well as playing live shows all around his local town. The connection of music and poetry is important to Samuel as he often records spoken word poetry with a backdrop of music he plays himself. You can acquire Samuel's music at bandcamp.com/samuelkaufman. Samuel believes that poetry has the power to change lives, and so he spends every day trying to write something worthy of that power.

STRANGE NIGHTS

Poems by Samuel S. Kaufman

Paperback: 120 pages

Publisher: Adelaide Books
(August 2018)

Language: English

ISBN-10: 1-949180-19-0

ISBN-13: 978-1-949180-19-0

Product Dimensions:
6 x 0,5 x 9 inches

FALL TENDERLY

Poems by Shari Jo LeKane-Yentumi

Paperback: 120 pages

Publisher: Adelaide Books
(August 2018)

Language: English

ISBN-10: 1-949180-18-2

ISBN-13: 978-1-949180-18-3

Product Dimensions:
6 x 0,5 x 9 inches

Shari Jo LeKane-Yentumi (B.A. English, Spanish; M.A. Spanish - Saint Louis University Madrid/St. Louis) lives in St. Louis, Missouri, writes articles, literary critiques, poetry and prose. She is a consultant for not-for-profit, business, community development, education, leadership development, disability, and elderly advocacy, and she teaches Spanish Language and Culture in a local university, and creative writing to men in a maximum-security jail and to special needs students. She wrote a novel in verse, Poem to Follow, two books of poetry, Fall Tenderly and Surviving Gracefully, and is featured in several poetry anthologies, including the Missouri VSA 2013 Anthology, Turning the Clocks Forward Again; Poetica Victorian; Red Dashboard Disorder Anthology: Mental Illness and Its Effects; Think Pink; The Muse India/Createspace Anthology Of Present Day Best Poems (Vols. I, II, III & IV); Bordertown Press Poetry of People on the Move; The Society of Classical Poets (Vol. I, VI); The Mas Tequila Review; Snapping Twig; The Lonely Crowd; Form Quarterly; Devolution Z; The Quarterday Review; Adelaide Literary Magazine; Adelaide Literary Awards Poetry Finalist Best of 2017 Anthology; Adelaide Voices Literary Award for Poetry Shortlist Winner for 2018; MacroMicroCosm Literary and Arts Review: Solstice; The Road Not Taken; The Faircloth Review; Bindweed; Halcyon Days; Lunaris Review; Iconoclast; The Poeming Pigeon; Unrequited: An Anthology of Love Poems about Inanimate Objects; and Literature Today International Journal of Contemporary Literature (Vols. I, II, & VI). Shari's poetry has been published in several literary magazines in the U.S., Canada, England, India, Ireland, Nigeria, Portugal, Scotland, Spain and Wales, and she has been featured in spoken word on the award-winning CD, 'How Live?' with LOOPRAT. Shari considers herself a modern formalist, addressing contemporary issues in poetic verse with a stylized language.

www.ingramcontent.com/pod-product-compliance
Lightning Source LLC
Chambersburg PA
CBHW080720020726
47502CB00009B/2484